Menu Musings

OF A MODERN AMERICAN MOM

2014
Julie May, PhD
menumusings.com

JULIE MAY

INDIGORIVER
PUBLISHING

Menu Musings
OF A MODERN AMERICAN MOM
OVER 150 RECIPES WITH "HOW-TO" PHOTOS FROM AMERICA'S TASTIEST FOOD BLOG
JULIE MAY
Menu Musings

Menu Musings of a Modern American Mom

Editors: Donna Melillo, Christian Pacheco, Hunter Brown, Kimberly Rooks, Adam Tillinghast

Interior Design: Rick Soldin / book-comp.com
Kevin Williamson / kevinwilliamsondesign.com

Line Art: vecteezy.com, freepik.com, flaticon.com

Cover Design: Jason Kauffmann / firelightinteractive.com

Photography: Julie May/menumusings.com

Indigo River Publishing
3 West Garden Street Ste. 352
Pensacola, FL 32502
www.indigoriverpublishing.com

Ordering Information:

Quantity sales: Special discounts are available on quantity purchases by corporations, associations, and others. For details, contact the publisher at the address above.

Orders by U.S. trade bookstores and wholesalers: Please contact the publisher at the address above.

Printed in the United States of America

Publisher's Cataloging-in-Publication Data is available upon request.

Library of Congress Control Number: 2014947163

ISBN: 978-0-9904857-1-1

First Edition

With Indigo River Publishing, you can always expect great books, strong voices, and meaningful messages.
Most importantly, you'll always find... words worth reading.

Proceed with Caution

Due to the overwhelming positive response I've had for these recipes, I can't guarantee you will be able to stop with making just one. In fact, you may even find yourself and your family spending more time in the kitchen working together. Since many of these recipes will instantly become family favorites, don't be surprised or alarmed if you are asked to make many of them again and again for your family and friends. ***You have been warned!***

To My Children:

those God gave me, and those I've managed to pick up along the way. The chairs around our table are rarely empty, and our hearts are always full because you are here.

And to My Husband:

who is the most amazing partner I could ask for.

Contents

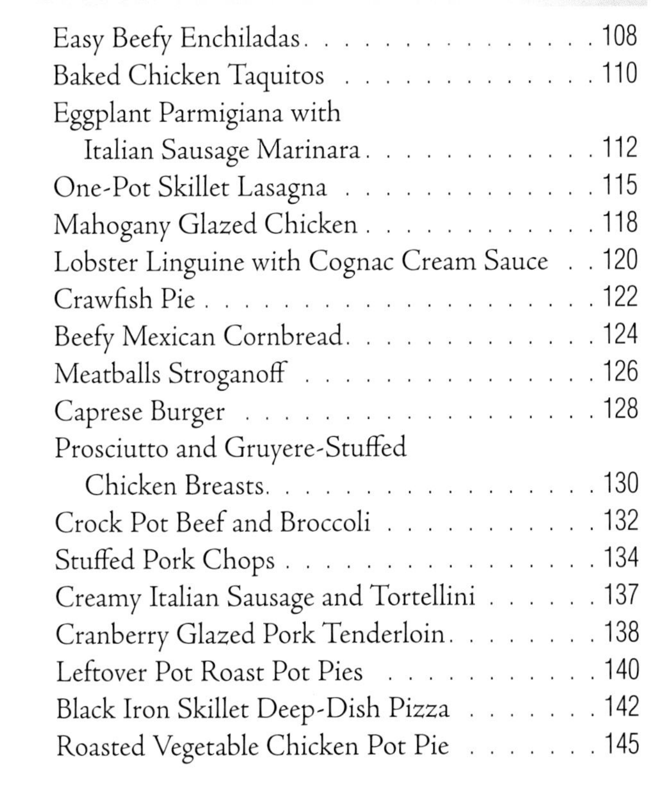

Soups and Such 84

Entrees 106

Side Dishes 246

A Few Notions and Knick-Knacks

All of the following are mentioned in multiple recipes. This brief section was designed for your convenience and to avoid repetitive information.

Peppers and Onions—
Saving Time

When you have the time and are cutting fresh peppers or onions, cut a little extra and put them in the freezer. Why? Because freezing swells the water in the cells of the flesh of the peppers or onions, which helps them break down a lot faster than the fresh ones. This translates into a shorter cooking time, which will be most appreciated when you are in a hurry.

Vanilla Beans —
For the Best Flavor

There is a world of difference between using a real vanilla bean and many of the prepared products out there. First, you don't want imitation vanilla in your house. That's a given. Pure vanilla extract works well; but when you want the ultimate flavor for your recipe, use a vanilla bean. The best flavor is in the seeds or "caviar" inside, so you need to split the bean in half lengthwise with a sharp knife. Scrape the edge of the knife along the inner surface of the vanilla bean pod to remove all the seeds. That "caviar" is used directly in your sauce. You can add the whole pod for a while to make certain you get all of those wonderful seeds in there, but then take the pod out. They are super fragrant!

Parmigiano Reggiano—
There is No Substitute for Fresh

There are many areas you can find to skimp on ingredients, but not the Parmesan cheese. Please do not use that powdered stuff that comes in a can. That bears no resemblance to this Parmigiano Reggiano—truly the king of cheeses! Also, cheeses that are "pre-grated" begin to oxidize very rapidly and lose a lot of flavor. So if you can, please make your cheese purchases in the block form and grate your own. Remember, great recipes start with great ingredients.

Rotisserie Chicken—
Another Great Time Saver

When you know you are pressed for time, consider this cheater ingredient—a rotisserie chicken. Pick one up on your way home. Often the chickens are discounted up to a dollar or more if they are refrigerated rather than still hot from cooking. You will need them cooled off anyway. These are flavorful and can be used in many of the recipes calling for cooked chicken. Just strip the meat from the bones and cut according to the directions.

Crawfish—
Washed or Not?

Washing your crawfish seems to be a hotbed of contention. Many people feel you should not rinse them, while others do not like the fishy smell. This is a personal choice. If you want all the flavor of the fat, don't rinse. If you bristle at the smell of the fresh crawfish or when you first open the package, then by all means, rinse them. Triple rinsing the crawfish tails will get rid any residual fat and take away any of the "fishy" odor. Then just let them drain off to the side in a colander.

Pillsbury Rollout Pie Crust— Always Reliable and Saves Time

For those of you who have limited time or do not wish to make piecrusts from scratch, there is a great alternative. For me, the Pillsbury Rollout Pie Crust comes out great each time I use it. Though I've tried other brands, I keep coming back to this one. If you have a favorite brand or want to make your own piecrust, go for it; but this one works great and saves me a lot of time.

Tasso Ham— Specialty of Southern Cuisine

Despite its name, Tasso ham is not typically eaten on its own. It may be found in dishes ranging from pasta to crab cakes to soup to gravy. In this case, "ham" is a misnomer since Tasso is not made from the leg of a pig, but the shoulder butt. This cut is typically fatty, though leaner cuts are often used, and has a great deal of flavor. The butt, which will weigh 7 to 8 lbs, is sliced across the grain into pieces about 3 in thick. These are then dredged in a salt cure, which usually includes nitrates and sugar. The meat is left to cure very briefly, only three or four hours, then rinsed, rubbed with a spice mixture that is sure to contain cayenne and garlic, and hot-smoked until cooked through. Appropriate to its roots, Tasso is most often found in recipes of Southern or Cajun/Creole origin.

Kosher vs. Table Salt— They Are Not the Same

Kosher salt can be used in nearly all cooking applications except for baking. Due to the larger grain size, unless you have sufficient liquid, some grains will be undissolved and you would be biting into them in the finished product. Kosher salt is not usually iodized, while iodine [an essential trace element for life] is added to most table salts. The most important difference to you relates to the crystal size. If my recipe lists 1 tsp of kosher salt and you use 1 tsp of table salt, it will be WAY too salty. A rough guideline would be to cut the volume of table salt in half. Of course, you should always go by taste. If necessary, you can always add additional salt.

Acknowledgments

Thank you to all of my faithful blog subscribers who kept asking me for a cookbook. Without your continued requests, I never would have had the guts to approach *any* publishers with a "pitch" for a cookbook idea in the first place. So this was really of your own doing!

I would like to thank Indigo River Publishing for giving me the opportunity to take these recipes, representing a portion of my blog, from the great big "cloud" of the Internet and put them into this hard copy medium... an actual testament that it really exists! ***WooHoo!!!*** A very special thanks to Adam Tillinghast, who has held my hand through every step of the process and answered countless queries via texts, e-mails, and phone calls. I hear about other publishers who are like the great wizard behind the curtain who can't be bothered to speak to you at all, but not mine. And for that, I am infinitely grateful.

Thank you to all of my friends, family, neighbors, and coworkers who have given me feedback on blog recipes over the years. You have been my "test group," although "guinea pigs" are what I've called you. I'm sorry for the times when my little ones have just come into your house, sometimes without even knocking, and left food on your counters. You know who you are.

Thank you to the following people who have helped me in various ways related to the blog and cookbook: Caitlin Steele, Brady Smith, Nicole Shelling-Mitchell, Jamie May, Jamie Lynch, Bubba Berlin, and my beautiful little cover girl and cooking partner—Lily Rogers. You each played a role in this thing, and I thank you for being there for me.

And I thank each of you for your patience with me as you read this book. I am not a professional chef, and I am not a professional photographer. I am a home cook with a passion. So if you see a photo that isn't quite "all that," please note that these are not captured in a studio, but in my kitchen. That means that you too can make these dishes! Remember, you can follow the QR code for each recipe back to the blog for the full step-by-step photos via your smart phone. I appreciate your support and friendship over the years; and I certainly appreciate your purchase and reading of this book!

Menu Musings of a Modern American Mom

The Modern Mom:

It's likely that you purchased this book, or were given this book, based off what you have seen on my blog—"Menu Musings of a Modern American Mom." That's a long title, huh? Where the heck did that come from? Well, it started as a way to get recipe ideas to my best friend, who is a super-busy mom herself. E-mailing the recipes then taking pictures to illustrate what I meant with certain techniques became too time consuming, so I just started up a blog. My thinking was that I could post the things I cook for my family on the blog, so when she wanted recipe options or instructions, they would be available at her convenience. I chose the phrase "Menu Musings" because not all of the recipes would be my original creations. I mean who cooks like that? I don't know about the rest of y'all, but many things I cook on a daily basis are things that I've grown up eating or were passed along from somewhere else.

Well I suppose now I should give you my definition of the Modern Mom (which consequently could easily apply to the Modern Dad). Back in the *Leave It to Beaver* days, there was June Cleaver who stayed at home and had all day to take care of the meal planning and cooking. But in our modern world, where there are so many diverse versions of the nuclear family, it's just a fact that a majority of families need to have a two-income household. Now whether you have made the decision to work outside the home or work inside the home, we all are required to perform a fine balancing act between the needs of our families, careers, and yes—let's not forget self-care!

So the Modern Mom likely has a day like this: She gets the kids up and off to school (even the home-schooled kids), goes to work, runs to the grocery store, and rushes home to start dinner. She oversees homework, drives kids to various practices (and recitals and ballgames), and considers herself lucky if she made it to the gym at some point before collapsing into a nice hot bath. Now in that scenario, many of those duties are non-negotiable. Unfortunately, the ones that *are* negotiable sometimes get thrown to the curb when we find ourselves short on time… like preparing a nutritious meal at home. Please don't get me wrong—our family does takeout sometimes too. But it's not a habit that I advocate on a regular basis.

Cooking at home, *with* your family, is something that has been deemed sacred since the beginning of time. It's almost the epitome of quality time together. It gives us the opportunity to bond and build relationships, rather than watching your kids fill out yet one more dot-to-dot coloring page at a restaurant after waiting for your table, then waiting for your order to come, then wondering what sorts of ingredients were used. Were they fresh? Were they full of preservatives? Did they add extra salt and fat beyond what may have been necessary? And why are the portions so HUGE?!

That brings me to one of my "soapboxes," which is the use of ingredients. One of the absolute best things about cooking at home is YOUR complete control over the quality and quantities of the ingredients. You can include or exclude ingredients according to your preferences, dietary needs, allergies, or whims! There's no way you have this much control over the food when it's left up to someone else—someone whom you don't even know. You'll find lots of tidbits of food trivia in this book. Call it a hazard of my professional career, if you will, but there's definitely that science nerd in me that likes to *know* some things about the stuff I'm eating or preparing for the people I love.

Since you are reading this, I presume that you consider yourself included in the category of someone having a crazy-busy, but purposeful life. Also, you are indeed concerned about your family, their nutrition, and the unique relationship that you are building together. It also tells me that you are interested in strengthening those ties by cooking some great meals at home with your family or friends. Did you read that line correctly? I said WITH your family. I am a huge proponent of involving the family in the meal preparation. The lessons that your children learn when they help you cook are so numerous that they can't all be illuminated here. In addition to the interpersonal, relational qualities of the process, they will be learning and practicing reading, writing, math, reading comprehension, etc. It is your opportunity to discuss life, to tell them of the food and stories from your youth, to teach them about nutrition and health, to have fun, to foster creativity, and all sorts of things!

Now here's the part where I get to tell you about my food. Oh yes, I'm definitely a Southern girl, but I don't just cook *all* Southern, or all any other regional or ethnic specialty, or all super healthy, or all super trendy, or all super indulgent. As a "Modern Mom," I pretty much cook all of the above. Sometimes it depends on who is eating at home and who is not. It may depend on the season, the weather, the amount of time I have available, our budget, or any manner of factors. I highly suspect it is the same with all of you. Because of that, I have included a wide variety of recipes in this book. I hope that you will find just the right thing for the occasion (or humdrum regular day) when you are at a loss for what to cook. My hope is that the instructional photos will give you the confidence to tackle any recipe you choose and that your families will shower you with rave reviews! Just channel your inner child—the one that used to do the paint-by-number projects. My cooking is sort of like that—we'll just re-label it as "cook-by-pictures!" Some of the photo steps may be abbreviated for the space available in the book, but you can always go back to my blog and see the full versions.

Diets:

I don't really believe in diets. Your diet is what you eat every day, so it should be something you are able to sustain; and it must be enjoyable enough that you want to continue. Life is way too short to exclude great food; so unless you have a specific dietary requirement for health reasons, I see no reason to! I truly believe in the saying "all things in moderation"—even moderation itself! That being said, I also believe in being smart about the choices that I make for myself and for my family. You really don't need someone to tell you that you shouldn't be having sweets every day or gorging on pizza before going to bed. You intuitively know when your choices aren't what they should be. But here's the thing: You have many more reasons to make good choices than poor ones... you only need to look around you at the smiling faces of your children, your parents, your family, and your friends to let you know that you are needed... and a healthier you can be a happier, more productive, and exuberant you! You are worth it. *They* are worth it.

So how can you make your "diet" more enjoyable? I think variety goes a long way toward an enjoyable experience. It can be so much fun to try new recipes, new combinations, and even the old familiar recipes made a little differently. When your family and friends start looking forward to dinner just to see what new sorts of things are going to be on the menu, it becomes sort of a game. I'm sure I learned this from my mother. She's the kind of person who enjoys browsing a farmers' market to see what's new, then trying to figure out what can be done with that ingredient. I've traveled to several different countries with her, and she always wanted to see what the local people really ate. She taught me the value (and the fun and adventure) in going to their markets and trying their foods. Alright, let's be honest—she probably tried more of their foods than I did. But I make a darn good observer!

Recipes as Concepts:

Aside from baking and candy making, which in my opinion are like science, recipes should be seen as concepts, not dictates. When you are preparing a recipe, you should feel free to add, delete, and substitute ingredients at will. Learn to see the whole picture for what it's worth. You wish a recipe had mushrooms? Add them! You don't want peppers in a dish? Delete them! You think it would be just perfect if a dish included toasted walnuts rather than pecans? Go for it! You don't like a particular cornbread mix that my family enjoys? Please feel free to use one that YOUR family likes. Over the years, I have received numerous comments that "a *real* Southerner would *never* use such and such" in a recipe. Really? Says who?! That sort of bullying is part of what makes new cooks feel intimidated to get into the kitchen. Using a particular brand or flavor is a matter of preference, not a litmus test for being *Southern* or any other group affiliation. We are not all made from a cookie cutter. If you and your family enjoy a recipe a certain way, that's great. Let me be the first to tell you that you shouldn't feel pressured to change it because I prepare it differently or because someone else tells you it's not "authentic." Authentic can be way overrated. No one is at your home grading you according to food rules. Don't feel as though you can't use dried basil because "real Italians would never use dried herbs." Geeez... Do it your way! If your family likes your food, isn't that all that matters? Aside from the endpoint of nourishing your family, cooking should be fun!

Balance:

Before going back to graduate school to earn my PhD, I was an occupational therapist. I vividly remember my first day of OT school up at LSUMC in Shreveport when the concept of balance was first introduced to us, and then continually drilled into our waking moments from there on out. There are three main components: WORK, PLAY, and SELF-CARE. If you don't have a good balance between these, something will be off in your life. You won't be able to be the happiest, healthiest, most productive you that you can be. I absolutely believe in this principle. It's a continual battle, but definitely worth the fight to work toward balance in my life... time with my spouse, children, work, blog, playtime, exercise, worship, down time, and sleep! Of course, life is hard with a career, a blog, and a large, active family. It has to be purposeful. Nope, I don't get much time to sit on the couch and watch TV, that's for sure. But I do know that I'm a better me when I'm enjoying a balanced life. So now, as a professor, you'd better believe that my students hear about balance a lot! It really is that important.

Brand Name Foods:

You wouldn't believe how many reader comments I've received in the past (usually signed "Anonymous") berating my choice of brands, rather than high-end, organic, pricey brands. I use many common store brand items in my recipes because I never want to hear, "Well if I could afford the fancy brands she uses, my recipes would come out better." With a few exceptions, I want to develop the recipes I use with the type of ingredients that the majority of people have access to. Of course I have some favorites; but in general, if I can make the recipes taste great using the less-expensive store brands, then when you use your favorite brands, just imagine how much you will enjoy them. Besides that, store brands have really come a long way since I was a young girl. I have a friend in the video production business, and he shoots many commercial spots for a large grocery store chain. He confirmed that many of the store brands *are* made by the "big" brand companies, then relabeled and sold to the stores. This means that in many cases, you are only paying for the name on the label. I'm not ashamed to use store brands, and neither should you be. We work hard for our money... and that money just might be better spent on a new music download or put toward a new movie for the kids than a name-brand box of beef broth! But again, it's your choice completely.

Originality Of Recipes:

Honestly, I don't think you CAN find an "original" recipe. I mean since the history of cooking, can you imagine that something you just put together has NOT been tried? I doubt it. We often see or hear about a recipe that sparks our interest. Sometimes it may even come to us in a dream (Or maybe that's just a strange quirk I have). We may make it exactly the same, or we may change things up to suit our needs or tastes, but really—it's probably been done at some point. But we don't need to think of that as a negative. It's actually great that there are so many wonderful ideas out there, and we don't have to reinvent the wheel so to speak. So why should you bother buying a cookbook? Good question. I think the answer lies in the convenience of having a recipe in your hand, presented to you in a way that gives you confidence to try it. Many of my recipes are great finds that I have picked up over the years. They have been gleaned from family, friends, neighbors, colleagues, students—you name it! And hey—I may have put a little bit of a different spin on it than you've tried before. I'm the sort of person who has recipes stashed all over the house in books, drawers, stacks, digital and handwritten form... it could be considered quite an illness if not for the fact that I grew up with my mom reading cookbooks as her nighttime reading material. As a matter of fact, I still have the first cookbook I ever made, from back in first grade, written in my own handwriting. The whole class contributed a favorite recipe, but you may have no trouble believing that mine was the first recipe in the book!

Salty vs. Sweet?

Definitely for me it has to be salty! When I cook something sweet—cake, pie, brownies, etc.—I'm sick of smelling it by the time it's done. I may have a *piece* of the product; but after that, I'm pretty much done with it. Salty bites, however, are another story. I could just about eat chips and salsa until I make myself sick. I don't, but I could. I know other people who are like that about freshly baked bread. Isn't it odd how we're all so different?

Serving Sizes and Nutritional Information:

You may notice that I don't have serving sizes on many of my recipes. Let's just be frank here—there needs to be some modicum of common sense. For example, the folks in my house range from kindergarten to adult and everywhere in between. One half-cup serving of something will mean something totally different to each member of my family depending on their age and size. I have no clue about who you are cooking for, but you do. Another huge factor in this issue is brand sizes. One chicken breast that came from a local free-range farmer may be a completely different size than one packaged by one of the huge chicken conglomerates where one *humongo* breast is about the size of your whole hand. You know best how much your family eats, so please let your knowledge of your family or dinner guests be your guide.

As far as nutritional information goes, pretty much the same principle applies. Different brands may vary in caloric and nutritional values, so I'll leave that up to you. Also, if you eat a half-cup serving of a recipe and your spouse eats two cups, obviously you will not be consuming the same amount of fat, calories, protein, etc. I firmly believe that recipes should be like concept guides. Again, with the exception of baking and candy making, you should absolutely feel comfortable adding, deleting, or substituting ingredients as you see fit. So if I use dry sherry and you substitute Marsala, again the recipe will differ.

Some of my recipes are really healthy, while others are decadent and rich. You will definitely know if you can afford to have one more serving of something or if you should have it in moderation or for a special occasion. I will not insult your intelligence by making that distinction for you. We all know that we should have balanced meals with lean proteins and lots of fruits and vegetables... and that we need to get exercise to be healthy. One of my pet peeves has to be companies that market their items as "This is low-fat/no sugar/etc, so you can eat ALL you want!" I personally think that is crazy advice. All that does is teach people that it's okay to eat lots of junk, and to get used to having that sensation of a stuffed, stretched-out belly. After that becomes a habit, you are no longer satisfied with a "normal" amount of something. I am definitely not anti-dessert or other fun foods, just anti-excess.

So now it's time for us to get you cooking! Have fun with your food. Have fun with your family, however your particular family is defined. Let me leave you with one of my favorite quotes. This one hangs in my kitchen.

> *"Do not spoil what you have by desiring what you have not; but remember that what you now have was once among the things you only hoped for."*
>
> —*Author unknown*

Appetizers, Party Foods, and Snacks
WARM UP THEIR APPETITES
Mozzarella Caprese Skewers
Buffalo
Tzatziki

Roasted Brussels Sprouts with Spicy Garlic Aioli

Roasted H
Pepper H

Chicken Dip

Steamed Asian Dumplings

Hoppin' John Fritters

Well these babies have a bit of an interesting story... On February 10, 2013, our city was hit by an EF4 tornado. Yes, that's a big one—170 mph winds! It passed a mile from our home, but fortunately left us unscathed. Many families were not so lucky. While we knew that severe weather was expected that afternoon, we really had no idea that the monster from the *Wizard of Oz* was coming our way. We were just minding our business passing the rainy afternoon hours away doing a little kitchen project.

My little one was pretty freaked out, so during the power outage, I wanted to make it as much like an "adventure" as I could... less like some terrible thing that had demolished homes, schools, and businesses. The threat of the weather had passed, and it was just a waiting game until our power came back on, so we carried on with these fritters. Some of the photos we did for the blog were made before we lost electricity. Others were made with candles and the flashlights on our phones, held over the stove!

I happen to love Hoppin' John. It just so happens to be one of the symbols of good luck eaten in this part of the country on New Year's Day, and it is typically served with cornbread. These fritters fuse both of these concepts... and we loved them! Not to mention they obviously brought us good luck! (But just between me and you, we nicknamed them Tornado Fritters.)

Ingredients

- ½ cup (about a 6-in piece) smoked sausage, cut into small cubes
- ⅓ cup canned black eyed peas, drained and rinsed
- ¼ cup chopped onions
- 1 box cornbread mix (I used Jiffy.)
- 2 large eggs
- ⅓ cup milk
- ½ cup whole kernel corn, drained
- 3 Tbsp melted butter
- ¼ tsp garlic powder
- ¼ tsp black pepper
- ¼ tsp kosher salt
- Canola oil for frying

How to...

Cut the smoked sausage into small cubes. I used about a 6-inch piece of sausage. Get the one with the smokiest flavor you can find! Rinse the canned black eyed peas. Chop the onion fairly small. Prepare your cornbread batter using 1 box of cornbread mix, 2 eggs and ⅓ cup milk. Add all the rest of the ingredients to the batter. Season the batter with the garlic powder, black pepper, and kosher salt. Green onions would also be an excellent addition to these.

Heat oil to 350°F. Drop the fritters by a large spoonful (probably about a tablespoon). I found that it worked better if I put the spoon down into the oil and allowed the batter to *slide* off into the grease rather than trying to "drop" the batter from a ladle or spoon.

You will use a spoon to turn them midway through the cooking to ensure even browning. *They only take a few minutes.* When they are golden brown, remove them from the oil with a slotted spoon. Allow the fritters to drain on a paper towel lined plate. Sprinkle them with a little salt if you'd like when they first come out of the oil.

Once they are cool enough to handle, break one of these little guys open! ***Yum!*** Cornbread nuggets seasoned up with great Southern flavor: corn, smoked sausage, black eyed peas, and onions!

Food Nerd Notes: *Hoppin' John is a dish served in the Southern United States consisting of black-eyed peas and rice, with chopped onion and sliced bacon or sausage, seasoned with salt. In the Southern United States, eating Hoppin' John on New Year's Day is thought to bring a prosperous year. Another New Year's Day traditional food, cornbread, can also be served to represent wealth, being the color of gold. Hoppin' John was originally an African-American food before spreading to the entire population of the South. Hoppin' John may have evolved from rice and bean mixtures that were the subsistence of enslaved West Africans en route to the Americas.*

As far as I can tell, a recipe for "Hopping John" in The Carolina Housewife *by Sarah Rutledge, which was published in 1847, is one of the earliest written references.*

Notes:

New Orleans BBQ Shrimp

This recipe for BBQ shrimp makes us feel like we are down at my parents' fishing camp in Cocodrie, Louisiana, where we sit out on the porch and watch the shrimp boats heading out into the gulf as the sun sets over the marshy bayou. In the mornings, after trolling all night, they head back up the bayou with their catch and sell the freshest gulf shrimp you can possibly get. So when we make these shrimp, it transports us to one of our favorite places, and we talk about "Papa's Shrimp." In addition to all that nostalgia, you can make these BBQ shrimp in the time it would take to get in the car, pick up take-out, and get back home. They are super easy, fast, and absolutely delicious. These are great for sitting around the coffee table watching a big game—just make sure you have plenty of crusty French bread on hand. You'll need it to dip in this fabulous sauce!

Let's just start off by saying that the title "BBQ Shrimp" is a bit of a misnomer because there is not barbecue sauce anywhere in the recipe, and these are not put on a grill of any sort. I have no idea where the BBQ Shrimp title came from originally, but folks down here in the Deep South know what you mean when you say it. Rather, the shrimp are simmered in a succulent sauce then allowed to sit and soak up the flavor for a while.

Ingredients

- 1 stick butter
- 4–5 garlic cloves, chopped fine
- ½ cup Worcestershire sauce
- ½ cup white wine
- 5–6 green onions, chopped
- 2–3 lbs shrimp
- Creole seasoning and/or red pepper flakes, *optional*

You probably have all this stuff on hand already!

Notes:

How to…

The basic idea is to throw everything together for the sauce, then add the shrimp last. So to a heavy saucepan, add the following together: butter, chopped garlic cloves, Worcestershire sauce, white wine, and chopped green onions.

Let all the sauce start boiling, then add the shrimp. The ones I used have been cleaned and deveined, and the heads have been removed. I just happened to have these in the freezer. However, if you have head-on shrimp, add those. The heads/shells will actually give you a richer depth of flavor to the sauce (although that's less kid friendly). Add the juice of one lemon. Throw the lemon in for extra flavor. Add Creole seasoning if you wish. I often use Tony Chachere's.

After cooking the shrimp for ONLY 3 minutes, turn off the heat. They will continue to cook in the gravy, and you do NOT want them to be overcooked and rubbery. They will have gone from still transparent looking (not cooked) to pink (cooked). That's how quickly they cook. *And that's faster than waiting for the order of fries to come out of the grease at that other place!* Now… allow them to sit in this "BBQ" sauce for 5–10 minutes. They will soak up the seasoning and all that great flavor in that time. While waiting, throw a loaf of French bread in the oven to get all hot and crispy. As my family will tell you, this is an important part of the recipe. You get a rich, lemony, buttery, spicy, deeply complex sauce bathing the tender little shrimp in goodness… followed by a big chunk of bread dunked in there!

Now, for all of about 10 minutes of work, we enjoyed a wonderful meal together that you would have a hard time going out and finding—and certainly not for this price! Aside from the shrimp, everything else is probably standard pantry items for most of you. And another thing, don't hesitate to buy a pack of frozen shrimp from your grocer. The shrimp are frozen almost immediately after being caught, and they are super convenient.

Note: *As told by the legendary New Orleans Brennan's restaurant… "Like proper barbecue, it's a spicy, succulent mess of a dish that is best eaten with your hands along with good company and cold beverages." Yep. That sums it up rather nicely.*

Grilled Zucchini Rolls

These Grilled Zucchini Rolls would be just perfect for a cocktail party, girls luncheon, etc.! They're very pretty and dainty, but they have BIG flavors! They are very simple to make and could easily be made up and refrigerated until time of service.

I happen to love the combination of herbed goat cheese and roasted red peppers together, and I've often served this combination on a crostini for an afternoon snack or simple appetizer with a nice glass of wine before starting to cook dinner. But since there are a ton of people out there right now who are trying to cut back on carbs, the bread gets the boot this time. Replacing the bread with the grilled zucchini keeps this low-carb but definitely not low flavor! As an extra bonus, both goat cheese and roasted red peppers are low-carb too! WOO HOO!!! *Not a goat cheese fan? Try replacing it with herbed Boursin or ricotta that you've seasoned up and maybe some crumbled bacon*... I'm thinking my kids may go for that one!

Ingredients

2 zucchinis (Each zucchini gave me about 10–12 slices.)

House Italian "lite" dressing

Herbed goat cheese, *If plain, season with kosher salt, black pepper, garlic powder, and Italian seasoning.*

Jarred roasted red peppers, finely diced

How to

Wash the zucchinis and slice them very thinly. For very thin and even slices, use a mandolin. This is not a job for the kiddos, as the mandolin is super sharp! Brush both sides of the slices with Italian dressing and grill for about 3 minutes per side. Allow to cool on a cooling rack placed over a bowl. This will allow them to cool, rather than steam. Once cool, smear a thin layer (less than a teaspoon) of goat cheese along the length of the zucchini slice. Add about ½–1 tsp of diced roasted red peppers along one end, then roll up from that side. The goat cheese is a perfect "glue" to keep your rolls together!

Tip » *After dicing the jarred roasted red peppers into small pieces, dry off all the extra liquid they give off so you won't have a soupy appetizer.*

Notes:

Tzatziki

I've never been to Greece. It's definitely on my list; but for now, I have to settle for the lovely food in the Greek restaurants and various street fairs selling gyros and such. But when you think about it, probably a LOT of the "ethnic" foods we enjoy here (Mexican, Italian, Chinese, etc.) are probably Americanized and may not be exact replicas of the real thing. The point is, this may not be the authentic Greek recipe for Tzatziki, but it's delicious nonetheless. And honestly, if you enjoy something, it really doesn't matter if it's exactly the way it would be done somewhere else around the world. You should make food that YOU and your family enjoy. Food should be fun! I adapted this a bit from one of Ina Garten's recipes.

Ingredients

- 2 cucumbers, peeled and seeded, minced
- 1 Tbsp kosher salt (not table salt)
- 2 cups plain Greek yogurt*
- ½ cup sour cream, *optional*
- 1 Tbsp champagne vinegar, *can use white wine vinegar*
- 2 Tbsp freshly squeezed lemon juice (about 1 large lemon)
- 1 Tbsp extra virgin olive oil
- 2 tsp minced fresh garlic
- 1½–2 tsp minced fresh dill
- Fresh ground black pepper, to taste

**I like the Greek yogurt for this recipe for a couple of different reasons. It's denser, thicker, and creamier than plain American yogurt (which you would have had to strain over a cheesecloth for HOURS to remove extra liquid). Additionally, it has almost double the amount of protein of regular yogurt. That's a definite plus.*

How to...

The only imperative in this recipe is to remove LOTS of the liquid from the cucumbers so the final dip will be nice and thick. Other than that, it's a dump-and-mix recipe. So let's start with that step first. Peel and seed the cucumbers. I used a small melon baller that worked great, but a small spoon would do the trick as well. Ina doesn't peel her cucumbers first; but for my tastes, I find the skins to be too tough in this recipe, taking away from the "smooth, creamy" feel. Cut the cucumbers and then mince them really, really fine.

Now you are going to add what seems like an absurd amount of kosher salt to them. This is going to draw out the liquid. *Okay, to all my former students reading this. What are you thinking right now? Yes! The water parties with the salt! Yep, I knew you wouldn't forget that.* The first time I did this, I only added about half the salt because this amount seems way too extreme. But I found myself adding more to the final dip. So if you are nervous about it, you can certainly go that route since you can always add more later. Put the salted cucumbers in a fine strainer over a bowl. Just let it hang out a while, so you can work on the other ingredients. I think I let mine drain for probably 20 minutes or so.

So while the cucumbers are draining, let's get on with the rest. Into a bowl, add your plain Greek yogurt. Next add the sour cream. This is where you get to make a decision. If you taste the Greek yogurt and the sour cream side-by-side, they are almost indistinguishable. The sour cream may be just a little bit stiffer. So if you are limited on what's in the fridge, you could just opt to add more of the Greek yogurt. I like that extra bit of stiffness and body for my dip, so I add the sour cream. To all this lovely creaminess, add the rest of the seasonings: champagne vinegar, lemon juice, olive oil, garlic, dill, and pepper.

By this time, let's go ahead and try to extract the rest of the cucumber water. Pour out the minced, salted cucumbers onto a clean tea towel. Gather it up and SQUEEZE!!! And then squeeze HARDER! You can see how much more of the liquid is coming out. It's the same thing you've done to spinach all these years. After you can no longer squeeze out any liquid from the cucumbers, add the cucumber "pulp" (well, that's what it looks like to me at this point) into the yogurt mixture. Now mix to combine. Taste and adjust any seasonings. More dill? Pepper? Salt?

It's best if you let the flavors marry for several hours or even overnight. If you are making it for a party, I would suggest making it the day before. Serve as you wish. I served it with pita bread triangles, sliced cucumbers, and strips of sweet yellow and red bell peppers. Oh, how I wished for some Turkish shawarma to eat with it, or a nice Greek gyro to slather it on! But that is way above my culinary expertise! ***Ha ha!***

Food Nerd Note: *By the way, ever wonder why fancy spas give you cucumber water and place cucumber slices over your puffy eyes? Extracts from cucumbers have been shown to have both antioxidant and anti-inflammatory properties.*

Notes:

Mozzarella Caprese Skewers

There is usually at least one night of the week where the others are dispersed to various places, so the little ones and I just get to play in the kitchen. And I don't know about the rest of you, but I really could just live on appetizers! One particular day was more stressful than usual, with a particularly LONG appointment at the pediatric asthma specialist for Lily, so something easy and comforting was just the ticket for me. Some years back, someone gave me a canapé set to make cute little hors d'oeuvres, so we pulled it out. They had fun making shapes out of the little breads and creating little stacked sandwiches to their own liking. Come to think of it, so did I! Of course it would be fine to just cut your bread into squares or rounds if that makes life easier for you.

These awesome little appetizer skewers are about two perfect bites each—crunchy toasted bread, fresh basil, melted mozzarella, juicy tomatoes, and a bit of Italian prosciutto. Seriously… all you need is a nice glass of wine and you are SET!

I would like to give you even ONE exact measurement, but there really aren't any. We just had fun as we went along. Make as few or as many as you'd like. Vary the ingredients to your liking. Make them straight-up cold and fresh, or hot and melty like mine. Have FUN!

Ingredients

- French bread slices (or country white bread)
- Extra virgin olive oil
- Italian seasoning
- Fresh mozzarella slices
- Sliced prosciutto
- Roma tomato slices
- Kosher salt and freshly cracked black pepper
- Fresh basil leaves

How to...

Cut bread into squares or whatever shapes you want. Brush them lightly with olive oil and season with Italian seasoning. Broil until lightly browned (about 3 minutes). Layer the toppings: toast, mozzarella, prosciutto, tomato, kosher salt and black pepper, fresh basil leaf. Repeat the layers, then end with a third piece of toast. Skewer them together.

Tip » *Consider soaking the skewers in water beforehand so they won't burn.*

Bake at 425°F for about 5 minutes or until mozzarella is "melted" the way you want it. Garnish with extra fresh basil and serve hot.

Notes:

Cajun Crawfish Bread

If you are not from the Gulf South part of the United States, it's very possible that you may not be familiar with crawfish. They look like little lobster impersonators! In the spring, "crawfish boils" can be found at many a social gathering down here on the coast. Imagine piles of ruby red crawfish, boiled in spices, dumped out into large tubs and onto newspaper-lined tables, and folks standing elbow-to-elbow peeling and eating them as fast as possible. This is our South!

That said, there are some occasions where you end up with leftovers. So we Southerners generally peel them and put them away in the freezer to make a delicious dish at another time. If you happen to be looking for something fabulous to do with your left-over crawfish tails, consider this Cajun Crawfish Bread as a great appetizer or even a small dinner. If you don't just happen to have crawfish tails left over, don't fret. You can purchase them cooked and frozen.

This recipe is a super easy and fast way to prepare an appetizer for those unexpected guests, or perhaps you are shuttling kids between ball games, music and dance lessons, etc. You just mix, spread, and bake until brown, bubbly, and melty! ***Mmmm!***

Ingredients — 8 servings

- ½ cup mayonnaise
- 4 Tbsp melted butter
- 1 cup shredded mozzarella
- ¼ cup freshly grated Parmigiano Reggiano cheese
- ¼ cup sliced green onion tops
- 1 tsp garlic powder
- 1 cup crawfish tails, finely chopped
- Kosher salt and ground black pepper, to taste
- 1 16-oz loaf French bread, cut in half lengthwise

I also think it would be fabulous with chopped, drained artichoke hearts mixed in. Perhaps about ¼ cup or so.

How to...

Preheat oven to 350°F. In a medium bowl, combine mayonnaise, melted butter, mozzarella, Parmesan, green onions, and garlic powder. *This portion can be made up ahead of time and refrigerated until you are ready to bake it.*

Fold in the chopped crawfish and season to taste with salt and pepper. Spread the crawfish mixture on the French bread and bake for 18–20 minutes. *To make cleanup a breeze, consider baking the crawfish bread on parchment paper.* For the last two minutes, I turn the broiler on high just to get a beautiful brown crispy edge on the bread and really toast up the cheeses in the mixture.

Cut into 2-inch pieces, garnish with a few more green onions, and serve while hot and gooey.

If you used leftover crawfish from a crawfish boil, you may not need to add additional spices. Taste first. If you used frozen crawfish tails from a seafood market or grocery store, you will definitely need to season them.

Food Nerd Notes: *If you do not have crawfish available in your area of the world, you may substitute cooked and seasoned chopped shrimp or lump crab instead.*

Notes:

Hot and Creamy Spinach Artichoke Dip

This is not my normal eating habit, but last night I just wanted to sit on the couch and munch while watching the Grammy Awards. I'm not an advocate for this type of mindless munching; but very occasionally, it can be nice. One of my favorite appetizers is spinach artichoke dip. It has color, texture, flavor, creaminess, and complexity—many of the elements I prize in a dish. That being said, sometimes when you order it, it can be bland and unexciting.

What's really nice about cooking for yourself is that you get to push the limits of the norm and make the dish with a little more razzle dazzle than you've had it before. What distinguishes this recipe from others I've tasted is a little more garlic and heat than some, and the addition of some chopped sun-dried tomatoes, which give it not only more color, but the unexpected tangy sweetness that compliments the velvety creaminess that you are used to.

It's an extremely easy recipe—just combine and bake—and could easily be made ahead of time and popped into the oven just before you need it. The other thing I kept thinking of while I was eating it is how great this would be as a filling for stuffed chicken breasts. Yep, you can find a recipe for that as well on my blog! ***Mmmm…***

Ingredients

- 1 package of frozen spinach, thawed, drained and squeezed
- 8 oz reduced-fat cream cheese
- ¼ cup reduced-fat mayo
- ¾ cup freshly grated Parmigiano Reggiano
- ¾ cup shredded mozzarella cheese
- 4 cloves garlic, chopped

Kosher salt and cracked black pepper, to taste
Crushed red pepper, to taste (about 1 tsp)

- 3 Tbsp sun-dried tomatoes, chopped
- 1 can drained artichoke hearts in water, chopped
- ¼ cup reduced-fat sour cream

Notes:

How to...

Thaw frozen spinach in the microwave (3–4 minutes) and drain. You'll still have to squeeze the liquid out, but this will give it a head start. Combine softened cream cheese and mayo in a large bowl. Add the freshly grated Parmesan. It *will* make a difference. Add the grated mozzarella. Chop and add the garlic. Season with salt, black pepper, and crushed red pepper. Chop and add the sun-dried tomatoes.

Wrap the spinach in a clean kitchen towel and squeeze all the liquid out of it that you possibly can. Yes, it will end up looking like the cud of a cow, which looks pretty gross, but it will taste great. And you don't want all that liquid in the dip. Break up the spinach and add it to the mix. Drain the artichokes. Chop them as fine or coarse as you would like them. This will determine the final texture. Round out the dip with the sour cream.

Combine, adjust seasonings, then add the dip to a casserole dish that has been lightly sprayed with cooking spray. Bake uncovered at 350°F for about 25 minutes. It will be lightly browned and bubbly around the edges. I served this with pita chips, but feel free to use whatever—bread chunks, crackers, chips, snow peas, pepper strips, etc.

Delicious! Now hurry up and share with your neighbors. This is my personal strategy for not sitting here and eating the whole casserole dish full!

Buffalo Chicken Dip

This is one of the easiest, fastest appetizers you can make. As a matter of fact, most of the ingredients are probably in your pantry right now. That makes it perfect for everything from guests who just happen to pop in, to throwing it in a crock pot and bringing it to a tailgating party. I serve the dip with celery, crackers, etc. No joke—the celery is awesome with it! Don't be fooled into thinking this is only for adults. It's really mild enough for a younger audience as well.

Ingredients for a crowd, 20 servings

- 1 lb cooked chicken breasts, *or 2 10-oz cans chunk chicken, drained*
- 2 8-oz pkgs cream cheese, softened
- 1 cup ranch dressing
- ¾ cup hot sauce or hot wing sauce (I used Moore's Buffalo Wing Sauce.)
- 1½ cups shredded extra sharp cheddar cheese

How to...

If using fresh chicken, add seasonings of your choice (I use salt, pepper, garlic powder, basil, and oregano). Pan cook the chicken in a little canola oil and butter. To make it easier, cut the chicken into small pieces first. Add hot sauce when chicken is cooked through. (If using canned chicken, heat the chicken and hot sauce in skillet over medium heat until heated through.) Stir in cream cheese and ranch dressing. Cook, stirring until well blended and warm. Mix in half of the shredded cheese and transfer the mixture to a slow cooker. Sprinkle remaining cheese over the top, cover, and cook on low setting until hot and bubbling, about 40 minutes.

Notes:

Fire-Roasted Corn Guacamole

This just may be the most awesome Fire-Roasted Corn Guacamole that I have ever had! Really! I had some at one of our favorite Tex-Mex restaurants, and it was really, really good—which prompted me to make this. But as I'm not making this for the "masses," I had more freedom to add bigger, bolder flavors.

Complicated? Nahhhh! It took me maybe 10 minutes to roast, chop, dice, grind, and mix this lovely dip. Now… don't we have a football game to watch?! Smooth and creamy avocado, big bright cilantro, roasted jalapeño, garlic, zesty lime, fresh pico de gallo, and sweet crispy fire-roasted corn. Can you taste it yet? Absolutely fabulous! Where are those chips?

Ingredients

These are ingredients are to make just a small batch (gotta have portion control around here). But for more than 2 people, I would consider doubling it.

- 1 ear of fresh sweet corn
- 1 jalapeño
- 2 ripe avocados, removed from peel
- ¼ cup prepared pico de gallo, *I just grab a fresh carton in the produce section.*
- 2 Tbsp lime juice (1 large lime)
- 1 tsp kosher salt
- 2 Tbsp fresh cilantro, chopped
- 2 large cloves of garlic, minced
- Black pepper, to taste
- Cotija cheese for garnish, *optional*

How to

Using long tongs, roast the corn and jalapeño over fire (either on a gas stove or on a grill) until blistered and charred on all sides (not burned, please). After cooling for a few minutes, cut the corn off of the cob.

Chop the avocados, mash or grind, then mix in the pico de gallo. Seed and mince the roasted jalapeño. Add the jalapeño, fresh lime juice, kosher salt, cilantro, the roasted corn, minced garlic, and pepper. Adjust seasonings and serve!

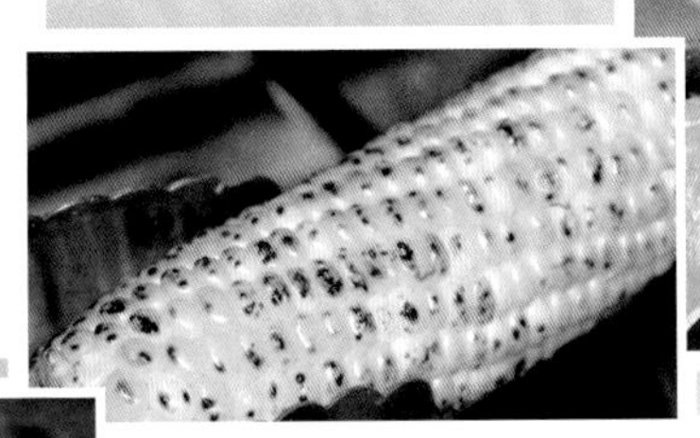

Notes:

Hot Parmesan Artichoke Dip

This hot, creamy dip has been a huge hit every time we have made it. It's extremely simple, easily transportable, and satisfies a wide variety of palates. As a matter of fact, I've never brought any home from a function… as it's usually gone in about 15 minutes!

Ingredients

- 1 cup Parmigiano Reggiano
- 1 cup sour cream
- ½ cup mayonnaise
- 1 8-oz package cream cheese
- 2 large cloves garlic, finely chopped
- 1 can artichoke hearts, chopped small (I used Reese artichoke hearts.)
- 1½ tsp white pepper
- 1½ tsp garlic powder
- 1 Tbsp fresh dill
- ¼ tsp kosher salt
- ¼ tsp cracked black pepper
- 1 large round bread to make the bread bowl, *either sourdough or Hawaiian*

How to…

I sort of wish there was more to this and I could say it was complex or something. But really, all you do is chop everything, mix together, and bake. That's the sum total of the difficulty. **The cheese should be pulverized** in the food processor until it's like sand. This happens to be the fun part of the recipe. After all, who doesn't love turning a big hunk of something into a fine, whirring powder in the food processor? That's the main key to this dish. It can then be mixed with the other ingredients. Add the sour cream, mayonnaise, cream cheese, and minced garlic. Drain and chop the artichokes.

Tip» *Use the artichoke hearts packed in water, NOT the marinated ones. Those have a totally different flavor.*

We've also used ½ artichoke hearts and ½ hearts of palm (also packed in water). The chopped hearts of palm also work really well. The final product just has a bit of a different texture but is delicious.

Add the artichokes, white pepper, garlic powder, fresh dill, kosher salt, and cracked black pepper into the mixture and give it a good stir.

Bake the dip: Spread the dip into an oven-safe dish. Bake for 30–35 minutes at 350°F until all hot and bubbly and slightly brown on the edges.

Prepare your bread bowl: Remove the "top" with a bread knife. Hollow out the bread, leaving a border around the sides and bottom, maybe about an inch.

Assembly: Spoon the dip into the hollowed out bread. Garnish with a little extra dill. Here we have a fork in the road. You can either serve now, or put it back in the oven just prior to serving, and let the whole thing get hot and bubbly (maybe about 15 minutes).

We've prepared this recipe with lower-fat versions of sour cream, cream cheese, and mayonnaise. The low-fat versions do work well and you won't miss the fat at all. It does **NOT**, *however, work well with the fat-free versions.*

Notes:

Roasted Brussels Sprouts with Spicy Garlic Aioli

You may not have considered Brussels sprouts as an appetizer before, but perhaps you should! Something about my mother mentioning to me that they roasted Brussels sprouts for lunch on Sunday really got me inspired. Some little bell went off in my head saying "Ooh... I have some Brussels sprouts in the fridge that need to get used." And that's all it took! We had this as our "appetizer du jour" while we watched the final moments of the Masters Golf tournament. *YUM!* Of course you could have this as a great side for your meal, but it really makes a great snack that you can mindlessly dip, dunk, and pop right into your mouth!

Ingredients

1 lb fresh Brussels sprouts
4–5 strips of bacon
1 Tbsp extra virgin olive oil

Spicy Garlic Aioli Dip

Kosher salt and cracked black pepper, to taste
1 cup reduced-fat mayonnaise
1½ tsp freshly minced garlic (about 2–3 cloves)
1 Tbsp Dijon mustard
⅛ tsp cayenne pepper
1 lime, juiced
1 Tbsp flat leaf parsley, chopped fine

How to...

Quarter the Brussels sprouts. Fry the bacon until crispy, adding a tablespoon of EVOO when about halfway done (to flavor the olive oil with the bacon flavor! yum!). Remove the bacon and use that flavored oil/grease to drizzle over the quartered Brussels sprouts. Turn them over and around in the oil until they are all coated equally. Season well with kosher salt and cracked black pepper. Bake cut side up at 400°F for about 23 minutes until golden brown and crispy. I put them on a parchment paper lined baking tray since it makes clean up super easy.

Tip» *If you heat the limes in the microwave about 15 seconds first, you get more juice out of them.*

Spicy Garlic Aioli Dip

While baking, mix up the remaining ingredients well (all but the parsley). Serve the sprouts hot and crispy with the spicy garlic aioli! Garnish with fresh parsley, a little bit more cayenne, and some cut limes. Taste and adjust seasoning to your liking.

Notes:

Meatball Stuffed Buns

These soft little pillows of goodness come with a surprise tucked inside—an Italian meatball and warm ooey-gooey cheese! They are great dipped in marinara and fun for kids and adults alike. These would be great as appetizers for a party tray, as they are super easy to make and super easy to eat. No utensils required! If you think about it, it's almost like having a meatball sub that you can eat with two fingers.

Ingredients

- 10 frozen fully cooked Italian style meatballs, thawed and cut in half
- 5 sticks string cheese, cut into 4 pieces each
- 1 can biscuits, each pulled into 2 layers (I used Pillsbury golden layers biscuits.)
- Cracked black pepper
- Dried basil
- Dried oregano
- Garlic powder
- Freshly grated Parmesan cheese
- Marinara sauce

Notes:

How to...

Heat oven to 375°F. For this recipe, make it easy on yourself! I love these frozen meatballs. They are well-seasoned, fully cooked, the perfect size, and very convenient; but feel free to use homemade meatballs if you have them handy! These are the ½-oz meatballs. I like to use the flaky "layer" biscuits since they separate well. Cut the string cheese "sticks" into four pieces each. You need 20 small pieces. Separate the biscuits into two layers each.

Cut each meatball in half. Add one meatball half and one string cheese piece to each biscuit. Wrap the dough around it and seal the edges. Place the seam side down into a round cake pan (or actually, I used the largest of my spring form pans). I find that it works best to put the meatball ***first*** with the cut side UP, then the cheese. This will put the rounded part of the meatball on the top when it's all said and done. Season the "buns" with pepper, basil, oregano, garlic powder, and a sprinkle of Parmesan cheese. Bake uncovered at 375°F until golden brown. These are great dipped into a bowl of warm marinara sauce.

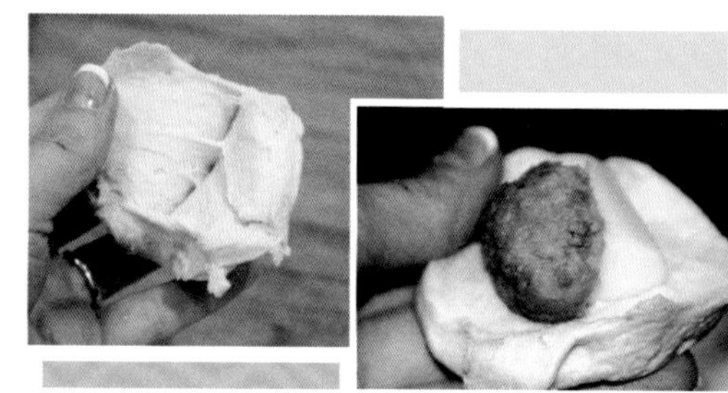

Dill and Sun-dried Tomato Cucumber Rolls

Oh my! These little cucumber rolls are soooo yummy... and fast... and easy! This is one of those recipes that you can throw together in about 10 minutes if you have unexpected guests, forgot you were supposed to bring appetizers to the company party, or just want something a little lighter for yourself or your guests amidst all the heavy holiday foods.

These are a delicate balance of crunchy cucumbers, smooth cream cheese, tangy yogurt, sweet and chewy sun-dried tomatoes, and the brightness of fresh dill. They are very delicate and fancy looking but hardly any work at all!

Ingredients

Use the amounts that you enjoy best, but here is what I used to make this small tray with one large cucumber.

1 large cucumber
Coarse salt
3 oz cream cheese, *Feel free to use the reduced-fat version.*
2 spoons crumbled tomato basil feta cheese
2 spoons plain, non-fat Greek yogurt
1–2 Tbsp sun-dried tomatoes, julienne cut
1 Tbsp chopped fresh dill
Cracked black pepper, to taste

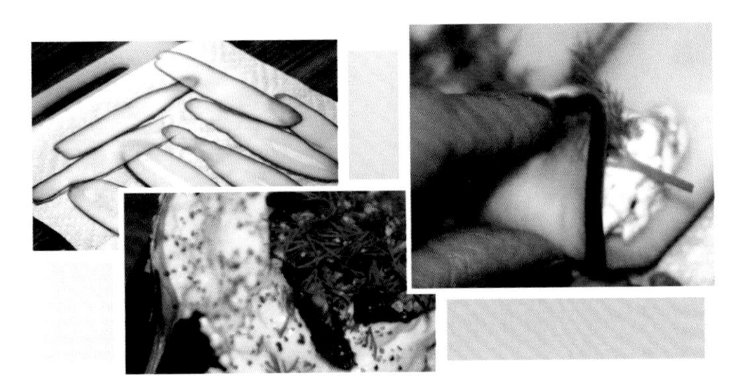

How To...

Slice the cucumbers very thinly. I used the #1 setting on my mandolin. Lay them out on a paper towel and sprinkle with salt in order to extract some of the water out of them.

To a small bowl, begin adding the ingredients for the filling. Add the softened cream cheese, crumbled tomato basil feta cheese, non-fat Greek yogurt, sun-dried tomatoes cut into small strips, and chopped fresh dill. Season with coarse salt and cracked black pepper. Stir well to combine.

Blot the cucumbers dry. Add between a teaspoon and tablespoon of filling. Add a sprig of fresh dill. Then starting on the thinner side, roll the cucumber around the filling. Secure the seam with a toothpick that has been broken in half, or go all the way through if you have some fancy party toothpicks you desire to use.

Notes:

Louisiana Crab Claws Bordelaise

This is quite possibly my oldest child's favorite dish in the entire world. Any time he sees it on a menu, he feels compelled to order it... and it usually says "Market Price" if you catch my drift. (By the way, they are only about half the price of what they charge in a restaurant when you make them yourself!) But if you only knew how ridiculously simple and fast this appetizer is to make, you would rush out and make some NOW! The entire dish is done in about 15 minutes! There's no way you can beat that for a ritzy, fancy-looking, delicious appetizer like this.

> **Note:** *Many restaurants call these "marinated crab claws," but some recipes for marinated crab claws are served cold. This dish is served hot.*

Now for some of y'all who aren't from the South, you may be asking, "What exactly is a Bordelaise anyway?" Well, think of an awesome scampi recipe and jack that up a few notches! A Southern Bordelaise absolutely demands that you sop it up (a term Southerners use) with some good crusty French bread. So we end up with big meaty crab claws swimming in a buttery garlic and green onion sauce with a hint of tang from the dressing and lemon. ***My, oh my!***

Ingredients

enough for about 6 people as an appetizer

- 1 Tbsp Creole (or Cajun) seasoning
- 1 Tbsp parsley, chopped
- 3 Tbsp green onions, chopped, plus more for garnish
- 4 tsp garlic, chopped
- 6 Tbsp butter, divided
- 16 oz fresh crab claws
- 6 oz chicken stock
- 2 oz Italian dressing

How to...

Add seasoning, herbs, garlic, and 4 Tbsp butter in a *preheated* skillet. Sauté until the butter is melted. Add in the seafood, chicken stock, and dressing. Increase the heat and cook until the seafood is cooked through (only about 5 minutes). Do not boil. Turn off the heat and stir in the remaining butter. Garnish with additional chopped green onions and a squeeze of fresh lemon juice. Serve hot with crusty toast or grilled French bread.

Food Nerd Notes: *Bordelaise sauce is a classic French sauce named after the Bordeaux region of France, which is famous for its wine. The traditional sauce is made with dry red wine, bone marrow, butter, shallots, and demi-glace sauce. Traditionally, bordelaise sauce is served with grilled beef or steak, though it can also be served with other meats that pair well with red wine demi-glace based sauces. The sauce has appeared on US restaurant menus since 1882, if not earlier.*

Now, let's get to the **New Orleans Bordelaise.**

A Bordelaise sauce in traditional New Orleans cooking is different from the French classical version. The basic flavor is garlic, rather than red wine and bone marrow. The sauce called Bordelaise in New Orleans is more like a fusion of French and Creole—and as early as a 1904 recipe calls for butter, olive oil, chopped shallots, garlic, and parsley. This combination is the foundation of the classic escargots bordelaises, a dish that was available in New Orleans restaurants in the early 1900s.

Notes:

Steamed Asian Dumplings

Well, so much for specificity in the title, huh? I have tried to research the origin of these dumplings and have managed to come across myriad stories, names, and explanations from multiple Asian cultures—Chinese, Japanese, Vietnamese, Cantonese, and Korean. At the very least, it seems everyone wants to claim a piece of these little guys. And who wouldn't? These fragrant, tender little dumplings are nothing short of delicious! We've probably all had them in one form or another at some point, whether they were steamed, fried, boiled, or simmered in a sauce. In reading the description from the various cultures, mine seem to be most closely aligned with the Chinese steamed dumplings, rather than the Japanese (which use a wonton dough that is quite a bit thinner).

Regardless, I think these are great. Truthfully, they are a bit time consuming, but they're not difficult to make at all. That said, the steps could definitely be broken down into several make-ahead parts and assembled later, or assembled early and frozen or cooked later. All the sites I visited reported that the homemade dough tastes so much better than using pre-made wontons, so I thought I would give it a whirl. I have watched several chefs on television fret over making the crimps and folds just right, etc., which just makes everyone scared to attempt them. I figured the worst that could happen is that we would make a huge mess and laugh about it later. No harm, no foul. But actually it was a lot of fun! We were VERY pleased with the outcome, the authenticity, the texture, and the flavors… and just plain proud of our little dumplings.

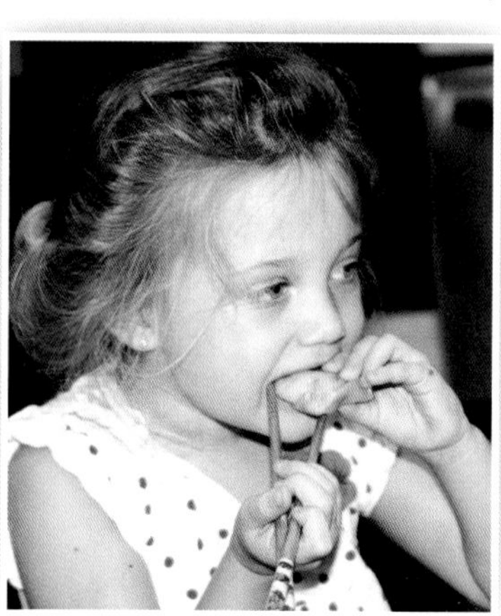

So next time you have some time with your kids, grandkids, neighbors, or friends, just make some! Good times, skill building, and making memories with the kids is ALWAYS worth it!

Oh, and one more thing—these share little resemblance to some of the deep fried, greasy dumplings that I've had in some of the restaurants. Steaming the dumplings is a totally fat-free step, and you can add as many healthy veggies as you want to them! Even my oldest teenager, who won't go near a vegetable, loved them… and he even looked inside and saw the green and orange. Ha! There's a new miracle each day!

Ingredients

Dough

4 cups all-purpose flour (plus more for working and rolling dough)
½ tsp salt
1¾ cups boiling water

Filling

2–3 cups Napa cabbage, chopped fine plus enough leaves to line steamer
½–1 tsp salt
1 lb ground pork
2 Tbsp plus 1 tsp fresh ginger, minced fine
2 Tbsp dried apricots, minced fine
A small handful of green onions, chopped fine (approx ¼ cup)
1 large carrot, grated
2 Tbsp soy sauce
1 Tbsp plus 1 tsp sesame oil
Black pepper, to taste, *optional*

Dipping Sauce

⅓ cup soy sauce
⅓ cup rice wine vinegar
1 tsp sesame oil
1 Tbsp brown sugar
⅓ cup chopped green onions or chives
Sriracha chili sauce for heat, *optional*

How to...

a. Prep

Dough: In a stainless steel bowl, mix 4 cups flour and ½ tsp salt. Slowly add boiling water to flour in ¼ cup increments. Mix until a ball is formed and the dough is not too hot to handle. The original recipes say to mix with chopsticks. That is probably over my head, so we Americanized this step with a spoon. On a floured surface, knead the dough until it becomes a smooth, elastic ball. Knead, push, fold over, then turn 90 degrees and repeat—again and again. This took me about 10 minutes. Place back in bowl and cover with a damp cloth. Allow to rest for at least 1 hour.

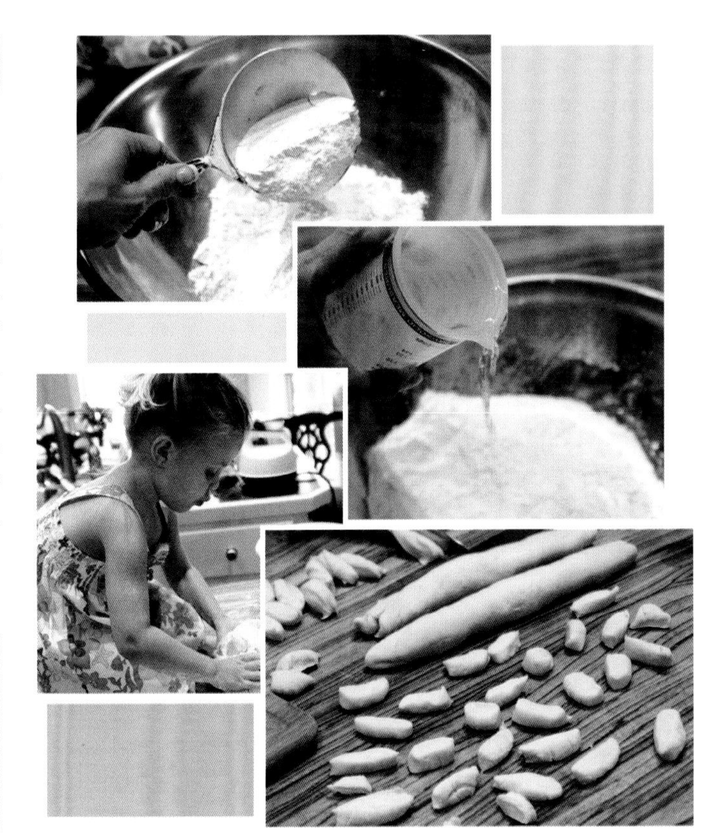

Notes:

Cabbage: Chop the cabbage and sprinkle with ½ Tbsp salt. Allow it to stand for 30–45 minutes to draw out the water. Place the cabbage on a clean dishtowel and squeeze out any water (just like when using frozen spinach). The drier the cabbage the better.

Filling: Combine ground pork, ginger, apricots, green onions, carrots, and wilted cabbage in a non-stick skillet. Break up the pork into small pieces while it is cooking. Add in the soy sauce and sesame oil and continue cooking until pork is cooked through. Check for seasoning. I think I also added a sprinkling of black pepper at the end. Turn off the heat and allow to cool so that you can handle it.

Sauce: Combine all ingredients and serve in a small bowl.

b. Assembly

Working on a floured surface with floured hands, cut the dough into several large chunks that are of manageable sizes. Roll out the dough to form long noodles, about 1 inch in diameter. Our noodle would have wrapped around the kitchen, so we cut it into chunks first. Cut the dough into ½-inch pieces and turn them over so the cut sides are facing up. Flatten them with your palm and roll out **thin** using a rolling pin. The dumpling wrappers should end up about 3–4 inches in diameter.

Place a small mound (1–2 tsp) of filling in the middle of the wrapper, being very careful not to touch the edges with the filling (this will prevent proper sealing of the dumplings). Wet one edge of the wrapper and fold in half over the filling to form a half-moon shape. Starting on one end, fold/pinch the wrapper tightly together. We found this worked better if we wet these edges as well. Proceed with this fold/pinch method until the dumpling is completely sealed. Some directions instructed that we should expect 10 to 14 folds per dumpling. ***Ha!*** Don't worry about how many you get. This isn't *Iron Chef*, and no one is judging you. Have fun! Allow the dumplings to rest with the folded edge straight up. My son got creative with his shapes and made several unique designs that we enjoyed.

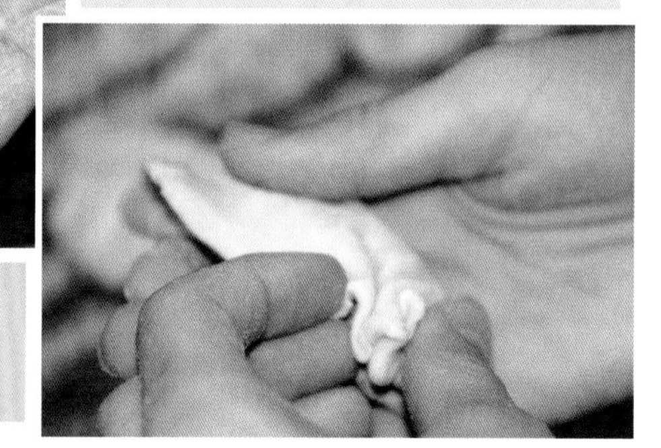

At this point, you can cover them and put them in the fridge to cook later or even freeze them. *If you freeze them, I recommend laying them out separately in a single layer on a sheet pan to freeze, then placing them in a zip-top freezer bag. If you put them in a bag while the dough is still a bit sticky, you may end up with one big giant dumpling clump! Not attractive.*

c. Cook

Add a small amount of water to the bottom of a wok (around 1 inch). Set a bamboo steamer down into the water. The water level should almost, but not quite, touch the bottom level of the steamer.

Line the steamer trays with Napa cabbage. This prevents the dumplings from sticking to the steamer. The steam will go up through the cabbage. I was worried about this, but it worked like a charm. Place dumplings on the cabbage and cover with the second filled "tray" and the cover. Allow the water to boil so that steam will rise up through the bamboo steamer. I steamed the dumplings for around 10 minutes (once it really started steaming). Serve on a bed of Napa cabbage with the dipping sauce on the side. Delicious! Light. Flavorful. Tender. NOT greasy!

I asked around at my local Asian market if you could just use an electric steamer (like the one I use for broccoli). He said, "Yes, you can; although it will not taste quite the same. The bamboo steamer is partly responsible for giving it its own unique flavor." Right now, I'm pretty darned happy about the $11 that I spent on the bamboo steamer. What a great price for authenticity!!

Footnote: *While I was in graduate school, my major professor was Dr. Yuan Luo. Dr. Luo, who was from China, made us many dumplings over the course of the years we worked together. Her dumplings had a way of making those long lab meetings a lot more enjoyable and brought us all together—regardless of the multicultural personalities working together. This is where I really learned to love these tasty bites. I can't believe it took me this long to attempt them on my own!*

Dr. Luo, if you are reading this… thank you. You taught me so much! Your encouragement and confidence in me meant so much… and I still remember you saying "Julie, make a plan." I wish you were here to taste these!

Roasted Red Pepper Hummus

My son asked me to send hummus to his school party since they were celebrating the end of a big Greek and Roman history unit. Interesting how you get "volunteered" for these things! Apparently it was a big hit because the container came back almost empty! Sure, you can pick some up at the market, but it is so insanely easy to make (not to mention tastes great) that there's no reason not to make it from scratch. Basically, you dump it all into the food processor and give it a whirl! That's it! A super-easy, healthy, and delicious appetizer!

Ingredients

- 1 15-oz can chickpeas (garbanzo beans), drained
- ¼ cup fresh lemon juice (about 1½ large lemons)
- ¼ cup tahini
- 2 large cloves of garlic, minced coarsely
- 1 tsp kosher salt
- ⅛ tsp cayenne pepper
- ½ tsp ground cumin
- ¾–1 cup jarred roasted red peppers, drained
- 2 Tbsp extra virgin olive oil plus more for serving, *optional*

Notes:

How to...

Drain the chickpeas. I used the reduced-sodium version, but feel free to use whichever kind you prefer. Add the chickpeas to the food processor, then all the other ingredients except for the olive oil. While the processor is doing its job, drizzle in the extra virgin olive oil. Process the mixture until it's creamy and smooth.

Garnish with extra diced roasted red peppers, a drizzle of olive oil, and a bit more cayenne. Serve with pita bread triangles or chips. Cover and store in the refrigerator up to several days. But it won't last that long!

Cooks

Party Foods

Family

Breakfast and Brunch

Honey Maple Granola

Granola is one of those things that's just so versatile! It's great as is for a snack, you can have it as any other cereal with milk, it's great on top of yogurt, you name it! When you pick up a package of granola at the market, however, the list of nonfood items in the ingredient list can be pretty long—there are many preservatives and such in there. Believe me, this is *such* an easy-to-make, healthy snack for your whole family! There is a ton of protein from all the nuts, a good source of dietary fiber and iron in the oats, and wheat germ is one of the most highly (naturally occurring) concentrated sources of vitamin E.

The other thing about making it at home is that you get to customize it any way you would like. So feel free to use your favorite dried fruit (apricots, raisins, blueberries, etc), change up the nuts as you see fit, and add or delete ingredients however you would like. Have fun with it and enjoy!

Ingredients

- 4 cups old fashioned oats
- ⅓ cup sunflower seeds, shelled and salted
- 1 cup rice cereal (I used Rice Krispies.)
- ¾ cup pecans, chopped fine
- ½ cup sliced almonds
- ½ cup walnuts, coarse chopped
- ½ cup wheat germ
- ¾ tsp table salt
- ¼ cup light brown sugar, packed
- 4 Tbsp maple syrup
- ¼ cup plus 2 Tbsp honey
- 1 cup coconut oil
- 1½ tsp ground cinnamon
- 2 tsp vanilla (I used clear Mexican vanilla.)
- ⅔ cup dried fruit (I used dried cherries.)
- 1 cup coconut

Notes:

How to...

Mix the first 7 ingredients together in a large bowl. In a separate saucepan, mix the salt, brown sugar, maple syrup, honey, coconut oil, cinnamon, and vanilla. Bring this syrup mixture to a boil for 2–3 minutes, then remove from heat and pour over the oatmeal mixture. Stir until well mixed. Pour out the mixture onto two parchment paper lined baking sheets and spread it out. Bake at 250°F and stir every 15 minutes for a total of 1 hour. *Every time I stirred the granola, I rotated the pans.* For the last 15 minute segment, add the cherries and coconut, divided equally between the two baking sheets. Remove from the oven and let cool.

Note: *It won't really crisp until it cools. Store in an airtight container once totally cool. Then watch it disappear!*

Orange Julius Smoothies

The other day I woke up with a craving for an Orange Julius. Do you all remember going to the mall many years ago as a teenager and having these? Where I grew up, they were hard to miss. It's the perfect eye opener in the morning with the bright sunny flavor of orange juice, yet creamy and frothy all at the same time. Really they are just one step away from being like an orange sherbet in a drinkable form.

Anyway, I happened to be gearing up for my morning run, and I needed something to get me going without being heavy enough to weigh me down. I have only recently been able to run with *anything* in my stomach at all. So I decided to give this a try as a pre-run meal. To get to the bottom line, I've done this a couple of times now and decided that it is perfect for me before a run. Each time, I've shaved off a minute from my run time. Now whether it was all in my head or not, these are great!

In less than 5 minutes, you can have one, too! Lots of vitamin C to bolster your immunity (here in the flu season), lots of calcium, and a secret ingredient to increase the protein count!

Ingredients

- 8 oz soymilk (I used Silk Very Vanilla Soymilk.)
- 6 oz orange juice concentrate
- 1 Tbsp egg white powder
- 1–2 cups ice, depending on how thick you want it

Notes:

How to...

Add all the ingredients into your blender and combine. The amount of ice you add will determine how thick the drink is. Serve immediately.

Now even if you aren't lacing up to go for a run, I'd be willing to bet you are running around trying to get your kids ready for school. These would be perfect to mix up, divide among the kids, and take them on the go as you drive them to school in the mornings, or to their practices and recitals in the afternoons. ***Cheers!***

Food Nerd Notes:

» *If you choose to use regular milk, you will probably want to add some sugar and vanilla, but the Very Vanilla Soymilk has both in it already, in addition to having twice the calcium of dairy milk. If you've never tried this product, give it a whirl… it's quite yummy! And the fact that it's sold in individual portions that do NOT have to take up space in the refrigerator is a big plus.*

This el cheepo brand of orange juice concentrate was fairly sweet, so in the end, I did NOT add any additional sugar. Other brands may differ in taste. Do not throw away the other half of the container. Just put it back in the freezer… you'll be making more of these!

» *Feel free to use a plain egg white in this drink if that is your preference. I have done that before, as well. (The chances of getting salmonella are like 1 in 30,000.) Neither the egg white nor the egg white powder changes the taste at all. They help to make the drink frothy, and they definitely increase the amount of protein in the drink. The egg white powder is pasteurized, comes in a can that is shelf stable for a long time, and can be added to other drinks or baked goods.*

Green Eggs and Ham in a Cup

I am one of the worst offenders for skipping breakfast. Somewhere between my morning cup of coffee and getting the kids fed and off to school and myself to work, eating breakfast often never makes it to my thought process. Well this is one breakfast that you can make in about 5 minutes with whatever breakfast ingredients are in your kitchen, and it is a pretty darn complete meal… with TONS of nutritional value to get your day started off right! You don't even have to sit at home and eat it—just grab the mug and go!

Ingredients

Let's just start by saying that you do NOT have to use the same stuff I did. This is just a recipe concept that you can personalize with whatever ingredients you have on hand, or your whim of the day.

For one large mug

1 Tbsp frozen bell peppers, chopped, *I used orange and green. Fresh peppers can be used.*
1 small shallot (about 1 Tbsp), *You can use a tablespoon of chopped sweet onion as well. This is just what I had on hand one morning.*
¼ cup fresh baby spinach, stems removed and chopped, *If you are anti-spinach, try a couple leaves of chopped fresh basil or even a little prepared pesto.*
1 stick of low-fat mozzarella string cheese, diced
1 oz reduced-fat sharp cheddar cheese, diced (about the size of a dice cube)
1 Tbsp butter-flavored spread (I used the Brummel and Brown Spread that is made with non-fat yogurt.)
2 slices of honey ham, chopped
2 slices of cooked bacon, crumbled, *You could use turkey bacon; I had leftover "real" bacon from the kids' breakfast.*
2–3 eggs, *You could use non-fat egg substitute.*
Splash of milk
Salt and pepper, to taste
A sprinkle of dried basil
Chives and cherry tomatoes for garnish

Let's see, have we included all of the food groups or what? This grab-and-go breakfast is definitely packed with nutrition! This may be one the easiest breakfast "meals" ever!

How to...

Grab your frozen veggies, etc. and give everything a chop. Add the butter or butter spread in the bottom of a mug, then start adding the vegetables. Cook for 1 minute in the microwave. They all cook down to almost nothing. Add in the ham and bacon. Combine the beaten eggs with a splash of milk, salt, pepper, and dried basil. Add the eggs to the cup.

Microwave for 1 minute, then give them a stir. Add the chopped cheeses and microwave for 1 minute more. Your eggs should be all set but still tender and fluffy after this. Now grab a fork, grab your mug of eggs, grab a carton of OJ, and you are OUT the door! You will NOT feel compelled to stop at Denny's after this! Go out and conquer the world!

Notes:

Strawberry Vanilla Bean Pancake Sauce

What could be better than waking up to the smell of pancakes in the morning? For my kids, it's THE breakfast of choice! Some people like great big pancakes, but my kids like the mini pancakes best. I make them about the size of a silver dollar. They've figured out that this is the ideal dipping size.

For my daughter, syrup on the pancakes is only a consolation prize. What she really wants is strawberry dipping sauce. And who can blame her? This sweet, fragrant strawberry vanilla bean sauce just begs for the pancakes to be dunked into. We can pretty much buy strawberries year-round these days, although they aren't always the sweetest when they are not in season. This is a great use for those that may not be perfect for eating out of hand. ***Mmmm***... warm, ooey-gooey goodness to get everyone's day off to an even sweeter start!

Ingredients

2 cups fresh strawberries, rinsed and chopped
⅓ cup sugar
Juice of ½ lemon
The "seeds" (caviar) from one vanilla bean, *In a pinch, use about ½ tsp vanilla.*
¼–½ tsp cornstarch plus 2 Tbsp water

Notes:

How to...

Cut up about 2 cups of fresh strawberries. To the strawberries, add sugar, lemon juice, and vanilla bean seeds. Cook on medium until thick and bubbly. The strawberries will release their juices, break down, and mush up. You can use a potato masher to break down the strawberries or leave them chunky if you want. You could also purée the sauce in a blender if you wanted it really smooth. Once the strawberries are broken down, add the cornstarch slurry. Mixing the cornstarch with a couple of tablespoons of water first to create a slurry will keep it from getting lumpy.

Then cook until thick, and that's it! Serve your pancakes and strawberry sauce with a dollop of whipped cream for breakfast perfection!

Food Note: *Vanilla is the second most expensive spice (after saffron) because growing the vanilla seed pods is labor intensive. Despite the expense, vanilla is highly valued for its flavor, "pure, spicy, and delicate," and its complex floral aroma. As a result, vanilla is widely used in both commercial and domestic baking, perfume manufacture, and aromatherapy.*

Funky Monkey Morning Smoothies

Even though I know it *should* be part of my routine, I won't even pretend that I'm a breakfast person. It's weird, because when we are on vacation, I love breakfast. But as a regular daily thing… eh. I'd rather just have my coffee and get on about the business of the morning (like making breakfast and lunches for the kids). I have been trying to do better with the occasional bowl of cereal or eggs and such. But one morning, I hit on something that I really enjoyed, so I'm passing it along to you!

These smoothies take less than 5 minutes to whip up, and that's just because you have to go to the pantry and such to get everything out. Lots of protein in here to keep your blood sugar stabilized, lots of potassium, and the best thing: they taste pretty similar to a Reese's Peanut Butter Cup in a drink! Woo hoo! And you can dump it in a glass and jump straight into the car without slowing down to actually sit and eat. Sorry, but time is a hot commodity! They would also be great after a workout or for an afternoon snack for the kids.

Ingredients for 2 glasses

- 8 oz soymilk (I used Silk Very Vanilla soymilk.)
- 1 large ripe banana
- 2 Tbsp peanut butter (I used 100% Natural Peter Pan honey roast creamy.)
- 1½ Tbsp unsweetened cocoa powder
- 3 Tbsp granulated sugar or raw sugar
- 1–1½ cups ice

How to…

Process everything together and serve immediately. If you don't have a blender with a strong motor, or if you want to make them up ahead of time so you won't wake up everyone in the house with the blender, you could make them without the ice and refrigerate, then serve over ice.

Notes:

Breakfast Casserole

I had this for the first time when I was expecting my oldest child and was in town looking for a home. I remember how special and welcome it made me feel as a guest. So in turn, this is a casserole that I like to make when I have special guests in for the holidays (like my parents). It's so yummy for them to wake up, smell the coffee, make their way downstairs, and get hit with the aroma of this casserole, some creamy grits, and maybe some fruit salad… ***Mmmm*** … starts the day off right!

Ingredients

- ¾ lb breakfast sausage, *your choice of pork or turkey.*
- 1½ Tbsp melted butter
- 3 slices white or wheat bread, crusts removed
- ¾–1 cup extra sharp cheddar cheese
- 4 large eggs, well beaten
- 1 cup heavy whipping cream
- ½ tsp table salt
- ½ tsp dry mustard
- ¼ tsp black pepper
- ¼ tsp dried dill
- ¼ cup red bell pepper, diced small
- ¼ cup green bell pepper, diced small
- ¼ cup yellow bell pepper, diced small
- ¼ cup sweet onion, diced small

Notes:

How to…

Cook sausage well and drain on a plate lined with a paper towel. If you need to save time, you can purchase breakfast sausage "crumbles" that are already fully cooked. Melt butter in glass casserole dish. (A 9-inch square casserole works great.) Tear bread in small pieces and sprinkle over butter. Sprinkle drained sausage over breadcrumbs. Add the onions and peppers to a microwave-safe dish and "sauté" in the microwave for about two minutes. Sprinkle these cooked vegetables over the sausage. Sprinkle cheese over the vegetables. Beat eggs and cream, add rest of ingredients, and stir together; pour over mixture.

Chill for 8 hours or overnight in refrigerator. Bake at 350°F in the oven for 40–50 minutes I find it best to cover with aluminum foil for the first 40 minutes, then remove the foil for the last 10 minutes to allow the top to brown slightly.

Cinnamon Spiced Banana Caramel Pancakes

Ingredients

1 cup buttermilk "complete" pancake mix
¾ cup plus 1 Tbsp water
2 Tbsp sugar
1 tsp clear vanilla
½ tsp cinnamon
1 banana, cut into slices about ⅓–½ in thick
Caramel sauce of choice
A bit of shredded coconut

This may seem like a lot of sugar, but my kids often like to eat "mini" pancakes with no syrup because they are sweet and have that great vanilla in them—and that makes for a lot less cleanup than with the syrup. Expect 6–9 pancakes depending on size.

Oh what a mouthful! You know how when you get home from your wonderful tropical beach vacation, and you are missing all the exotic breakfast items from that humongous buffet, regular pancakes just don't seem as exciting? Or maybe you are just dreaming of that vacation! Nonetheless, these pancakes will bring you back to the sounds of the ocean waves lapping up on the beach, seagulls swooping through the salty air for a lost chip on the sand, the smell of sunscreen, and new paperback novels laid out on carefully reserved cabana chairs at six o'clock in the morning just so you can't get one for the rest of the day. (But that's a whole different story.)

Snap out of it! You are at HOME! There are kiddos to feed, laundry, dishes, and floors to be tended to. But all that will be a lot easier to stare down if you start the day off with a fabulous breakfast. You know I'm right! These cinnamon spiced pancakes are extra special with the banana slices getting all roasted and gooey in the middle and topped off with a little caramel sauce and coconut. You can at least pretend for five minutes that you are somewhere special while the kids are watching cartoons.

The bottom line is that I often buy too many bananas; and when they get really sweet and ripe, the kids decide that they no longer want any. Sigh. So this is sort of like a food recycling program.

Please be advised, these are not totally from scratch. There is no time for that in the mornings.

How to...

Mix the pancake mix, water, sugar, vanilla, and cinnamon. I use clear Mexican vanilla (the best you can find). I like my batter to be fairly "loose" for the pancakes that my family prefers. Do not overmix the batter, or the pancakes will be tough. There will probably still be some lumps in it. That's okay. They'll cook out.

I like to spray a nonstick pan with butter-flavored cooking spray and heat until a droplet of water shaken into the pan starts sizzling. On a medium-high heat, add some sliced bananas to the pan. Pour the batter over them. This will allow the bananas to come in direct contact with the hot pan so they will sort of caramelize on their own. When the batter looks fairly dry on top and the bubbles "stay," the pancakes are ready to be flipped. *You can probably turn down the heat to medium from here on out. Once my first pancake is about done, I always lower the heat.*

Top pancakes with caramel sauce and shredded coconut. ***Yum!*** Okay, so if you don't like coconut, leave it off. More for me!

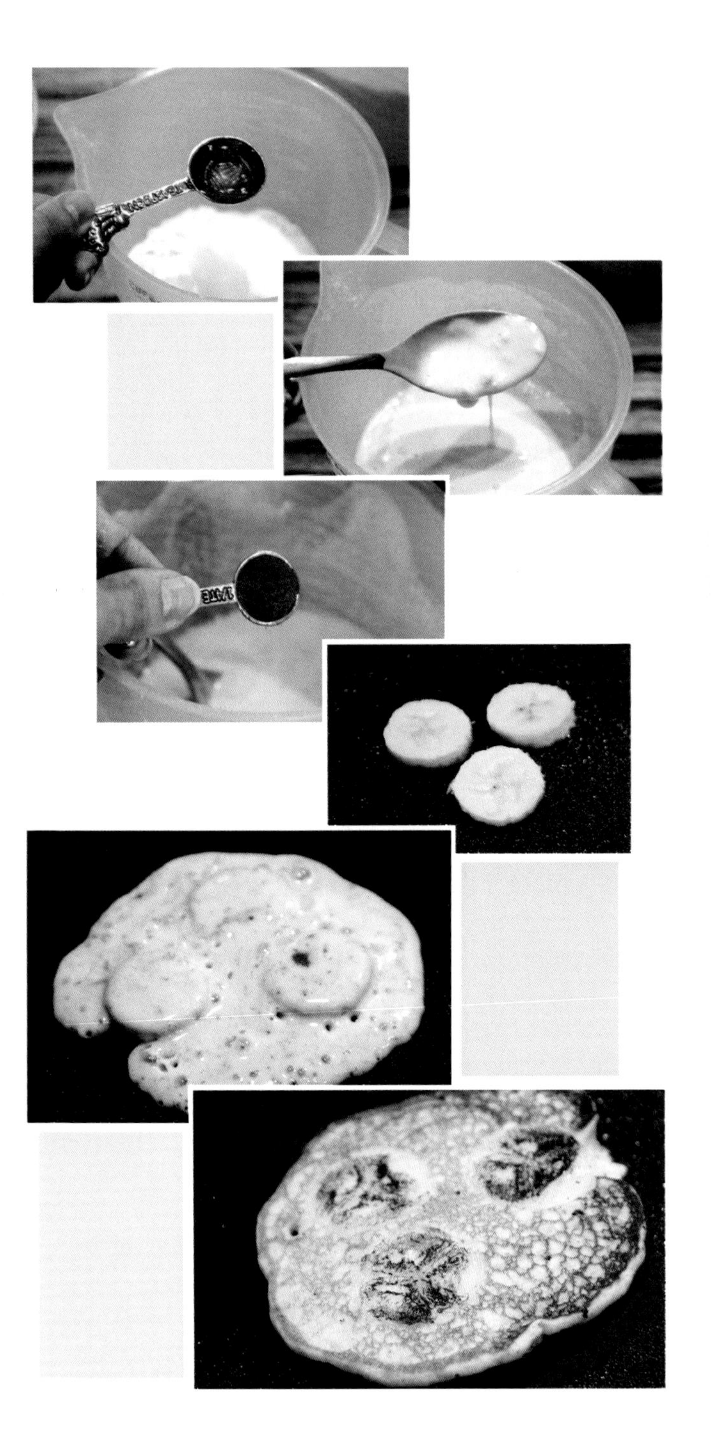

Food notes: *While you are cooking, notice the cinnamon in the batter and stop to smell the aroma. Watch as the bananas start caramelizing in the pan. They are soft and sweet and delicious. Enjoy the process as well as the food!*

Notes:

Andouille Breakfast Potatoes

These breakfast potatoes are one of my kids' favorite weekend breakfast choices. At our house, we call them "Papa Potatoes" because Papa makes these for the grandkids when we visit. The flavor experience is this: a perfectly cooked potato that is slightly crispy-crunchy on the outside, but buttery soft on the inside; sweetness from the almost-caramelized onions; smokiness from the Andouille sausage; then the assertively pine-like fragrance and pungent flavor of rosemary that brightens the whole bite! Are you interested yet?

Ingredients

Enough potatoes to feed your "crew", *at least enough to fill the bottom of a black iron skillet*
½ cup sweet onion, diced
½ lb smoked Andouille sausage, cut into small chunks, *or good smoky pork sausage*
1 Tbsp vegetable oil
Creole seasoning, to taste (I used Tony Chachere's.)
1 sprig of fresh rosemary, stripped from the stems

How to...

Cut the potatoes into half-inch chunks. I like to use the small red potatoes. The point here is to parboil them before adding them to the skillet. Raw potatoes would burn on the outside before the inside was cooked. Chop, cover with water, and then pop them into the microwave for about 10 minutes until they are fork tender but still firm (but not breaking apart). Drain the cooked potatoes. Chop up a small sweet onion. Use the smokiest pork or Andouille sausage your grocer has to offer. It doesn't necessarily need to be spicy (that is entirely up to your palate), but you do want to go for SMOKY. Slice the sausage in whatever size you desire. I prefer "coins" because they stay a little softer when you render the fat and cook them. My kids prefer the coins cut into quarters because they get crunchier.

Cook: Add the sausage to a black iron skillet to start rendering the fat. This smoky fat will be an important factor in flavoring our potatoes! When the sausage is starting to crisp, add the chopped onions to them. You may need to turn down the heat to medium and cook the onions a little lower to get them to a nice caramelization level without burning them. Once the onions are soft and brown, remove the sausage and onions to a bowl… but keep as much of the sausage grease as you can in the pan. To the sausage grease, add maybe another tablespoon of canola oil to the pan and then add the drained, cooked potatoes. You ideally want the potatoes to fit in a single layer covering the bottom of the skillet. Once you get them in there, DO NOT mess with them for a while! You want to sort of sear them to create that crunchy crust. Also, if you stir them around too much, they will mush up.

Season with Tony Chachere's Creole seasoning or your Creole seasoning of choice. Remember, this can get pretty spicy. I think there may be a light version of this in the seasoning aisle of the grocery store if you are sensitive to heat. Alternatively, you could use salt, pepper, and garlic and onion powders. Cook them on medium to medium-high heat until the bottom of the potatoes are golden brown. Then turn them with a metal spatula.

While the potatoes are putting on that golden coat of crispy crunchy goodness, strip the rosemary from the stems and chop them (medium-fine). *The rosemary brings the flavor palate to a whole new level. If you are rosemary adverse, you could use fresh oregano or parsley, but our family likes the rosemary. I use about a full sprig.* To strip the rosemary, hold the stem at the end and pull back on the tender leaves towards yourself with your thumb and index finger. Remember: It's essential that you continue to season at each step. These are potatoes. Potatoes need lots of seasoning or else they will be bland! Do not under-season them, or you will be disappointed.

Once the potatoes are golden brown, crunchy on the outside, and soft on the inside, add the sausage and onions back to the skillet. Turn off the heat and add the chopped rosemary to the potatoes. Check for seasoning again.

Serve: After removing the Andouille sausage breakfast potatoes to a plate, while the potatoes are cooling down from molten lava status to just hotter than Hades, consider frying up a couple of eggs. As a more grown-up option, consider frying up a couple of eggs in a little butter-flavored cooking spray, salt, and pepper. Gently turn after all the whites have just set and add that soft-medium fried egg on top of the potatoes. Garnish with a tiny bit more of the chopped rosemary. When you cut into the egg, the rich yolk will ooze down into the potatoes. Now can you just taste it?

Note: *My mother does an alternate version of this where she leaves the potatoes in the pan, makes a well in the center, then breaks the eggs in the middle. She lets the egg cook right in the middle, like a nest. So many endless variations! Isn't cooking fun?*

Ham, Caramelized Onion, and Gruyere Quiche

These individual quiches are an excellent option for a light lunch or dinner or perhaps a special brunch menu. You all know how much I love caramelized onions—so sweet and almost creamy—and they pair so well with the smoky ham, the nutty Gruyere cheese, and the bright, verdant flavors of fresh thyme. You have lots of protein represented here; and afterward, you won't feel like you've had a big heavy meal.

These can easily be made ahead of time, refrigerated, and reheated to serve. Have you have seen what they charge for individual-sized quiches in a bakery or sandwich shop? They are so easy to make; and chances are, you probably have most of this in your kitchen already!

Ingredients

for 5–6 individual tart quiches

Refrigerated "roll out" pie crust
1 medium-large onion, cut into medium slices
2 Tbsp butter
¼ cup smoked ham, cut into small pieces
⅓–½ cup Gruyere cheese, grated
3 eggs
¼ cup milk
¼ cup evaporated milk or cream
1 Tbsp fresh thyme, stripped from the stems, *or ½ tsp dried thyme*
¼ tsp dry mustard
½ tsp kosher salt
¼ tsp black pepper

Notes:

How to...

Roll out the pie crust on a lightly floured surface. Cut the pastry a little larger than the tart pans and press into the pans. Cut off the excess so that the dough is flush with the top of the pans. Prick the bottom of the dough with a fork several times. Now bake the empty shells at 400°F for about 9 minutes. You'll want them to be set with only a tiny bit of color. *If you allow the dough to come to room temperature rather than baking it while it's still cold, I think it may "shrink" less.*

Let's move on to the onions. Sauté sliced onions in the butter low and slow until caramelized. This is really the only "slow" step. They will probably take 20–25 minutes. *This step could also be done ahead of time. You can caramelize the onions and store them in the refrigerator until you need them.*

Prepare the other ingredients. Chop your ham into small pieces and grate the cheese. Combine the eggs, milk and cream, thyme, dry mustard, salt, and pepper.

Assembly time! Add a healthy tablespoon or so of cheese to the bottom of each pastry. Add some ham. Add some of the caramelized onions. Now ladle some of the egg mixture over each tart—approximately 1 ounce to each tart, ladled right over the filling.

Bake uncovered at 350°F about 20–25 minutes. A clean knife inserted into the center should come out clean, but you don't want too much color on the egg. Allow them at least 5 minutes or so to rest before cutting into one.

Food Nerd Notes: *A quiche is a savory, open-faced pastry crust dish with a filling of savory custard with cheese, meat, fish, or vegetables. Although known as a classic French dish, the quiche originated in Germany. The word quiche means "cake" which came from the German word Kuchen. Today, quiche is considered as typically French. However, savory custards in pastries were known in English cuisine at least as early as the fourteenth century. Recipes for custards baked in pastry containing meat, fish, and fruit are referred to as Crustardes of flessh and Crustade in the 14th and 15th century cookbooks as well.*

Cranberry Orange Muffins with Brown Sugar Pecan Crumble Topping

On one particular trip down to the New Orleans Jazz and Heritage Festival, I popped into a coffee shop and picked up a cranberry orange muffin. Oh, my! I realized how long it had been since I had enjoyed one of these. The sweet, tender muffin is a joy when paired with the juicy burst of tangy cranberries and the sweet crunchy topping. It's a nice balance without having just an overly sweet muffin. But WOW, they are so pricey! So after getting back home, I dug through a bunch of old handwritten recipes that I had collected over the years, remembering a recipe given to me by a dear friend for cranberry bread when we were in professional school together. I adapted it a bit to make these muffins with a crunchy brown sugar pecan crumble topping. My mother was the one who showed us her love by making everything just a bit extra special; and my friend Jackie was the one that showed me that you could do it all— be a great mom, wife, friend, and professional… and STILL find the time to cook at home!

Ingredients

Brown Sugar Pecan Crumble Topping

- ¼ cup oatmeal
- ¼ cup all-purpose flour
- ¼ cup pecans, finely chopped
- 3 Tbsp brown sugar
- 1 tsp cinnamon
- ⅛ tsp salt
- 3 Tbsp melted butter

Muffin Batter

- 2 cups sifted all-purpose flour
- 1 cup sugar
- 1½ tsp baking powder
- ½ tsp baking soda
- 1 tsp salt
- ¼ cup butter, slightly softened
- ¾ cup orange juice
- 1 egg, well beaten
- ½ cup chopped pecans
- ½ cup whole cranberries

Tip–*They are pricier, but if you need a time-saving step, you can purchase the pecans already chopped.*

How to...

Preheat oven to 375°F. I like to prepare my pans before making the batter when I'm baking. That way, I am ready to go! Spray your muffin tins with non-stick cooking spray. I use a butter-flavored spray.

Make the crumble first. Just dump all the topping ingredients together, butter being the last thing. Mix all ingredients with a fork until it looks like coarse sand. It's a no-brainer. Set aside the topping.

Now make the batter. Mix all of the dry ingredients for the muffin batter together. Remember to sift your flour, as it makes them airy to help avoid packiness. Cut in the butter until the mixture resembles coarse cornmeal. Add in the beaten egg and the orange juice all at once, then prepare your cranberries. I like to dredge mine in a bit of flour first. It helps absorb some of the juice as they bake, and it also keeps them from "dropping" to the bottom. Then add the whole cranberries and nuts to the mix. Just blend them in. You do not want to overmix the batter, or they will be tough. It will be thick and pretty lumpy. That's fine.

Spoon the batter into 6 jumbo muffin tins. Divide the crumble topping evenly over the top of the batter and push down slightly. Bake in the preheated oven for about 35 minutes or until a toothpick inserted into the center comes out clean.

The added benefit » *Your house will smell divine!!*

Notes:

Note: *You could cook these faster by making them into the standard size muffins rather than the jumbo muffins. Adjust the baking time accordingly (probably 25–30 minutes). Conversely, you could also spread the batter into one bread pan and make into a loaf, baking for 50–60 minutes.*

Let them cool for a few minutes in the muffin pan. To remove them, run a knife around the edges first before inverting the muffins. You WILL lose some of the topping. Expect it. But it's fabulous to clean up—feel free to snack on what falls!

Now cut one of these tender, fragrant muffins open. ***Oh, MY!*** Tart juicy cranberries, the slight orange flavor, the sweet and crunchy topping of brown sugar and nuts! ***OH, YEAH!*** That will definitely make someone's breakfast or brunch sweeter!

Ham Cups

So it's always a little difficult cooking eggs for a crowd, right? At least for me they are. My mother drilled into my head that one of the most important considerations in cooking is timing everything such that all the dishes are ready at the same time. No one wants cold eggs!

Well, this is a super-easy way to make really cute eggs for everyone that will all be done at the same time. These are so easy to individualize to each person's taste with the fillings. The fact that the oven does all the work frees you up to cook the other things… or refill juice cups… or change the channel to a different cartoon… AND they are delicious!

Ingredients

It's a little hard to say what ingredients should be used because you could add any ingredients under the sun to these, but basically, I allowed about ½ egg per cup.

Onions and peppers, diced small
A small pat of butter
Ham slices, a little thick
Grated cheese
½ egg per cup
A little heavy cream (or milk)
Salt and pepper, to taste
A couple of young green onions

Notes:

How to…

Sauté the onions by adding a bit of butter to frozen onions and peppers, and microwaving for 2 minutes. *I told you this was a no-brainer recipe!* Spray muffin tin cups with non-stick cooking spray and line each with a slice of ham. Add the cooked onion and peppers, and then sprinkle in some shredded cheese of your choice. Combine eggs, cream, salt, and pepper and beat well with a fork. Pour in the egg mixture. Chop the green part of a small green onion and divide onto each. Feel free to add your fillings of choice (perhaps fresh baby spinach and tomatoes with a little feta). Bake at 350°F for 20–25 minutes.

So your final ham cups are just perfect! Fluffy, cheesy, eggy filling—salty, crunchy outside. So… Sam-I-Am, I believe even Dr. Seuss would be proud of these Green Eggs and Ham!

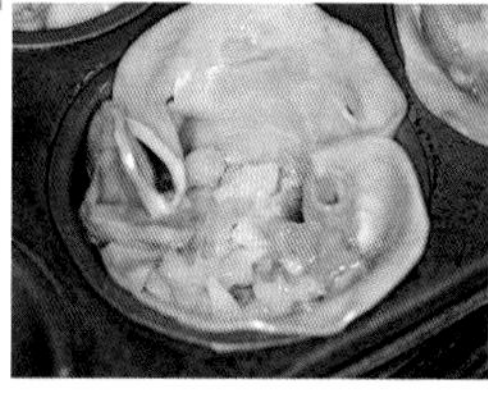

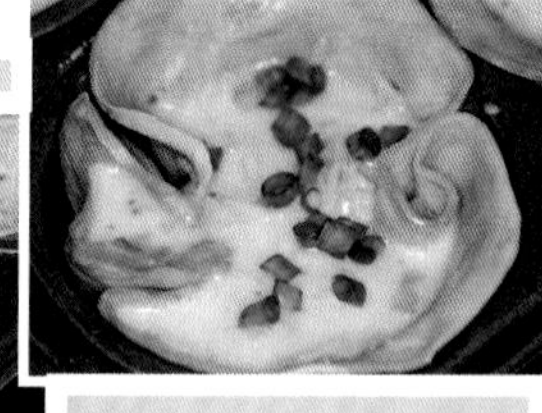

Bacon Pancakes

When I was a girl, we often had breakfast for dinner. Something about breakfast food just embodies comfort. You certainly don't have to have these for dinner. These would be great as a "make-and-take" breakfast while driving the kids to school. I just really love having that salty and sweet taste together. And I bet your kids or grandkids would think they were an awful lot of fun, too!

Has it been one of those days? Need I say more? You know, a day that requires either some lovely libation or some comfort food? Maybe this evening, it's the latter.

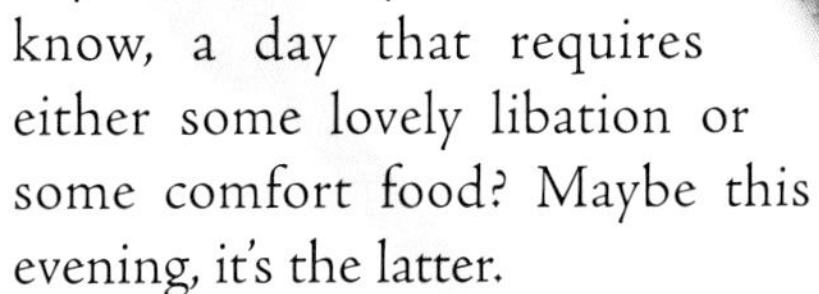

How to...

There is no recipe for this. Just cook some strips of nice smoky bacon, then pour your favorite pancake batter over it along the strip. Flip when the top gets bubbly and slightly dry around the edges. Dip into syrup. ***Yum!** Try it with maple bacon for that great salty/sweet maple flavor!*

Notes:

Breads, Salads, and Sandwiches

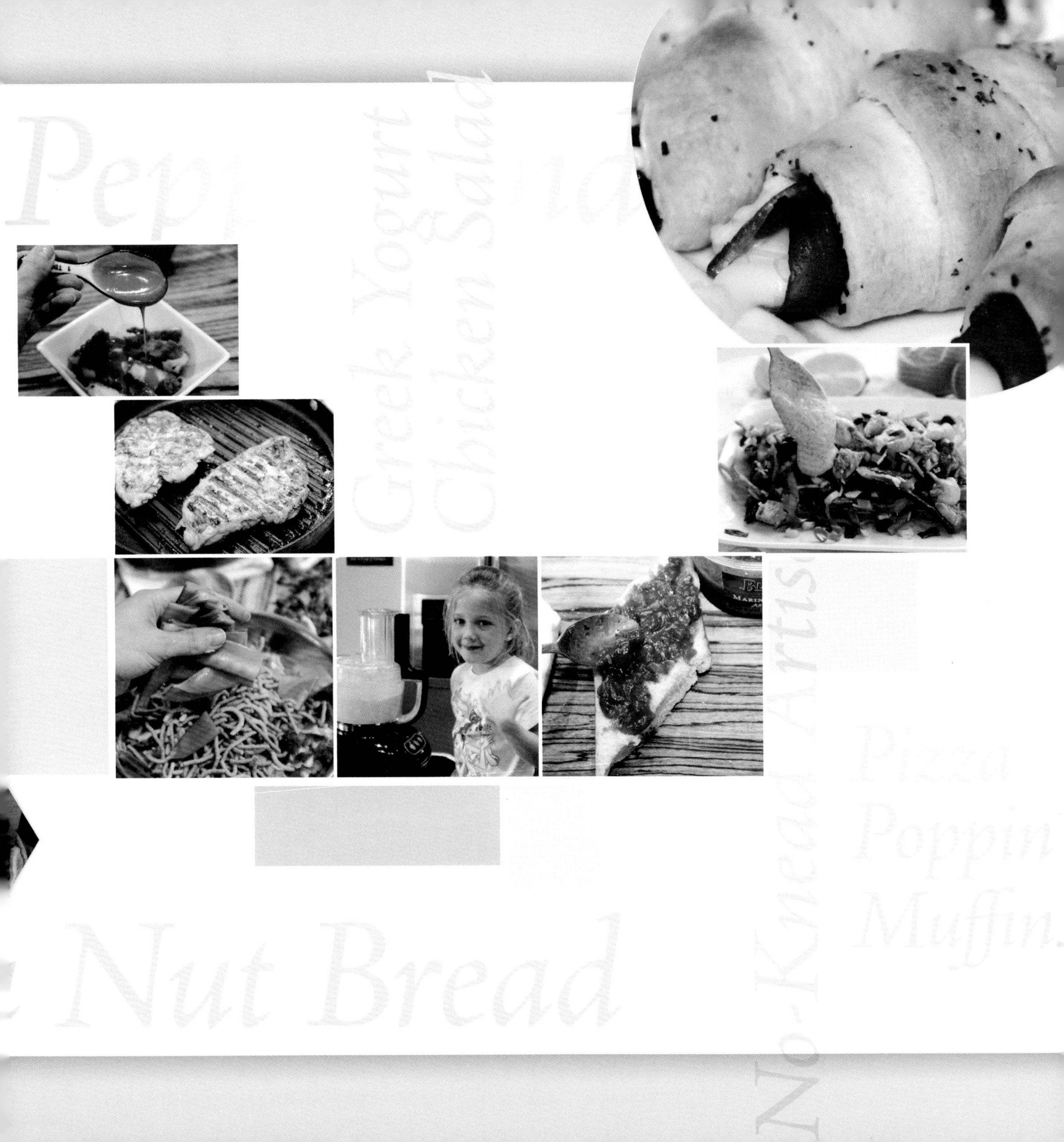
Greek Yogurt
Chicken Salad
Nut Bread
Pizza

Greek Yogurt Chicken Salad

Love chicken salad but find yourself wincing at the thought of all that mayo wrecking your diet? Well, you won't find one drop of mayo in this one! The Greek yogurt is a great substitute for the mayo, especially when you consider that it has NO fat and TONS of protein! The roasted chicken is complimented by the zing of the sun-dried tomatoes and champagne vinegar, the crunch from the pecans and celery, and the sweetness of the grapes. This would be perfect for your brown-bag lunch for the office!

So if you are like me, and you are always looking for something healthy to bring for lunch (really to avoid the temptation of the drive-thru window), this one hits the spot!

Ingredients 4–6 servings

- 2 cups roasted chicken, *Pick up a rotisserie chicken from the market. I used only the breast meat.*
- 2–3 Tbsp sun-dried tomatoes
- ½ cup chopped pecans
- ¼ cup chopped celery (1 stalk)
- ⅔ cup halved red grapes
- ⅔ cup plain Greek non-fat yogurt
- 1 tsp champagne vinegar, *can substitute a good white wine vinegar or apple cider vinegar*
- Kosher salt and cracked black pepper, to taste

If you would like more or less of any particular ingredient, go for it! The point is to make it your own and have a great, balanced chicken salad with lots of taste and lots of texture that is healthy and enjoyable!

How to...

Remove the breasts from the rotisserie chicken and chop into bite-sized pieces. Mix in the rest of the ingredients! Yes—it's that easy!

Serve as you like it. The possibilities are only limited by your imagination! You could try it on a bed of mixed salad greens, with crackers, with celery sticks, in a hollowed out tomato or avocado, in a pita pocket, rolled into a wrap or flatbread, on sandwich bread… YOU decide and have fun with it!

BLT Buffalo Chicken Wrap

This happened to be one of "those days." I woke up before daylight with a headache, which persisted the entire day on and off. I could just tell this was not going to be a cooking night! Chicken tenders and mac-n-cheese for the kids. Yes, really. I know that every parent out there has those kinds of nights every once in a while! But anyway, from the leftover chicken tenders, I made myself a really awesome buffalo chicken wrap, so it wasn't entirely a bad evening.

This is a fabulous way to use up extra chicken tenders from the kids, or whatever cooked leftover chicken you may happen to have. Adding all the salad ingredients into the mix really gives this wrap a fresh crunchiness, and the garden spinach tortilla makes me feel like I'm incorporating even more veggies into this quick meal.

Don't get me wrong—these made a very satisfying (and filling) dinner, but they would be just awesome to fix for your brown-bag office lunches, picnics, tailgating, etc.! Don't worry—even the guys will enjoy these. After all, what guy doesn't love buffalo chicken?!

Ingredients — makes 1 wrap

About 3 oz cooked chicken, *Yes, I used leftover chicken tenders!*
Buffalo chicken sauce of your choice (I used Moore's. It's not too incredibly hot. About 2 Tbsp per serving.)
Garden spinach wraps, *Sure—use whatever kind you want!*
Prepared buttermilk ranch dressing
Romaine lettuce blend
Blue cheese crumbles, *I used the reduced-fat kind.*
Shredded cheddar cheese, *I used a reduced-fat Mexican blend.*
Diced fresh tomatoes
Diced avocado spritzed with lime juice
Chopped cooked bacon

Notes:

How to...

Let me first say that making any type of sandwich (or wrap) is a very personal thing. With four kids, I know all too well that each person has their own preferred balance of flavors and ingredients. So I have intentionally left off amounts from the ingredient list. A recipe is meant to be a guide, not a Bible, so definitely make this to your taste!

Cut your chicken into strips and drizzle it with a couple of tablespoons of buffalo chicken sauce to coat. Layer your ingredients onto your tortilla. I begin with a nice smear of the ranch dressing so it will sort of hold all the ingredients to the wrap. Layer on the lettuce, buffalo chicken, and all the rest of your ingredients. Wrap and roll, baby! Then slice and serve with a side of ranch for dipping.

These have so many great textures, big flavors, crunchy ingredients, smooth ingredients, my beloved cheese, and tangy and creamy flavors. ***Woo Hoo!*** And don't forget that these are mobile, which means that your lunchbox will be the envy of the office.

Thai Chicken Salad Cones

This is a fabulous wrap for your brown-bag office lunches! With lean protein and Thai-inspired salad fixings, this wrap comes with lots of crunch and textures, rather than lots of guilt from fast food! The flavors are big and bold and sure to be palate pleasing. Either way you look at it, I assure you, you aren't going to find this in a drive-thru window. I think you're really going to like this!

Ingredients

makes 6–8 wraps

- 4 oz (1 handful) of snow peas, blanched 2 minutes
- 3 cups Napa cabbage, rough chopped
- 1 cucumber, peeled and seeded, diced
- 3 green onions, snipped (only the green parts)
- ½ cup fresh cilantro, chopped
- ½ cup dry roasted peanuts, rough chopped
- 1 cup crunchy chow mein noodles
- 2 cups rotisserie chicken breast meat, cut into chunks
- Garden spinach herb tortillas
- Asian Toasted Sesame Lite dressing (2 Tbsp per wrap)

How to...

To prep for this salad: Blanch the snow peas briefly, only about 2 minutes. Then remove them and let them cool. Then just start throwing it all together. Mix together the Napa cabbage, cucumber, green onions, cilantro, peanuts, snow peas cut in half, and chow mein noodles. Debone the chicken and give it a rough chop into bite-sized pieces. Toss to combine. Wait to dress the salad until you are ready to prepare the wraps.

To assemble: Divide each tortilla in half, which will create a semi-circle. Add ½ cup of salad mix to each spinach tortilla semi-circle. Add 2 Tbsp dressing and roll up into a cone. ***Enjoy!***

Variation: For making into wraps, rather than cones, keep the tortillas whole. Add 1 cup salad mix, 4 Tbsp dressing. Roll up burrito style, wrap in waxed or parchment paper, and cut on the diagonal.

So we have a wrap that is super fresh, balanced, and very flavorful, with lots of crunch and texture. It has lots of lean protein and big flavors! And it's healthy and fast! PERFECT for your lunch box!!

Note: *If you are making enough wraps or cones to use up all of the salad mix at once, you can add dressing to the whole salad. But if not, add the dressing to each individual portion so the salad doesn't become wilted.*

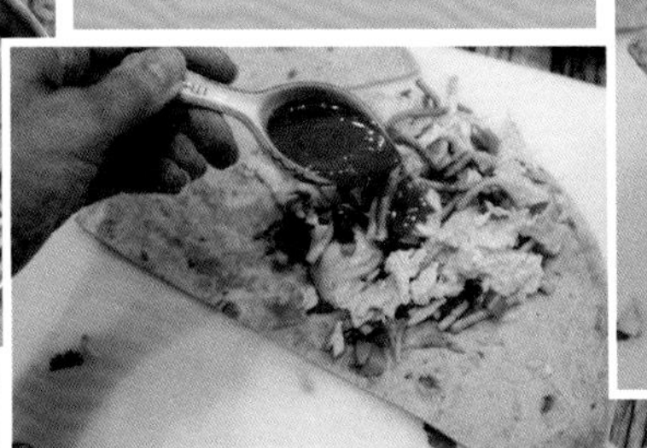

Toasted Couscous Salad with Asparagus and Tomatoes

One thing I love about visiting my parents is that I can experiment on them! They are up for pretty much any new recipe I throw at them, which makes them excellent test subjects. On this particular visit, I was looking to make something light and healthy, but really flavorful and easy. I settled on this toasted couscous salad, and it was a big hit! We ALL went back for seconds!

Couscous may look like a grain, but it is really tiny pasta. Toasting it first makes it fragrant and gives it a slightly nutty flavor. We added enough protein and veggies to make it a full but light meal, and the flavorful vinaigrette adds a LOT of flavors to bring it all together! This would be perfect lunch or a light and healthy dinner dish when you don't want to feel weighed down—and it couldn't be much easier. You could easily make this a vegetarian option with vegetable broth and maybe some big, meaty mushrooms.

Ingredients

- 4 cups chicken broth or stock, *Feel free to use a broth base or even bouillon cubes.*
- 2 cups couscous
- ½ bundle of fresh asparagus, cut into 2 in pieces
- ¼ cup lemon juice
- ½ cup extra virgin olive oil
- 3 Tbsp capers, drained
- ⅓ cup fresh basil, cut into thin ribbons
- Zest of 3 lemons
- ½ pint grape tomatoes, cut in half
- 6–8 thinly sliced green onions (scallions)
- 2 cups cooked chicken, cut into bite-sized chunks
- 1 Tbsp kosher salt
- 1½ tsp black pepper

Notes:

How to...

Begin by heating up the chicken broth. While broth is coming to a boil, toast the couscous. Over moderately high to high heat, dry toast the couscous in a wide pan, stirring as you go, until golden brown and fragrant (about 5 minutes). Once the broth has come up to a boil, stir in the couscous, toss in the asparagus spears, cover, and turn off the heat. After 5 minutes, the broth should be absorbed and you can fluff it with a fork.

During that 5 minutes, prepare the vinaigrette: combine lemon juice, olive oil, capers, basil, lemon zest, tomatoes, green onions, cooked chicken, salt, and pepper. Now, combine the cooked couscous and asparagus with the vinaigrette and stir gently to combine. I prefer it served hot; if you would like to serve it as a cold salad, of course that is up to you. If you will not be serving it immediately, consider making additional vinaigrette. This is a pasta, and it will soak up all the vinaigrette. You don't want it to be dry when you serve it!!!

As for our synopsis? Yes—it was DELICIOUS! Yes—it is healthy! Yes—it was fast and easy and would fit into the "under 30 minutes" category quite nicely! And it was a fabulous way to recycle some leftover chicken. I think it would also be really great with some pan-sautéed shrimp.

Food Nerd Notes: *So, just what exactly IS this couscous pasta? Archaeological evidence dating back to the 10th century, consisting of kitchen utensils needed to prepare this dish, has been found in North Africa. To this day, couscous is known as "the North Africa national dish." In the Sahelian countries of West Africa, such as Mali and Senegal, pearl millet is pounded or milled to the size and consistency necessary for the couscous. In Algeria, Morocco, Tunisia, and Libya, couscous is generally served with vegetables (such as carrots, potatoes, turnips, etc.), cooked in a spicy or mild broth or stew, and has some meat added in (generally, chicken, lamb, or mutton).*

In preparation, semolina is sprinkled with water and rolled with the hands to form small pellets, sprinkled with dry flour to keep them separate, and then sieved. This process is very labor-intensive. In the traditional method of preparing couscous, groups of women would come together and make large batches over several days. These would then be dried in the sun and used for several months. Couscous was traditionally made from the hard part of the durum, the part of the grain that resisted the grinding of the relatively primitive millstone.

Nutritionally, couscous is among the healthiest grain-based products. It has a glycemic load per gram 25% below that of pasta. It has a superior vitamin profile to pasta, containing twice as much riboflavin, niacin, vitamin B6, and folate, and containing four times as much thiamine and pantothenic acid. In terms of protein, couscous has 3.6g for every 100 calories, equivalent to pasta, and well above the 2.6g for every 100 calories of white rice.

Grilled Ginger-Sesame Chicken Salad

I found this recipe from celebrity chef Curtis Stone in one of my magazines, pulled it out, and knew I had to make it. I am SO happy that I did! The salad was easy to make, FULL of HUGE flavors, and very little fat. This dressing doubles as the marinade for the grilled chicken, gives us salty soy, sweet hoisin, spicy Sriracha, and rich sesame oil, all dancing together in this amazing dressing. In short—***Yes! It's amazing!*** What a hit this would be at a potluck gathering!

Notes:

Ingredients

Marinade and dressing

- ¼ cup soy sauce
- 3 Tbsp fresh ginger, peeled and finely chopped
- ¼ cup canola oil
- 2 Tbsp hoisin sauce
- 1 Tbsp sesame oil
- 1 tsp Sriracha sauce
- 1 tsp kosher salt
- 2 large chicken breasts, boneless and skinless
- ¼ cup red wine vinegar
- ¼ cup finely chopped green onions (white and green parts)

Salad

- 1 lb Napa cabbage, very thinly sliced
- 2 carrots, grated
- 3 green onions, thinly sliced and cut on the diagonal
- ⅔ cup freshly cut cilantro leaves, coarsely chopped
- 1 tsp white sesame seeds, toasted, divided, hold some for garnish
- 1 tsp black sesame seeds, toasted, divided, hold some for garnish
- ½ cup slivered almonds, dry toasted, divided, hold some for garnish

How to...

Marinade

Whisk together the soy sauce, ginger, canola oil, hoisin sauce, sesame oil, Sriracha, and salt to make the marinade. Wow, you HAVE to smell this! Put the two chicken breasts in a gallon sized zip-top bag and add 3–4 Tbsp of the marinade over the chicken. Reserve the rest of the marinade for the dressing. Squeeze the air out of the bag so that the marinade comes into contact with the meat. With a meat pounder (or heavy pan, or empty bottle), pound the breasts to a uniform thickness. This will allow them to cook more evenly and also help tenderize the meat. Allow the flattened chicken breasts to marinade 30 minutes.

Dressing

To the reserved marinade (which never touched the raw chicken), add in the vinegar and green onions. Now we have the dressing.

Grill the Chicken

To a hot grill pan (yes, an outdoor grill or "regular" pan is fine), add the marinated chicken breasts. Cook them about 4 minutes per side or until there are no signs of pink and juices run clear when pierced with a small, sharp knife. Transfer the chicken to a cutting board and allow them to rest 15 minutes. Please don't cut them right away. All the juices will run out leaving you with dry meat! After the 15 minutes, you will cut them crosswise into ¼-inch slices. It doesn't matter that they are cool after this amount of time. They are going into a salad!

Salad

In a large bowl, add the cabbage, carrots, green onions, cilantro, half of the sesame seeds, and half of the almonds. Add the chicken strips and mix together. Add just enough of the dressing to coat the salad lightly and toss together.

Serve

Distribute salad to 4–6 plates. Re-whisk the dressing and drizzle a little over each salad. Garnish with the remaining almonds and sesame seeds on each salad.

Cajun Chicken Salad

This chicken salad has a smoky flavor because of the sausage, sweetness from the sun-dried tomatoes and apples, crunch from the celery, and brightness from the lemon juice. It's great as a sandwich, alone with crackers, or over mixed salad greens.

How to...

Sauté chopped onions and Andouille sausage in butter until onions are soft and translucent. Add the chopped chicken, sausage, and sautéed onions to food processor and blend until desired consistency. Add other ingredients and then season to taste.

Ingredients

- ½ cup onions, chopped fine
- ⅓ lb smoked Andouille sausage, *or really smoky pork sausage*
- 1 Tbsp butter
- 3–4 cups cooked chicken, minced into small pieces, *Feel free to use a cooked rotisserie chicken or cook your own.*
- 4 green onion tops, finely chopped
- 1 stalk celery, finely chopped
- ⅓ cup apple, finely chopped
- 1 handful sun-dried tomatoes, chopped small
- 1 lemon, juiced
- 1 cup light sour cream
- ¼ cup mayonnaise
- Salt and pepper, to taste
- Creole seasoning, to taste

Notes:

Cranberry Pecan Chopped Autumn Salad

So occasionally there are those nights when we don't have everyone home. No hubby. No big kids. Just a quiet night to play, with no practices to shuttle to and no big production of a meal. So I grab a rotisserie chicken from the supermarket (one of my favorite "go to" pick up items). It's much healthier than picking up fast food, feeds more people, and costs less. For the little kids, of course they wanted something to go with the chicken, like buttered noodles with freshly grated Parmesan cheese and basil. For me, I turned some of that rotisserie chicken into a lovely and satisfying autumn salad. (And then I ate their leftover pasta. Shame, shame, shame. Pasta will probably be my downfall.) Anyway, I digress.

How to...

So basically, you throw all the stuff together and enjoy! In a large salad bowl (or individual plates), combine the lettuce, pears, cranberries, pecans, bacon, and feta cheese. Tear the rotisserie chicken and add on top. I actually mixed the poppy seed dressing WITH the balsamic vinaigrette first, and then drizzled them generously on top. I probably used a 2:1 ration of poppy seed to balsamic dressing. Toss and enjoy!

You have just had a generous serving of dietary fiber, vitamins and minerals, oleic acids (an essential monounsaturated fatty acid), antioxidants, protein, and goodness! Now you can go eat some pasta!

Notes:

This salad is a very nutritionally balanced dish. We have the fruits and veggies category covered, proteins in the nuts and meat, and dairy from the feta. As a flavor and mouth-feel description, that translates to crunchy, bright lettuce, sweet caramel flavor of the glazed nuts, creamy and tangy feta, crisp, sweet brightness of the pears, smoky bacon and savory chicken, and little pops of sweetness from the cranberries. Can I get an ***"Amen?!"***

Ingredients

I made only one portion, but here are the ingredients to feed about 4 people, using this as a main course.

- 6–8 cups chopped romaine lettuce blend, with carrots and purple cabbage
- 2 medium pears, peeled and chopped
- 1 cup dried cranberries (I used Craisins.)
- 1 cup chopped glazed pecans
- 8 slices of good smoky bacon, crisp-cooked and chopped
- 4–6 oz tomato basil crumbled feta cheese
- Rotisserie chicken, torn into bite-sized pieces
- Poppy seed salad dressing
- Balsamic vinaigrette

Sour Cream Banana Nut Bread

This is the perfect cure for buying too many bananas! In our house, I usually only buy a few bananas at a time, as our family rarely eats a whole bunch of them; but sometimes when I send my sweet husband to the store with a grocery list, he comes back with practically the whole tree! When bananas are really ripe and sweet, there are few things better to do with them than this. Banana nut bread is a great snack with a great balance of nutrition. This recipe will make 1 large loaf, but these little individual loaves are super cute and just the right size for a bake sale, teacher gifts, neighbor thank you gifts, a quick breakfast, etc.

This recipe came from one of my favorite cookbooks, *Celebrations on the Bayou*, given to me some 20 years ago by a dear friend. I've been making this ever since then. When my oldest child was a toddler, it was sometimes the only thing I could get him to eat. These days, he's way bigger than I am, but he still loves this great recipe. Just the smell alone is enough to bring him bounding down the stairs, which tells me that the allure of this super-easy recipe still works like a charm!

Ingredients

- ½ cup butter
- 1 cup sugar
- 2 eggs, beaten
- 1½ cups flour
- 1 tsp baking soda
- ½ tsp salt
- 1 cup mashed bananas (about 3 bananas)
- ½ cup sour cream, *I use the "light" version.*
- 1 tsp vanilla
- ½ cup chopped pecans

How to...

Cream together the butter and sugar. Add eggs and mix well. Sift together: flour, soda, and salt. Combine the flour mixture with the butter mixture. Add the bananas, sour cream, and vanilla and mix well. Add the chopped nuts. Pour the batter into a greased 9 × 5 × 3 loaf pan or several smaller loaf pans (or muffin tins). Bake in 350°F oven for 1 hour for 1 loaf, or around 20 minutes for muffins or small loaves. ***Mmm!***

Pizza Poppin' Muffins

These are great for an afternoon snack, make a cool lunchbox choice, and are perfect for having kids over for sleepovers, movies, and game night. You get the idea, right? KID FRIENDLY! Not only are they a great snack, but they carry a heavier nutritional punch than most snack foods! You can load these babies up with the meat of your choice, and maybe even hide a few veggies!

Scared of the idea of making pizza dough? Don't sweat it—this recipe requires no kneading at all! The whole kitchen will smell like a pizza parlor between the yeast, pepperoni, and oregano all baking together… but the texture is more like a muffin, with a tender, moist crumb. I'd be willing to bet that your kiddos would be thrilled to come in from school in the afternoons to these hot pizza muffins, fresh and steamy out of the oven, dipped into some warm pizza sauce. But don't be surprised if the neighbor kids start migrating over, too!

Notes:

Ingredients

- 2¾ cups all-purpose flour
- 1 envelope "quick-rise" yeast
- 2 Tbsp granulated sugar
- 1 tsp table salt
- 1½ tsp dried oregano
- ½ tsp dried basil
- 1¼ cups very warm water, 120–130°F
- 1 Tbsp canola or vegetable oil
- 1 Tbsp butter
- ¼ cup finely chopped bell pepper
- ¼ cup finely chopped onion
- ¾ cup mini pepperoni, *could use chopped deli meats*
- ¼ cup chopped cooked bacon
- 1 cup shredded mozzarella cheese, *could use small ½ in cubes*

A sprinkle of red pepper flakes, *optional*

Tip: *don't forget to check the expiration date on your yeast!*

How to...

Combine 1½ cups AP flour, the packet of yeast, sugar, salt, oregano, and basil in a large mixer bowl. Add the water. *I heated my water for a minute in the microwave. Worked perfectly!* Add the oil, then beat 2 minutes on medium speed. While that's mixing, add the butter to the chopped vegetables in a microwave-safe dish and cook on high for two minutes to sauté the vegetables. Gradually add in the remaining 1¼ cups flour to make the dough. It will be really sticky and fairly stiff. Now stir in (by hand) the pepperoni, bacon, sautéed vegetables, and cheese. Add in the red pepper flakes if you desire. Careful—these pack a lot of heat! Cover this bowl and allow the dough to rest for 10 minutes.

After it rests, portion the dough into 12 standard-sized (2½-in) muffin cups that you have generously greased with nonstick cooking spray. I don't recommend you use paper liners, as we want the outer crust to get a little crispy. Now cover the whole muffin tin and allow the dough to rise somewhere a little bit warm for about 45 minutes. You can expect some amount of rise, but not double.

Bake these in a preheated 375°F oven for 20 to 25 minutes (I went 22 minutes for the ones in the photo) until they are a golden brown color. You should also be smelling them by now. Let them cool a couple of minutes on a wire rack, then remove them from the pan by running a knife around the edges of each muffin. Serve them warm with pizza sauce and maybe a sprinkling of freshly grated Parmesan cheese!

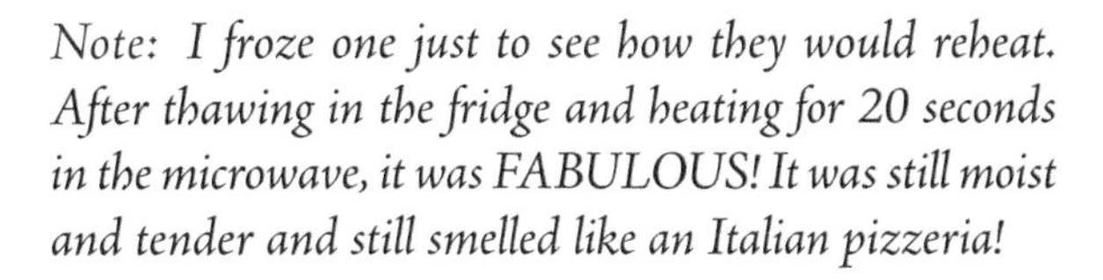

Note: I froze one just to see how they would reheat. After thawing in the fridge and heating for 20 seconds in the microwave, it was FABULOUS! It was still moist and tender and still smelled like an Italian pizzeria!

Rosemary Black Pepper No-Knead Artisan Bread

Isn't this a gorgeous loaf of bread? To think that you can just mix this up, let it sit overnight, then bake it in a pot the next day with this beautiful result just blows my mind!

To the best of my knowledge, the originator of this bread concept is Jim Lahey, owner of Sullivan Street Bakery. He figured out that you can use a heavy cast iron or cast enamel pot *with* a lid to recreate a baker's steam oven to give the bread this gorgeous crust. What a GENIUS!

So here is my experience making this bread. I have added some extra stuff to my loaf. You can CERTAINLY make it plain or add your favorite ingredients to it.

Ingredients

- 3 cups all-purpose flour
- ¼ tsp yeast
- 1¼ tsp kosher salt
- 1 cup Gruyere cheese, grated
- Zest of 1 large lemon
- Fresh chopped rosemary (about 2 Tbsp)
- ½ tsp cracked black pepper
- 1½ cups water
- Oil (for coating)
- Extra flour, wheat bran, or cornmeal (for dusting)

Notes:

How to...

Mix all of the dry ingredients in a medium bowl. Add water and incorporate with a wooden spoon for 30 seconds to 1 minute. Lightly coat the inside of a second medium bowl with oil and place the dough in the bowl. Cover the bowl with plastic wrap and let the dough rest 12–18 hours at room temperature (approx. 65–72°F).

Tip » *Use a marker to write the beginning and ending time on top of the plastic wrap.*

Remove the dough from the bowl and fold once or twice. Let the dough rest 15 minutes in the bowl or on the work surface. Next, shape the dough into a ball. Generously coat a cotton towel with flour, wheat bran, or cornmeal; place the dough seam side down on the towel and dust with flour. Cover the dough with a cotton towel (not terrycloth) and let rise 1–2 hours at room temperature, until more than doubled in size.

Preheat oven to 450–500°F. Place the pot in the oven with the lid at least 30 minutes prior to baking to preheat. Once the dough has more than doubled in volume, remove the pot from the oven and place the dough in the pot seam side up. *Careful—the pot is now 450°F!* Cover with the lid and bake 30 minutes. Then remove the lid and bake 15–30 minutes uncovered, until the loaf is nicely browned.

Food Nerd Notes: *This is an excerpt from* The Minimalist, *in the* 2006 NY Times:

Mr. Lahey's method is striking on several levels. It requires no kneading (Repeat: NONE). It uses no special ingredients, equipment or techniques. It takes very little effort.

It accomplishes all of this by combining a number of unusual though not unheard of features. Most notable is that you'll need about 24 hours to create a loaf; time does almost all the work. Mr. Lahey's dough uses very little yeast, a quarter teaspoon (you almost never see a recipe with less than a teaspoon), and he compensates for this tiny amount by fermenting the dough very slowly. He mixes a very wet dough, about 42 percent water, which is at the extreme high end of the range that professional bakers use to create crisp crust and large, well-structured crumb, both of which are evident in this loaf.

The dough is so sticky that you couldn't knead it if you wanted to. It is mixed in less than a minute, then sits in a covered bowl, undisturbed, for about 18 hours. It is then turned out onto a board for 15 minutes, quickly shaped (I mean in 30 seconds), and allowed to rise again, for a couple of hours. Then it's baked. That's it.

The long, slow rise does over hours what intensive kneading does in minutes: it brings the gluten molecules into side-by-side alignment to maximize their opportunity to bind to each other and produce a strong, elastic network. The wetness of the dough is an important piece of this because the gluten molecules are more mobile in a high proportion of water, and so can move into alignment easier and faster than if the dough were stiff."

And, as Mr. Lahey himself notes, "The Egyptians mixed their batches of dough with a hoe."

Ham and Cheese Crescents—for kids, by kids

Looks like we've had a mutiny around here, as my kiddos have taken over. These two are always up for a little kitchen experimentation, so when I suggest we try something new—count them in! I have been wracking my brain about new things to include in little kids' lunchboxes. Since these are so easy and quick to throw together (obviously I wasn't needed for much of the process), I thought we could bake these up in the morning and jazz up the standard lunchbox ham and cheese sandwich.

We gave them a little more pizzazz with a sprinkling of Italian seasoning.

Ingredients

makes 8

- 4 sticks mozzarella string cheese
- 8 slices ham
- Canned crescent roll dough
- Italian seasoning, to taste

How to...

Preheat the oven to 350°F. Line a pan with aluminum foil or parchment paper for super easy cleanup. Cut the cheese sticks in half. Pat dry each side of the ham slices. The moisture could result in soggy rolls. Sprinkle the crescent dough with Italian seasoning and then separate them into triangles. Roll each piece of cheese into a piece of ham, and then roll into the dough—starting at the wide end. Arrange them on the foil-lined pan and bake. I baked these about 15 minutes until golden brown. You can expect some of the cheese to start oozing out of the ends. Allow them to cool briefly if handing them out to toddlers.

*I'm thinking these would be great slathered with basil pesto, filled with rotisserie chicken, sun-dried tomatoes, and mozzarella. **Yum!** There are endless variations!*

Notes:

Oriental Coleslaw

Let me start by saying that I am NOT a big fan of mayo, so I don't usually enjoy coleslaw. This recipe, however, does not have mayo. It's fast, fresh, crunchy, and totally addictive. My parents love it! It comes together in a snap and is great for large crowds or potlucks. In the times that I've brought it to potlucks, I've only come back with empty containers! It's also perfect for summer picnics. Since there's no dairy in it, you don't have to worry about letting it sit out.

Ingredients

serves 10–12

- ½ cup butter
- 2 pkgs Ramen Noodles (Remove seasoning packet.)
- ½ cup slivered almonds
- ½ cup sesame or sunflower seeds
- ½ cup green onions chopped
- 1 14-oz pkg prepared coleslaw, shredded
- 2 cups shredded purple cabbage
- 1 cup sugar
- 1 cup vegetable oil
- 2 Tbsp soy sauce
- ¼ cup red wine vinegar

Tip: *You could make this a complete meal with the addition of some cooked chicken or shrimp!*

Notes:

How to...

Melt butter in a skillet. Crumble Ramen noodles and brown them along with the nuts and seeds. Cool and drain on a paper towel. Mix onions, nuts and noodle mixture, coleslaw mix, and the purple cabbage.

Dressing: Mix sugar, oil, soy sauce, and vinegar in a jar and shake well! At the very last minute, add the dressing to the slaw and toss so everything won't get soggy!

Tip» *This recipe can easily be cut in half for a normal household.*

Black Pepper and Gruyere Popovers

On a recent vacation, I had some of the most amazing popovers. They were so rustic and awesome, and so I've had them on my mind ever since. The other day I was in a kitchen supply store looking for something entirely different, and this popover pan called me over and demanded that I purchase it. I make it a practice to not turn down requests from talking pans, so it came home with me.

I seriously don't know why I haven't made these before! They are so easy. They are comical to look at as they pop up tall out of the pan like a bread version of a jack-in-the-box. They have a rustic, crunchy exterior and a delicate and light interior. And you could probably flavor them with any combination of herbs or spices you want. Lovely Lily and I made these, and we figured out that they were perfect for pulling apart and running them through the gravy of the pot roast we were serving—I mean THE perfect gravy vehicle!

If you tend to be intimidated by making bread because of the kneading, rising, etc., this is the way to go! It's no more complicated than throwing all the room-temperature ingredients into the food processor and then pouring the batter into the preheated pan. Seriously. I love that kind of thing!

Ingredients

- 2 large eggs, room temperature
- 1 cup whole milk, room temperature
- ½ cup grated Gruyere cheese
- 1 tsp freshly ground black pepper
- 1 cup all-purpose flour
- 1 tsp kosher salt
- 1½ Tbsp melted, cooled butter plus 1 tsp room temp for pan
- ½ tsp baking powder

How to...

Preheat oven **and** popover pan to 400°F. While the oven is heating, take out the eggs and milk to warm and grate the cheese and pepper. Combine all ingredients except cheese in a food processor. Process the mix for 30 seconds. Carefully remove the hot popover pan from the oven and add a piece of the reserved 1 tsp of room temperature butter to each of the 6 wells. Please don't touch the hot pan and burn yourself. Pour the batter immediately into the wells. It should come at least halfway up the pans. If you are using cheese, sprinkle it over the batter now. You could also sprinkle fresh herbs, etc. Bake them for 35 minutes, and don't peek—this makes them fall. They will be golden brown with a beautiful, crunchy exterior.

Serve with your choice of spreads or toppings.

Grilled Chicken Southwestern Chopped Salad with Creamy Cilantro Dressing

I'm sure you know this, but salads do NOT have to be boring!!! On the contrary, it seems that the more stuff you pile on there the better. I learned that from my mom, who makes the most amazing salads with lots of colors and textures. So let's see... The star of the show would have to be the sliced Southwestern-flavored chicken breast strips, which top a bed of romaine lettuce, shredded red cabbage, carrots, and a little coleslaw mix. Topping that are the beautiful colors of the season, with vine-ripened grape tomatoes, sweet summery corn and black beans, sweet peppers, green onions, and big bold cilantro. Of course, I threw in some goodies with a blend of Monterey Jack and cheddar cheeses, and some colorful tortilla strips for crunch. It's essentially the rainbow, on a plate! Now of course you could top this all off with ranch dressing or something, but NO! We are going to make a cool creamy cilantro dressing that will blow your socks off, from a base of Greek yogurt!

Now this may look like a long list, but you just dump it all together! This salad would be perfect for bringing to a family reunion, a work party, neighborhood block party, etc. You could even layer it in a trifle bowl for a pretty presentation. Just be sure everything is well drained so it will be crisp. And let everyone dress their own portion at the end, so you won't wilt the salad beforehand. Of course you can cut down the amount and have a killer salad to bring to work for yourself, too! And as always, feel free to change it up any way you want to. One of the joys of cooking is that you can make something how YOU want!

Note: *If you are making this to take to a function, or just for eating later, keep the dressing separate!*

Ingredients

Creamy Cilantro Dressing

- ½ cup plain Greek yogurt
- 1 cup cilantro leaves, loosely packed
- 2 Tbsp fresh lime juice
- 1 avocado
- 2 cloves garlic
- ⅛ cup olive oil
- ⅛ cup canola oil
- 1½ tsp white vinegar
- ⅛ tsp table salt
- 1 tsp ground cumin
- 1 tsp chili powder

Salad

- 1 large head romaine lettuce
- 1 cup shredded red cabbage
- 1 cup shredded carrot strips
- 1 cup canned black beans, rinsed and drained well
- 1 cup canned corn niblets, drained
- ½ cup orange bell pepper, diced
- 1 cup coleslaw mix
- 1 pint grape tomatoes, halved
- ½ cup cilantro leaves, loosely packed and rough chopped
- 5 green onions, chopped
- 2 6-oz packages Southwestern grilled chicken strips
- 1 cup Monterey Jack/cheddar cheese blend
- 1 cup colored tortilla strips
- 1 packet taco seasoning, *optional*

Notes:

How to...

Let's do the dressing first. Then we can stick it in the fridge so all the flavors can marry together while we do the salad. Or the dressing could obviously be made up ahead of time.

For the Dressing: Combine all ingredients in a food processor. Give it a whirl until smooth and creamy. Adjust seasonings as you desire. The final dressing is smooth, cool, creamy, but BOLD! I usually put it in a dish, covered, and refrigerate it until I want to dress the salad.

Now for the Salad: Really, you just dump it all together. Nothing more complicated than that. Add the dressing when you are ready to serve your salad. Add a wedge of lime to the plate as a splash of freshness!

Quick Chicken Parmigiana Panini

This is a shortcut recipe to getting all those great flavors of chicken parmigiana without spending a long time making the original. For this super-quick lunchtime or light dinner treat, you can pick up a few convenience items at the grocery on the way home and have a gourmet, deli-worthy panini in only a few minutes! And since you aren't staring down a breaded and fried dinner with a pile of pasta, you won't be too weighed down to get out and take that walk after dinner that you've been promising yourself.

I want to preemptively say (again) that this is a shortcut recipe. No, I'm not making the components from scratch. It's for a ***fast*** and easy meal. Of course you can use your delicious homemade sauces, chicken, etc.

Ingredients

French bread
Prepared marinara
Freshly grated Parmigiano Reggiano
Cooked, grilled, and sliced chicken breast strips
Fresh basil leaves, *or dried basil*
Shredded, part-skim mozzarella
Sliced provolone
Just a bit of mayonnaise

How to...

It feels a little silly giving you a method to make a sandwich, but here goes, as some people like having explicit directions. The short version: make the sandwich, grill it, and press it!

The longer version: Find yourself some lovely French or Italian bread. Apply store-bought marinara to the inside of each piece that you will be using. Starting with the "bottom" bread, add grated Parmigiana Reggiano, your pieces of cooked chicken, some basil, shredded mozzarella, and provolone. Top with the second "top" bread that also has marinara spread onto it. *I like the chunkier marinara because I like having the pieces of tomatoes. I'm sure you can find a smoother version if that's your preference.*

Now to get this beautiful golden brown color, spread a little mayonnaise to the *outside* of each bread. You can use butter or cooking spray, but the mayo really browns beautifully, and no—it won't taste like mayo. You can grill them on a grill pan, on a panini machine, on a George Foreman-type grill, on a black iron skillet, or just a plain old non-stick skillet. Pressing them, however, gets all the ingredients glued together. *I LOVE my grill pan and use it all the time!* If you are using just a skillet, consider putting a second heavy skillet on top of the sandwich to press it.

Serve with a side of marinara.

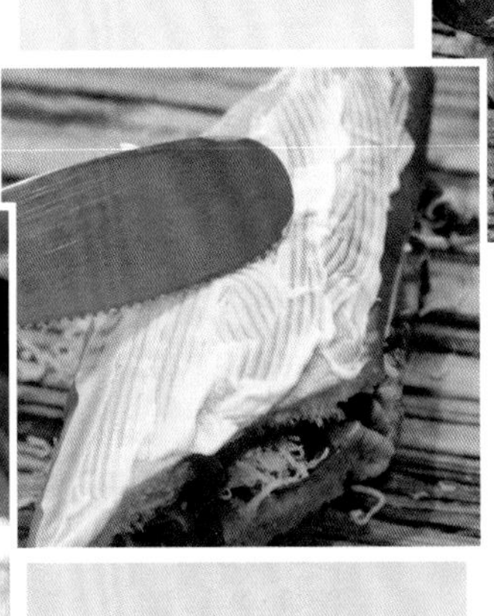

Cranberry Cherry Chicken Wrap

If you are looking for a quick and healthy lunch wrap, here's one you might try on for size. This wrap comes together in a snap, thanks to convenience grocery items, and packs a punch with a whole-grain flatbread wrap and lots of protein to keep you going strong! Studies show that people get more satisfaction with crunchy foods, so I've included a crispy lettuce/carrot/cabbage blend as well as nutrient-dense pecans to cover that category. To balance out the flavor profile, we have sweet dried cherries and cranberries, tartness from the Greek yogurt and tarragon vinegar, and the spicy bite of Southwestern seasonings on the lean chicken strips. What's not to like?! Your brown-bag lunch never tasted so good!

Ingredients

- 3 oz Southwestern-seasoned chicken breast strips
- 1 Tbsp sun-dried tomatoes
- 2 Tbsp cherry cranberry pecan mix
- A couple of shakes of tarragon vinegar, *You could substitute other acids such as lemon juice or apple cider vinegar.*
- 1 Tbsp plain non-fat Greek yogurt
- Kosher salt and black pepper, to taste
- Lettuce/carrot/cabbage blend
- Multigrain flatbread

Notes:

How to...

Add the chicken, diced sun-dried tomatoes, and the cherry cranberry mix together and chop. Add the vinegar. Combine with the yogurt and season with salt and pepper to taste. Add the lettuce blend and chicken salad to the flatbread, and wrap these guys up! It's a fresh, crunchy, filling, healthy, FLAVORFUL lunch!

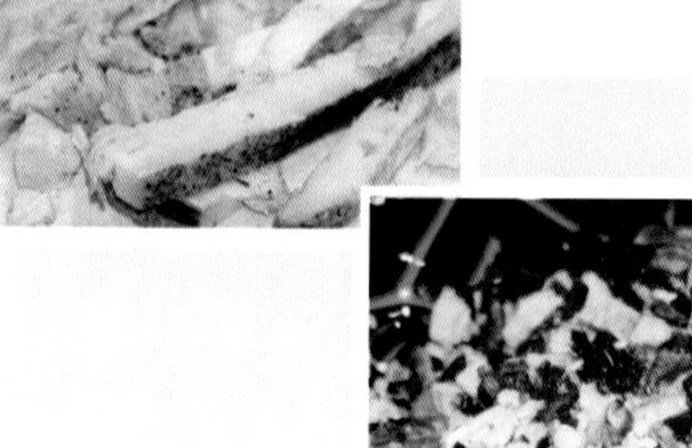

Tea
Party

LOVE

family

Sweet

elegance

Soups and Such

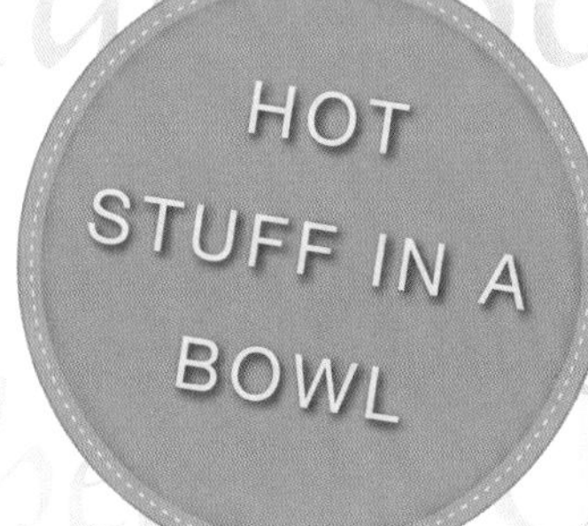
HOT
STUFF IN A
BOWL

Cheater Cheater Chicken and Dumplings

Ingredients

A rotisserie chicken, *Almost every grocery store has them hot nowadays...just waiting for you.*
A box of low-sodium chicken broth
Salt, pepper, and poultry seasoning, all to taste
Flour
A can of biscuits, *Doesn't matter what kind. Get the cheap ones!*
3 Tbsp butter
⅔–1 cup evaporated milk in the can
A few sprigs of thyme for the broth and garnish, *optional*

Notes:

Now before anyone starts yelling at me, I will fully admit that my recipes run the entire gamut of "made from scratch" and "right from the garden," all the way to "cheater cheater" recipes that take liberal advantage of convenience foods that you can pick up quickly on your way home from work. Some readers have been aghast at my use of canned biscuits and store-bought meatballs. Well, you know what? There are times when you have TIME, and other times when you have NO time but still want to cook for your family. There are also times when a novice cook wants home-cooked comfort but is intimidated by certain techniques. For those times, there is absolutely nothing wrong with incorporating convenience items! Believe me...the kids will still much prefer that to picking up takeout.

Well this is one of those "cheater cheater" recipes. On nights when you have four baseball games scheduled, then torrential rains moved in, all you want is comfort food. Nope, this may not be Grandma's cook-all-day, made-from-scratch chicken and dumplings, but who cares? They are easy, good, and the kids love them! They also required very few kitchen skills, so you may recommend them to someone just getting started in the kitchen.

How to ...

Strip the meat from the bones of the rotisserie chicken. *Seriously, aren't rotisserie chickens one of the best things around? They are hot, juicy, well-seasoned, already cooked, and actually less expensive than buying a whole raw chicken!* Cover the meat in a bowl and throw the bones into a pot with enough chicken broth and water to cover the chicken. Season the water with salt, pepper, and a little poultry seasoning. Get that on first and let your broth "build" flavor while you go about your afternoon business—putting up groceries, checking homework, getting hugs and kisses, etc. Boil for about an hour and a half to extract the flavor out of the bones, skin, etc. Using the parts that you would have thrown away (skin, bones) to make the broth really stretches the buck out of that 5–6-dollar chicken!!! If you want, you can add a few sprigs of fresh thyme. Just throw them in whole. The little tender leaves will separate from the stems, which you can fish out later. You could also do this part ahead of time and have the broth ready in the fridge when you get home.

For the dumplings, liberally sprinkle your work surface with all-purpose flour. Arrange the biscuits on the flour. Sprinkle the biscuits with a mixture of salt, pepper, and poultry seasoning. *It may seem odd to you that I season the dough, but this ensures that I have seasoning at every level of the dish.* Roll the dumplings out very thin (larger than your hand) and make easy work of cutting them by rolling over them with a pizza wheel. *That's a great job to let the kids do, by the way. Don't worry if they aren't all the same. This isn't the* Food Network. *Anne Burrell isn't going to fuss at you if your knife cuts are not all the same (No offense, Anne. Love ya!). You are spending time together and they are learning skills and having fun. Period. Keep it all in perspective.*

Gather up the dumpling pieces *with* the flour and let them rest while you fish out all the "stuff" from your broth, using a spider or strainer. The more flour you pick up with them, the thicker your final broth, so adjust according to the preferences of your family/guests. You could also make these dumplings ahead of time and put them in the fridge.

Bring the broth to a boil and add the dumplings. At first, they will puff up and get super fluffy. Don't worry...they won't stay that way. Add the butter and evaporated milk and give them a good few stirs. Let them cook on about a medium to medium-high boil for about 15 minutes. The dumplings will thin out and drop down, and the broth will thicken. It's like magic.

Now, you can turn off the heat (or turn to low heat) and add in the cooked rotisserie chicken. At this point, we have done very little real work and have thick creamy broth and tender dumplings. Adding the chicken back at the end ensures that it won't be overcooked and dry, and that it won't break up into shreds (we prefer nice healthy hunks of chicken).

Serve to some people you love. Stay dry and cozy.

Enjoy family time.

Man Chili

Down here in the Deep South, we get absolutely giddy when it gets cold enough to light the fireplace, as the cooler weather is *such* a relief! On one such particular occasion, I was all set to make a nice, light turkey chili. My husband, however, said he would prefer the traditional beef. After all, he's a MAN. He needs MAN CHILI! Ha. Well, anyone who knows him would agree that he is such an amazing person and would pretty much do anything I asked of him—so conceding to make "Man Chili" was a very easy request. That got me thinking. There are a ton of alternative chili recipes out there, but when it comes down to comfort food, most people I know want the real deal. So this is a basic recipe for regular, comfortable, delicious Man Chili.

The awesome thing about chili is that after the meat is browned, you basically dump the rest of the ingredients together and just let it do its thing. That's great for people who have tons of other things going on. It's also great because a recipe like this is just begging to be brought to a good tailgating party or for little Trick-or-Treaters to come in from the cold streets. This chili is equally comfortable in a big steaming bowl, or ladled over big, juicy hot dogs. So go ahead—make a big batch of it. It freezes beautifully, and it takes the same amount of time to make a big batch as a small one. May as well have an extra meal waiting for you in the freezer, right?

Note: *This chili is well seasoned and flavorful, but it is NOT spicy hot. So this one IS appropriate for your whole family, including heat-sensitive kids.*

Ingredients

6–8 very generous portions

- 2½ lbs ground beef (85/15)
- 1 large onion, chopped
- 1 cup mixed bell peppers, chopped
- 1 Tbsp chopped garlic
- 2 pkgs chili seasoning
- 1 can red kidney beans, *I used the ones that say "with chili gravy."*
- 2 28-oz cans whole tomatoes, chopped ***with*** the juice
- 1 6-oz can tomato paste
- 1 8-oz can tomato sauce
- 1 Tbsp cumin
- 2 tsp kosher salt (Use much less if using table salt.)
- 1 Tbsp ground mustard
- 1 tsp cinnamon
- 1 12-oz bottle dark amber beer
- 1 Tbsp apple cider vinegar

How to . . .

Begin by browning your meat. I used 85/15 because I think it needs that amount of fat in it. If you want to go leaner, go for it. After the meat is browned and crumbled, add in the onions and peppers.

Let them cook down until softened, and then mix in the other ingredients. Then just let it simmer on about medium-low for a good long while (at least 30 minutes) until all the veggies are tender and all the flavors are married together. Really, the longer the better.

Note: I'm not a fan of chili with TOO many beans in it, so a single can gives me enough beans to see and to have that change of texture, but not so many as to have "bean chili" as I've seen some places.

Food Notes: *Why start with whole tomatoes then chop them? Whole canned tomatoes are held to a higher standard than chopped ones (which can just be bits and pieces). By doing this, I know I'm getting the really good ones. But feel free to use what is convenient.*

Why the beer and vinegar? The beer adds a molasses note, and the vinegar wakes the flavors up.

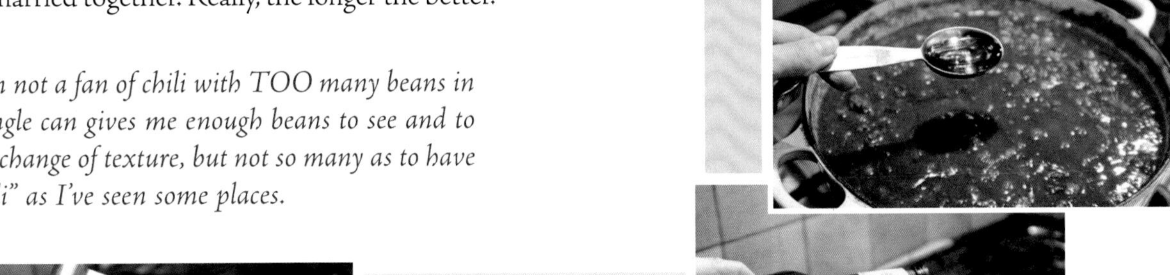

Chicken and Sausage Gumbo

If you are from the Southern part of the United States, you undoubtedly know that gumbo is the ultimate comfort food, and a sure sign that the crisp autumn weather has graced us at long last with a breath of cool air. Autumn means football, beautiful leaves, marshmallows, and hot dogs roasting out on the back deck with the kids...and gumbo with friends!

Ingredients

- 2 medium yellow onions, chopped
- 3 large cloves chopped garlic, *You can use garlic powder if you need to.*
- 2–3 celery stalks chopped
- ¼–½ cup bell peppers
- 2 smoked sausage links (approx. 12-16 inches long), sliced on a bias
- 1 whole chicken, *It can be already cut into pieces.*
- ⅔ cup vegetable oil
- 1 cup flour
- Salt and pepper, to taste (at least 1 tsp each, probably more)
- Ground, dried thyme, to taste (approximately 1½ tsp)
- Fresh green onions
- Gumbo file' (2–3 tsp for whole pot, a sprinkle over individual bowls)

Notes:

How to ...

Note: *I highly recommend having all of your ingredients chopped and ready to go before you begin. Once you start the roux, you CANNOT leave it or stop stirring it.*

Chop onions, garlic, celery stalks, and bell peppers. Slice the sausage links.

For the Chicken: Cover bone-on chicken pieces in a large stockpot with cold water. Bring to a boil, and reduce down until the chicken is fork tender. When the chicken gets tender, debone the chicken. You can either toss all the skin and bones (if you are in a hurry), or replace them in the stock pot to enrich the stock. If you do this, let them boil another 15 minutes or so to get a richer stock. Then you can strain them or fish them out with a spider/slotted spoon. I don't really like to put my chicken meat back in just yet because it can both overcook the chicken and make it shred... and I prefer my meat to be in larger pieces.

For the Roux: Preheat a cast iron skillet. Add ⅔ cup of oil to skillet. Heat oil for a while. Add approximately 1 cup of flour, stirring constantly. When roux starts to really brown, lower heat to medium. When roux is a *dark chocolate* or close to color of skillet, add chopped vegetables and sausage (It should be the color of the Nutella chocolate hazelnut spread). It might be necessary to increase the heat when the vegetables are added. They will bring down the temperature of the roux immediately when you add them. Cook down several minutes more until veggies are wilted and soft. Be careful, the preservatives in the sausage might cause the roux to stick and burn.

Once the stock has come to the desired state of richness and the bones have been removed, add the roux to the stockpot. Continue the roux in the stock at a hard boil. Correct the seasonings. Add the chicken to the gumbo and let it simmer for a while for all of the flavors to marry. This part really takes a while. If you taste it and it just doesn't taste like anything, just let it continue to simmer for a while. This part really can't be rushed. Don't bring it to a hard boil because the chicken will start breaking up.

If you have time, let the gumbo cool and remove the grease that will rise to the top. Add fresh green onions after you remove the grease. Add gumbo file', if desired. Do not add it to the whole pot, but to individual bowls to avoid making the gumbo stringy. Serve hot over white rice.

Food Nerd Notes: *Gumbo is a stew or soup that originated in southern Louisiana during the 18th century. It consists primarily of a strongly flavored stock, meat or shellfish, a thickener, and the vegetable holy trinity of celery, bell peppers, and onions. Gumbo is often categorized by the type of thickener used: the African vegetable okra, the Choctaw spice file' powder (dried and ground sassafras leaves), or roux, the French base made of flour and fat. The dish likely derived its name from either the Bantu word for* okra *(ki ngombo) or the Choctaw word for* filé *(kombo).*

Several different varieties exist. Creole gumbo generally contains shellfish, tomatoes, and a thickener. Cajun gumbo is generally based on a dark roux and is spicier, with either shellfish or fowl. Sausage or hams are often added to gumbos of either variety. After the base is prepared, vegetables are cooked down, and then meat is added. The dish simmers for a minimum of three hours, with shellfish and some spices added near the end. If desired, filé powder is added after the pot is removed from heat. Gumbo is traditionally served over rice.

The dish combines ingredients and culinary practices of several cultures, including French, Spanish, German, West African, and Choctaw. The dish is the official cuisine of the state of Louisiana.

Taco Soup

I adapted this recipe a bit from one my cousin Donna makes. It is absolutely the simplest thing in the world and amazingly delicious, not to mention very healthy! The protein here is ground beef, but the flavors are so big in this soup that you could certainly substitute ground turkey for an even healthier, lower-fat version. On a dark, rainy evening, this soup is sure to take the chill out of your bones. Cornbread muffins would be just perfect as an accompaniment, or you could simply serve the soup with corn chips for dipping. I just thought what a great soup to serve on Halloween after trick or treating. I can see the kids' smiles already.

Ingredients

- 2 lbs lean ground beef (90/10)
- 1 chopped onion
- 1 14½-oz can chili-style tomatoes
- 1 17-oz can whole kernel corn
- ½ 15-oz can kidney beans, rinsed
- ½ 15-oz can black beans, rinsed
- 1 8-oz can tomato sauce
- 1 8-oz can water
- 1 14-oz can tomatoes with chilies, mild (I used Ro-tel.)

If you don't have access to these, you could use another can of diced tomatoes and 1 small can of diced green chilies.

- 2–3 cups chicken broth
- 1 pkg taco seasoning mix
- 1 pkg ranch dressing mix (I used Hidden Valley Ranch.)

Suggested Toppings

Sour cream, grated cheese, corn chips, or tortilla chips

Notes:

How to ...

Sauté ground beef and drain well. I did NOT add any additional oil. *I line a colander with paper towels to drain the fat.* Even in the lean 90 percent version, there is plenty of fat in the meat. Feel free to cut back to only 1 lb of meat if you desire a soup that is a little thinner. Depends on your audience.

Return the meat to the pot. Add all the other soup ingredients. *We added kidney beans AND black beans and cut the quantity to ½ to ⅔. In this recipe, it really doesn't matter. Add in as much as you wish.* Simmer 1 hour. Serve over chips and top with sour cream, corn chips, and grated cheese. And we have a beautiful, healthy, very flavorful soup!

I could also see this as being a great candidate for a crock pot soup!

Cajun Corn Chowder

If you are a novice in the kitchen, making soup is an excellent place to start. Soups are super easy, super flavorful, and very comforting. This recipe requires very little actual skills in the kitchen, yet tastes like you spent hours making it. The soup is wonderfully textured, sweet from the corn, smoky from the spiced ham, and warms you up from the inside.

I grew up with my Mom making a lovely corn soup, usually from a leftover ham. It's so perfect on a cold and rainy evening. Even now when I'm leaving work and it's dark and rainy, my mind drifts to some type of soup. It also freezes wonderfully.

Ingredients

makes 8–10 cups

- 1 cup finely chopped onion
- 1 Tbsp (about 3 large cloves) garlic, finely chopped
- ½ cup (about 2 large ribs) celery, finely chopped
- 1 stick butter (8 Tbsp)
- 1 slightly rounded cup (1 pack) highly seasoned, very smoky ham (I used Tasso.)
- 2 15-oz cans cream-style corn
- ½ 15-oz can white/yellow whole corn niblets, drained
- 2 cups diced potatoes, peeled if using large potatoes, *For small, thin-skinned "new" potatoes, you can just wash them and leave the skins on.*
- 3 cups chicken broth/stock
- ½ cup tomato sauce
- 1 tsp kosher salt
- 1 rounded tsp sugar
- ¼ tsp black pepper
- Heavy cream, *optional (For finishing, NOT added in with the other ingredients during cooking.)*

Notes:

How to …

Sauté the onion, garlic, and celery in the butter until soft and the tiniest bit brown. While sautéing the vegetables, chop your Tasso (or ham). I cut them into about ½-inch pieces. When the vegetables are soft, go ahead and add the Tasso.

Add in all the remaining ingredients (except the cream). Yep, just dump them in and give it a good stir. It is quite thin now. Bring this to a full boil for a couple of minutes, then turn down to simmer. Simmer uncovered for an hour. The starches in the corn will do a lovely job of making this creamy and thick. Bring to a boil over medium heat, then simmer for about an hour without the lid. The potatoes should be soft by now.

Tip » *A regular smoked ham will work for this recipe if you can't locate Tasso. However, if you ARE using Tasso, be careful in adding additional pepper. The one I used was not, but Tasso can be very spicy from some smokehouses.*

After an hour, the soup should have reduced and thickened somewhat. At this point (after the hour), you can add some cream to the soup for an even creamier (LOL) texture and taste. But it really is quite nice without it. If you do add the cream, warm it up gently a bit before adding it. You don't want to boil it or the cream will break on you and curdle.

Garnish simply—some parsley, a chopped tomato, a bit of black pepper. Lovely when accompanied by some cornbread muffins!

Crock Pot Chicken Tortilla Soup

I think soup, in all its forms, may be one of the best food groups there is! Every ancient text and historical account has people gathering around a big pot of communal soup—warm, nourishing, healing, and practically magical. Remember the story of "Stone Soup" that we were told as children? The great thing about soup is that you can use practically any ingredient in a wonderful marriage of slow-cooked flavors, and it's a great way to stretch a dollar!

I have adapted my normal stovetop soup recipe for this dish into a slow cooker recipe for all of you who are super busy with kids, work, after school activities and appointments, and all the wonders of life that make your family tick. The morning prep for this recipe takes only 10–15 minutes and it will pretty much be ready and waiting for you when you walk in the door in the evening.

It's basically an open-and-dump fun fest where everything just gets thrown into the slow cooker. The finishing touches include options (Don't we love options?!). You can eat as-is after shredding the chicken, or take it a few steps further if you'd like. I puréed my soup in the food processor, as my kids are really picky about having vegetables in their food. As for toppings, I like fried tortilla strips, shredded cheese, chopped cilantro (a must!), and a squeeze of lime. A dollop of sour cream and slice of avocado are lovely with this as well.

The soup is very flavorful, but not hot (spicy). After it's all said and done, you have a very healthy, economical, and fast dish. For just the soup part (exclusive of the toppings), there is almost no fat at all, lean protein from the chicken, and tons of vegetables (vitamins, minerals, healthy fiber) from all the tomatoes, corn, and beans. Feel free to substitute fresh tomatoes, corn, homemade chicken stock, etc., but I chose these items in the canned version for the speed of putting the soup together in the mornings.

Notes:

Ingredients

- 2 chicken breasts
- 1 can fire-roasted diced tomatoes
- 1 can mild enchilada sauce
- 1 cup diced onions
- 1 can diced chilies
- 2 cloves minced garlic
- 4 cups low-sodium chicken broth (1 box)
- 2 tsp cumin
- Kosher salt and black pepper, to taste
- 1 bay leaf
- 1 small can sweet corn niblets, drained
- 1 can black beans, drained and rinsed
- Corn tortillas (2 for soup, more for garnish)
- 1 can tomato paste

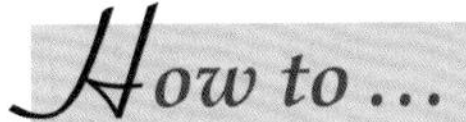

How to ...

To Prep: Dump all of the ingredients into the crock pot. Set on high for 4 hours or low for 6–8 hours depending on your crock pot.

To Finish: Remove chicken when cooked and shred with a fork. If you are puréeing the soup, keep the chicken out and covered to stay hot. *Don't forget to pull out the bay leaf.* Add a little of the liquid to prevent it from drying out. If not puréeing, add the shredded chicken back to the soup, and you are ready to eat.

For the Tortilla Strips: Cut tortillas into uniform strips. Drop carefully into hot oil. The oil should IMMEDIATELY start sizzling when you add them. Once light/golden brown, remove them with a spider or slotted spoon, drain on a paper towel lined plate, and sprinkle immediately with salt.

Garnish: Because you might as well do it up right! Fried tortilla strips, shredded cheese, a squeeze of lime, a dollop of sour cream, chopped cilantro, a slice of avocado.

I serve my chicken tortilla soup with cheese quesadillas, as I enjoy having something to dip into my soup!

Shrimp and Corn Soup

I got this recipe passed down from a lady way down in Cocodrie, LA, who used to make it for a restaurant there. It's super simple and the kind of thing where you just basically dump it all together.

For a smaller family, consider cutting the recipe in half, because it makes a TON (like 8–10 cups)! This would be good for a football party or something where you have a LOT of people dipping into the pot!

Ingredients

1 stick of butter
1 onion, chopped
5 cloves garlic, finely chopped
2 cans cream-style corn
1 can tomatoes with chilies (I used Ro-tel.)
2 lbs shrimp (60–70 size)
1 can whole kernel corn, *optional*
1 pint half and half
1 pint whipping cream
1 lb cheese (I used the Velveeta 2% fat version.)
⅓ lb cooked bacon
Garlic salt, to taste
Black pepper, to taste

Garnishes: chopped green onions, fresh parsley, corn kernels, and cooked bacon (about ⅓ lb)

Notes:

How to ...

Sauté butter with chopped onion and finely chopped garlic. Add cream-style corn and diced Ro-tel tomatoes. *Vary the heat with the type of Ro-tel you buy, from mild to spicy.* Add shrimp. Place on medium heat and bring to boil until shrimp are cooked (8–10 minutes). You can add a can of whole kernel corn to soup for extra "corn" texture.

Add half and half and whipping cream, heat on low until hot. Add Velveeta cheese. *I know...try not to have a heart attack just looking at it. It IS very rich, but I did use the 2% milk lower-fat cheese if that makes you feel better.* Stir and heat until cheese is melted. You don't want to keep boiling it after the cheese is in there, or it will scorch on the bottom. Can you see how full the pot has become? Add bacon.

Add garlic salt and pepper to taste. If soup is too watery at this point, bring up to a boil for a few minutes to thicken. I didn't season it earlier because the cheese and bacon can be very salty.

Garnish with chopped green onions or parsley, some whole corn kernels, and a little extra chopped bacon.

Creamy Tomato Soup

Down in our part of the world, we have more than our share of tropical storms and hurricanes—with LOTS of rain and howling winds! When it's horrible, nasty weather like this, there's something extra comforting about a big steamy bowl of soup. One of my favorites is this Creamy Tomato Soup with a good old grilled cheese. A comfort food extraordinaire!

Ingredients

Soup Preparation

1 cup heavy cream

Seasoning Blend

1 Tbsp sugar
2½ tsp salt
2 tsp paprika
1½ tsp dried sweet basil
½ tsp white pepper
¾ tsp garlic powder
½ tsp onion powder
½ tsp black pepper

Soup Ingredients

4 Tbsp unsalted butter
1½ cup chopped onions
½ cup chopped celery
2 28-oz cans whole peeled tomatoes
1½ cups chicken stock
¼ cup fresh parsley

Notes:

How to . . .

Bring the cream just to the boiling point in a small saucepan. Turn the heat down to low to just keep warm.

Combine the seasoning mix thoroughly in a small bowl. Melt the butter in a heavy pot, **not** cast iron. Add the onions and celery. Cook over high heat for 12 minutes. Chop the tomatoes and add to the pot, using only the juice from one can. Add the rest of the seasoning mix. Stir in the seasoning. Cover and bring to a rolling boil. Uncover the pot, stir well, and cook hard, about 3 minutes. Stir in the stock and bring to a boil. Cover, reduce the heat to low, and simmer 10 minutes.

Uncover, turn the heat to high and cook for an additional 10 minutes.

Put the soup into a food processor in 2 batches and process until coarsely puréed (but not quite smooth). You can also use an immersion blender (shown below). Stir in the reserved warm cream.

Of course this soup BEGS to be served with a good grilled cheese sandwich.

French Onion Soup

A rich beef broth enhanced by red wine, fresh thyme, caramelized onions, toasted French bread croutons, and gooey melty cheese! This is one of my all-time favorite soups, and what a classic! ***YUM!***

Ingredients

1½ Tbsp butter
1½ Tbsp extra virgin olive oil
1 large onion, thinly sliced
1 Tbsp flour
2 cloves garlic, finely chopped
½ cup red wine
2 cups low-sodium beef broth
2 tsp fresh thyme, stripped off of the stems
Salt and pepper, to taste
2 thick slices of French bread, *Consider cutting them into large croutons.*
Handful of fresh mozzarella, cut into cubes or grated
4 slices of cheese, *I recommend Gruyere, but you can also use Swiss or provolone.*

Notes:

How to . . .

Heat saucepan over medium-high heat, then add both butter and olive oil. Slice the onions thinly and uniformly. Add onions and sweat them until caramelized down to darkish-brown color (20 minutes). Here is the progression you can expect. You will go from having a whole pan full of firm, crisp onions, to soft but still white, and then to buttery soft with caramel coloring. *Expect this to take a minimum of about 15 minutes.* Add flour, stir into onions, and cook a couple of minutes. Add garlic and cook until fragrant (about a minute). We are essentially creating a roux with the hot fat and the flour. This will thicken the broth part of the soup. You want to cook this until it's not floury in taste. Your fire should be low...please don't burn the garlic!

Add wine to deglaze and cook until thick and bubbly. Deglazing just means that we are adding liquid to this pan, which brings up all those caramelized yummies on the bottom of the pan. They will essentially all dissolve into the liquid, thereby making ourselves a gravy of sorts. The wine will turn it pink (for now). Don't worry, it won't stay that way. You won't have to explain to your husband why you are serving him pink soup! Can you see how thick it is? That's because of the roux that we built in there.

Slowly add beef stock. Incorporate well into the all the pinkness! Season to taste with fresh thyme, salt, and pepper. I suppose you could use dried thyme, but I almost always have the fresh stuff growing in my garden. If you use dried, you will NOT need as much. Dried herbs are much more pungent. Cook for a while until you reach the desired consistency. Give the flavors time to develop. You can continue here or freeze this soup until it's time to serve later. See, I told you it wouldn't stay pink! Ladle broth into bowls.

Now for my bread:

I am not a big fan of just having one big piece of toasted French bread on top. I don't like wrestling with it...and trying to separate one bite from the rest. So to circumvent this, I cut my bread into nice chunks. Maybe the size of 1-inch cubes. That way, I can get one bite at a time. But hey—do it however you fancy it! Throw them in a pan and put them under the broiler until nice and toasted.

Soup assembly for serving:

So this may just be my cheese fetish, but I enjoy having chunks of mozzarella in my soup. For one thing, melty cheese is heavenly to me. But additionally, I think the cheese creates a waxy layer that helps to prevent the bread from getting soggy too quickly. Add the toasted bread cubes. Add your top cheese layer and put in oven under the broiler until cheese is melted and bubbly. After all, what is French Onion Soup without melted cheese smothering the whole thing?!

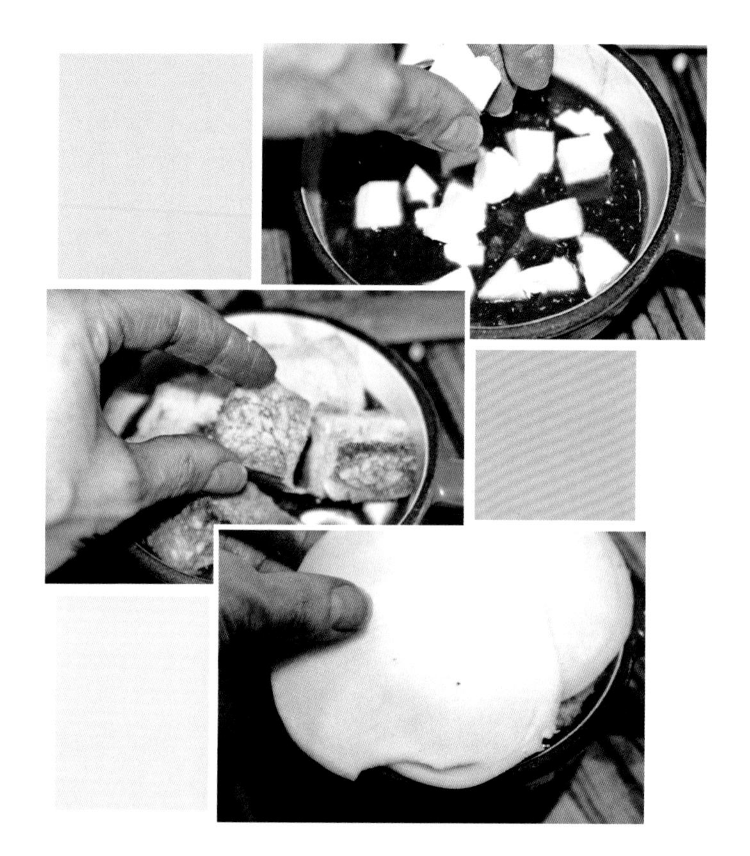

Food Nerd Notes: *Onions have long been a part of cooking, and were often identified as food used by the poor since they stored well, grew easily, and were plentiful. The legend of the creation of this soup is that King Louis XIV or XV of France created the dish at his hunting lodge after returning from a hunt and finding the cupboard bare of much beyond some stale bread, onions and champagne.*

Classic French Onion Soup begins with beef stock. Onions are sliced thin and then caramelized, which allows them to become sweet. They are then added to the heated stock. A little red wine may also be added to the stock to yield a richer flavor. Often, the soup is topped with a toasted crouton, and then is layered with cheese (typically Gruyere). The soup may be placed in ramekins or ovenproof crocks so the cheese gets bubbly, brown and melty, when broiled for a minute or two, before being served. When served in large portions, the heartiness and richness of French Onion Soup is a meal in itself. It can also make a lovely beginning soup course when served in smaller portions.

You can make a vegetarian version of the soup by omitting beef stock and using a hearty vegetable stock instead. Moreover, you can use tofu cheese or omit the cheese entirely for vegans.

Cooking icon Julia Child is said to have eaten French Onion Soup as her last meal before she died. I can't say that I disagree with that at all!

stuff in a bowl

Hot

Soup

teamwork

Yummy!

& Such

Entrees

Ritzy Cheddar Baked Chicken

Leftover Pot Roast Pot Pies

Tomato Basil Chicken

Black Iron Skillet Deep-Dish Pizza

Stuffed
Pork

Easy Beefy Enchiladas

A few shortcuts for this recipe lead up to big flavor with minimal effort! Okay, so maybe this isn't THE family-friendliest meal in the world, depending on your family. For the little ones, this enchilada sauce may be a little spicy. For the picky ones, there are onions and black olives in there to fuss about. *Sigh*... sometimes a girl has an urge to cook something that SHE wants. There's always mac-n-cheese in the house, right? I need a few guilt-overriding votes of "Amen, Sister!" here.

All that said, it *is* a very tasty and really easy recipe. It would be great for a potluck function, would freeze nicely, and will be great for your lunch tomorrow. It could also be put together one evening or morning to be popped into the oven when you get home from work. My honest opinion is that they are even better the next day than when they are initially made. ***Yum!***

Ingredients

1 lb lean ground beef
½ large onion
Salt, pepper, ground cumin, to taste
1 4-oz can chopped green chilies
1 Tbsp canola oil
1 Tbsp flour
1 can red enchilada sauce, *I use mild.*
1 cup heavy cream
10–12 corn tortillas, *or flour tortillas if you prefer*
Partial small can of chopped black olives
4 cups shredded Monterey Jack and cheddar cheese
Fresh cilantro
Sour cream
Lime wedges

Notes:

How to...

Crumble and brown a pound of lean ground beef in a skillet. When it's about half done, add the chopped onion. You could save time here with the frozen chopped onions that I'm always telling you about. Once the onions and ground beef cook down, add seasoning. I like LOTS of cumin, ground pepper, and salt. Add a can of chopped green chilies, another time saver.

Make a quick roux of equal parts oil and flour (1 Tbsp each). Stir until is just gets a little brown and nutty, not dark. This is going to give our sauce some additional body instead of just being thin and runny out of that can. Add the can of prepared enchilada sauce. I'm sure some Mexican grandma has a wonderful recipe of how to make this from scratch; but hey—this is an after-work meal! Let the sauce come to a complete boil. Turn down to medium and let it cook for a few minutes to thicken. Add the heavy cream. The reason I like the cream in it, if you must know, is that I think enchilada sauce can be a bit acrid. I want a rounder, softer mouth feel and a creamier consistency.

Ladle a bit of the thickened sauce into a casserole dish. Set up an assembly line: tortillas, sauce, meat, olives, cheese, casserole dish. Briefly dip the tortillas into the sauce. Add a spoonful of meat onto the tortilla. *Caution:* it's going to start getting pretty messy here. Add a few pinches of chopped black olives. Add a BIG glop of cheese. Roll the enchiladas. Place them seam side down in the pan. Squish them together as you go. Pour all the remaining sauce over the enchiladas. You don't want them to be dry after you bake them. Spread the remaining cheese over the enchiladas. Here is another time-saving thing: I am one of the biggest proponents you will find for buying cheese in a big hunk and grating your own. It just tastes a LOT better. The shredded cheese oxidizes and gets a little bit hard, and I don't think it's as good. But again, this is the shortcut version, so alas, I used the cheese in the bag.

Bake uncovered for 20 minutes at 350°F. This gives you time to make a side dish. Add a dollop of sour cream and sprinkle the top with fresh cilantro. Oh, how I love cilantro! The flavor is so big and bright and Mexican-y! Now don't forget to squeeze that lime over the enchiladas before you dig in. The acid from the lime juice further brightens the flavor profile.

Baked Chicken Taquitos

Who doesn't love Mexican food?! These chicken taquitos can be filled with anything you want and easily customized to the palates of your family. They would be great fried, I'm sure we all agree on that. But by baking them, it really cuts down on the fat! You could make these ahead of time and pop them into the oven (or fryer, if you wish) when you are ready for afternoon snacks, a fun dinner, tailgating, or even putting together an appetizer platter.

Ingredients

It's hard to put amounts on ingredients that should be added to the taste or to the consistency that you like, but here's a rough guide.

Rotisserie chicken, fully cooked and seasoned
⅔–1 cup of jarred or fresh salsa
1 cup shredded "Mexican blend" cheese
⅓ cup sweet white and yellow corn niblets
⅓ cup canned black beans, drained and rinsed well
1 tsp ground cumin
Salt and pepper, to taste
Large pinch of chopped fresh cilantro
1 pack of egg roll wrappers

I'm thinking that a little chopped baby spinach would be good in here, too. So much nutrition... but that would totally depend on whom you are making them for.

Notes:

How to...

Remove the chicken from the bones and chop into small, bite-sized pieces. Mix the next seven ingredients into the chicken and mix well. Add a few spoonfuls of the chicken mixture to an eggroll wrapper. Fold in the sides first, and then roll them up. Wet the far end with water so it will stick to itself. Egg roll wrappers are so easy to work with! *You could also experiment with oiled and heated corn tortillas if you prefer.*

Spray a cookie sheet with butter-flavored nonstick spray and arrange the taquitos. Spray the tops of them with the butter-flavored spray and sprinkle with black pepper and extra cumin. Bake at 375°F for about 25–30 minutes or until golden brown. It would be nice to turn them onto their sides if you can remember. Serve with condiments of choice, like light sour cream and salsa.

Mmm... chicken... gooey cheese... sweet corn and black beans... bright cilantro... smoky cumin... and a crunchy shell covering! A perfect after-school snack!

Note: *To reheat these, pop them into the toaster oven! They get totally crispy again!*

Eggplant Parmigiana with Italian Sausage Marinara

So eggplant parmigiana is one of those dishes that you make when you really love someone. Why? Because honestly, once you are committed to making it, you should plan on being in the kitchen a while. Is it hard? Nope. Just multi-step. That said, it is an amazingly delicious dish that anyone would be proud to serve—whether to family, guests, or even just your sweetheart. Also, you could break this into several make-ahead steps and just assemble and bake at the end. I guess my point is that it's awesome, and you should try it! And don't worry about all the steps, because you know I'm going to walk you through it each step of the way! Not only that, but I'll discuss steps for making this as individual servings as well as family-sized. So stick with me!

Oh—and what, you may ask, makes my recipe different from the rest? Well for one, this is usually a vegetarian dish. But this time, I'm going to be making it with an Italian sausage marinara. I happened to be making this for my parents, and I knew that going meatless was not going to be an option for the response I was hoping for. There are just some folks out there (usually men, let's face it) who prefer having some meat in the meal. If you prefer a meatless version, by all means, omit the meat. My favorite thing about cooking is being able to control every aspect of the dish.

Ingredients

Italian Sausage Marinara

¼ cup extra virgin olive oil (EVOO)
2 onions, diced fine
6 cloves of garlic, minced fine
Kosher salt – generous pinch
1 Tbsp red pepper flakes, adjust to taste
2 Tbsp granulated sugar
3 28-oz cans whole peeled tomatoes
1 tsp dried oregano
2 tsp dried basil
1 lb mild Italian sausage

Eggplant

1 large eggplant, firm and heavy
Generous amount of kosher salt for pulling out the bitterness

Breading station # 1

½ cup all-purpose flour
Kosher salt and cracked black pepper, to taste

Breading station # 2

2 large eggs
3 Tbsp buttermilk, *You can use regular milk if you prefer.*
Kosher salt and cracked black pepper, to taste

Breading station # 3

2 cups Italian bread crumbs
1 Tbsp dried oregano
2 Tbsp fresh thyme leaves, rough chopped
Canola or peanut oil for frying
6 slices provolone cheese
A generous handful of freshly grated Parmigiano Reggiano cheese
2 cups fresh basil, cut into thin ribbons
2 cups shredded mozzarella cheese

Marinara

I put the marinara on first, because I think one of the keys to a good marinara is giving it time to just simmer a long time. I honestly think that the longer it cooks, the better the flavors marry together.

To a heavy pot, add the EVOO. Add the chopped onions and garlic to the oil and let them start cooking down. Add in a generous pinch of kosher salt and red pepper flakes. Add in the sugar (to cut the acidity of the tomatoes). Add in the tomatoes and your dried seasonings. In a separate pot, crumble the sausage as it browns, then add it to the marinara. Now just let that simmer.

Eggplant

Cut the eggplant into ½-inch slices. Generously salt both sides and allow them to sit for an hour. Set them on a paper towel-lined baking sheet because a lot of water will come out of them. After an hour, rinse all that salt off of the eggplant thoroughly. Then just allow them to drain, pat them dry, and set them on paper towels.

Now begin to prepare your breading stations:

- » *Station 1:* **The flour station.** Mix flour, salt, and pepper.
- » *Station 2:* **The egg station.** Mix eggs, buttermilk, salt, and pepper.
- » *Station 3:* **The seasoned breadcrumbs.** Mix bread crumbs, oregano, and thyme.

Dip both sides of your eggplant rounds into each station. Then set them somewhere to hang out while you get your oil hot. You will need enough oil to provide about 2 inches of depth. You want the oil to be around 350–365°F. I have a candy thermometer clipped to the pot so I can keep it at this temp. Add about 3 breaded eggplant rounds per batch. You don't want to crowd the pan, as it will drop the oil temperature too much. They will only need a couple of minutes per side until they are golden brown and gorgeous. When you take them out, set them on a paper towel-lined baking sheet to drain, and sprinkle with salt if you'd like.

Assemble!

The same steps will apply here whether you are making these as individual servings or "family style." First, put a little of the marinara in the bottom of a baking dish that you have prepared with a little cooking spray. Then, layer in the following order: eggplant, provolone, Parmigiano Reggiano, basil ribbons, and mozzarella.

For the family-style casserole, do the same thing, but repeat for a total of three delicious layers. Add a layer of that gorgeous marinara in between each layer. For the individual serving, just make one layer.

Bake at 350°F for 35–40 minutes until the top is bubbly and brown. The individual servings will take *quite* a bit less time. When it comes out of the oven, garnish with more fresh basil right before serving. The heat will wilt the basil down in just a couple of minutes.

So here we have delicious layers of the golden-brown eggplant, the Italian sausage marinara, gorgeous ribbons of sweet basil, and don't forget the cheese—glorious cheese!

Food Note: *Whole tomatoes are held to a higher standard in the canning process than diced tomatoes (which are basically left over pieces and parts); so when you use whole tomatoes, you can be confident that these were the best.*

One-Pot Skillet Lasagna

I'm willing to bet that you are super busy right now. This recipe is a great way to have that home-cooked flavor, whole-kitchen-smelling-awesome aroma, and comfort food extraordinaire feeling in a ONE-POT MEAL! You asked for fast and easy, but delicious? You got it! But wait, you say—lasagna takes forever, not to mention all that layering and all those dishes! Not this one, my friends! Oh, and one more thing. We are going to make it just a tad bit healthier with a few tweaks along the way. Don't look worried—***you'll love it!***

Notes:

Ingredients

- 1 cup diced onions (about half of an onion)
- 1 Tbsp minced garlic (about 5 medium cloves)
- 1 medium-sized zucchini, peeled and grated
- 1 Tbsp extra virgin olive oil
- 1 tsp kosher salt
- ½ tsp black pepper
- ¼ tsp crushed red pepper flakes
- 1 tsp Italian seasoning
- 1 lb lean ground beef
- 12 lasagna noodles
- 1 8-oz can tomato sauce
- 1 28-oz can diced or crushed tomatoes
- ⅓ cup red wine, *Or substitute this much beef broth.*
- 2 cups beef broth
- 1 tsp sugar
- 1 cup 1% fat or fat-free small curd cottage cheese
- 1 cup low-fat shredded mozzarella
- ⅔ cup freshly grated Parmigiano Reggiano
- 1 egg
- Additional ½ tsp kosher salt, sprinkle of black pepper, and Italian seasoning for cheese mixture
- A fresh mozzarella ball
- Fresh basil for garnish and grated Italian seasoning

How to...

Chop/prep your ingredients first, as this goes pretty quickly. Sauté diced onions and garlic in EVOO until soft and fragrant. Add in the seasonings: kosher salt, black pepper, red pepper flakes, and Italian seasoning. Add in the peeled and grated zucchini. *This is one healthy addition that your family will not even notice. We are adding them early so they completely cook down.*

To the sautéed vegetables, add in the ground beef. *This is one of the leanest packages of beef out there! You could also add ground turkey or Italian sausage.* Break apart the ground beef while it's cooking.

Once the beef is cooked through, break apart the raw lasagna noodles into pieces. I suppose mine were in about 2"–3" pieces.

One top of the noodles, let's add in the liquids (red wine and beef broth). You will want this to be really soupy because it will reduce and be soaked up by the noodles as they are cooking. Add the sugar to the sauce. This is not enough sugar to make it sweet, but it will cut the acid of the tomatoes. Adjust any seasonings and bring up to a boil, making sure that the noodles are down in the sauce. Then reduce the heat down to medium and allow it to simmer for about 20–25 minutes so the noodles can get all tender. *These noodles will have more flavor than noodles boiled in water, as they will be absorbing all those great flavors!* Give it a good stir every few minutes or so. If it seems like it's getting too dry, add a little more beef broth.

While the noodles are cooking, throw together the cheese mixture: low-fat cottage cheese, low-fat shredded mozzarella, and freshly grated Parmigiano Reggiano. Add in an egg. Season with a nice big pinch of kosher salt, black pepper, and Italian seasoning. *Healthy substitutions: the cottage cheese rather than the ricotta and the low-fat mozzarella rather than full-fat mozzarella. Please see the nutritional information below.*

Once the noodles are cooked, turn off the heat. Drop the cheese mixture by big globs onto the meat and noodles and coarsely stir them in. I didn't want it to be too mixed, as I like seeing pockets of cheese.

Now cover with slices of fresh mozzarella and a sprinkling of Italian seasoning (because you want it to be pretty) and pop this whole skillet into the oven under the broiler until everything gets all melty and bubbly and just the slightest hint of brown. Garnish with some freshly chopped basil leaves and serve to some people that you love!

Cottage Cheese vs. Ricotta?: *Here are some stats I pulled up. I think you'll understand why I went with the cottage cheese!*

226 g low-fat cottage cheese has 163 calories, 2 g fat, 6 g sugars, and 28 g protein.

246 g part-skim ricotta cheese has 339 calories, 19 g fat, 1 g sugars, and 28 g protein.

Comparing cup for cup, the cottage cheese is less caloric (123 calories vs. 200) and has more protein and fewer carbohydrates. The full-fat versions of each of these are a little different. One cup of cottage cheese at full-fat has 9.6 g fat (6.0 g saturated) while one cup of whole ricotta has 31.9 g fat (20.4 g saturated). That's a huge difference.

In terms of what they are, cottage cheese is made from milk curds, so it contains casein, a slower-digesting protein. Ricotta is made from whey, so it is a faster-digesting protein. If you're looking primarily for a source of protein, cottage cheese has ricotta beat. If you're looking at full- or reduced-fat variants, then cottage cheese still has an edge over ricotta.

Mahogany Glazed Chicken

My kids ask for this one when they want to cook something special for someone. It's super easy and has big, bold flavors. Aren't we always looking for something new to do with chicken? This is a very flavorful and healthy meal that really satisfies. It offers exotic tastes of the Orient and down-home comfort all at the same time.

Ingredients

Chicken breasts, *or breasts and thighs (whatever combination you prefer)*
5–6 Tbsp apricot preserves
2–3 Tbsp balsamic vinegar
2–3 Tbsp soy sauce
1½ tsp fresh ginger, grated and peeled
4 tsp Dijon mustard
1 cup chicken broth
Salt and pepper, to taste
1–2 mandarin orange "fruit cups," *optional*

Notes:

How to...

Preheat oven to 450°F. If using bone-on chicken, place chicken pieces bone side down in pan. Otherwise, arrange in a baking dish.

In small bowl, stir preserves, vinegar, soy sauce, ginger, and Dijon until blended. Pour broth around chicken in the pan. Brush one-third of glaze over chicken pieces. Sprinkle with salt and freshly ground black pepper. Roast chicken pieces 10 minutes, then brush with half of remaining glaze. Repeat every 10 minutes, glazing pieces until thermometer inserted into meat (without touching bone) reaches 160–165°F. The cooking time will be extended with bone-on chicken a bit, and the glaze will be a little more caramelized.

Remove chicken pieces to a plate and let stand at least 5 minutes so juices can redistribute. While chicken is resting, stir pan drippings over stove to thicken and reduce. You can add a little cornstarch to cold water and add to drippings if they are not thickening. When sauce is consistency that you want, add about 2 handfuls of oranges (optional). Pour over chicken and serve.

Food Notes: *If you prefer, you can also use ⅔ of a navel orange, peeled and white pith removed, coarsely chopped. The mandarin orange snack pack is less time, less prep, and less cleanup.*

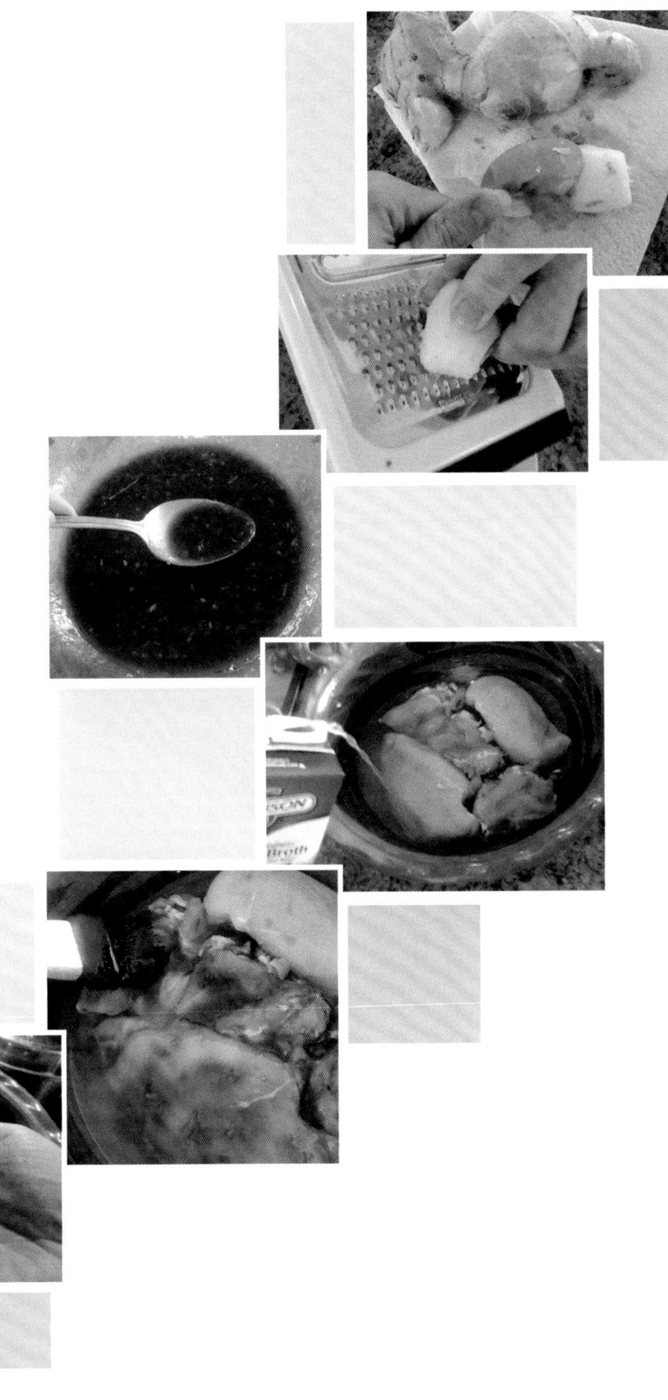

Lobster Linguine with Cognac Cream Sauce

Oh, my! Cognac and crimini mushrooms are a classic pairing. The crimini mushrooms are earthy and full-bodied, while the cognac gives a subtle, oak-barrel smokiness to the silky sauce. The little bit of acidity in the tomatoes balances out the richness, and the fresh chives and parsley bring a fresh, grassy tone to the finished dish. Don't worry about it tasting like alcohol, as the cheese and cream soften the flavor and reduce the sharpness. And what can you say about the lobster? Mmmm… it is really delicate and sweet. This is a very simple and quick, yet elegant dish that is sure to please your special guests! Feel free to substitute other proteins in place of the lobster, such as shrimp, scallops, or even chicken.

I'm sorry the measurements aren't more exact. I was sort of playing around with the recipe, and it just came out so nicely that I felt I must share.

Ingredients

serves 3 or 4, depending on what you serve it with

Handful of chives, chopped (about 3 Tbsp), *Or use green onions if you prefer.*
1 shallot, minced fine
3 cloves garlic, minced fine (about 1 Tbsp)
1 handful of grape tomatoes, halved
1 handful of sliced crimini mushrooms (about ¼ cup)
1 lb of lobster tail meat, cut into 1" pieces (2 or 3 tails)
1–2 Tbsp extra virgin olive oil
3 Tbsp butter, divided
½ cup cognac
½–⅔ cup heavy cream
⅓ cup Parmigiano Reggiano, freshly grated
Kosher salt and black pepper, to taste
Enough cooked and drained linguine for 3 to 4 people

How to...

Chop all your seasonings, start heating the pasta water, and remove lobster meat from the tails. You need all of this done first because this recipe goes really fast! To remove the tail meat, I just run my thumb between the meat and the shell and pull it out. It's okay if it doesn't come out all in one piece. You're going to chop it into pieces anyway. *This is the point at which I feel obligated to tell you that I made the fish guy kill the lobsters for me. We all have our personal limitations, and I know mine well.*

Sauté the shallots and garlic in the EVOO/butter for a couple of minutes until soft. Add the sliced mushrooms and cook for 3–4 minutes until there's only a little liquid left in the bottom of the pan. Deglaze the pan with the cognac, allowing it to come up to a nice bubble. Throw in the lobster pieces and add the remainder of the butter. Cook the lobster for 2–3 minutes until no longer translucent. Remove the meat to a bowl for later so it won't overcook. Add in the cream, tomatoes, and chives. Bring to a boil and then reduce heat to medium until sauce has thickened and reduced to a silky, creamy consistency (maybe around 5 minutes). Next add the freshly grated Parmesan cheese, kosher salt, and black pepper to your taste, then turn off the heat. Add the lobster back to sauce, then toss with the cooked/drained linguine. Garnish with a little fresh parsley if you'd like. Serve immediately.

Notes:

Crawfish Pie

One of the most unique things about the people from South Louisiana is their sheer enjoyment of getting together and talking about food. Many of us literally grow up in an environment of growing, catching, trapping, fishing, hunting, and preparing excellent and well-seasoned food. Needless to say, at large events, such as family reunions, we pass a good time by enjoying an abundance of great food and excellent fellowship. I made this recipe for just such an occasion, and it was a huge hit! My contribution to this smorgasbord was a couple of savory crawfish pies—a flaky crust containing the spicy goodness of tender crawfish swimming in an étouffée of smothered spices, vegetables, and seasonings. This is not for the faint of heart! This is a "stand up and take notice" pie. While this dish does take a while, there is *nothing* hard or technically difficult about it at all. I will walk you through each step so that you can take your bows at your next "bring something special" event.

Notes:

Ingredients

Yes, it does look like a long list, but it is mostly seasonings and spices that are already in your kitchen.

- 2 bunches of green onions
- 1 green bell pepper, chopped (about 1 cup)
- 2 cloves garlic, minced
- 1 onion, chopped (about 1 cup)
- 1 cup celery, chopped
- 1 bunch parsley, chopped
- 1 stick (8 Tbsp) butter
- ½ cup flour
- 3 Tbsp tomato sauce
- 2 tsp salt
- 1 tsp paprika
- ¼ tsp white pepper
- ¼ tsp onion powder
- ¼ tsp garlic powder
- ¼ tsp dry mustard
- 1 tsp cayenne
- ¼ tsp black pepper
- 3 cups water
- 3 lbs crawfish tails
- 2 boxes Pillsbury fold-out pie crust, *Feel free to make your own.*

How to...

Prep first by chopping green onions (separating tops and bottoms), bell pepper, garlic, onions, and celery. In a separate pile, chop parsley leaves and mix with the green onion tops. In a saucepan, melt the butter. Add flour and brown lightly, stirring constantly. Add the garlic, green onion bottoms, onions, green pepper, celery, and tomato sauce. Cover and simmer about 1 hour, stirring frequently, to keep from sticking. Add seasonings and water. Now simmer for an additional 2–3 hours. If mixture thickens too much, add more water. Mixture should be creamy and as thick as paste when tails are added.

Add the crawfish tails (or tails and fat if you prefer) to the mixture. Cook about 15 minutes or until tails are tender. Add chopped parsley and onion tops. The mixture will still be thick and creamy.

Pour filling into two pie shells. Cover with another layer of dough. Cut slits in the top.

Bake the pies at about 400°F for 35–45 minutes or until crust is golden brown without any translucent spots in it. I like to cover the edges for the last 15 minutes or so to prevent them from over-browning.

After removing them from the oven, it is important that you allow the pies to cool for at **least** 20 minutes or so. If you don't let the filling set, it will run out all over the place, which is not pretty!

This recipe works best for a "make ahead" situation. You can make the filling a day ahead and fill the pies on the day you wish to serve them. Or you can fill and freeze ahead of time, baking on the day of serving. You can also serve the étouffée filling over rice. The filling freezes well.

Beefy Mexican Cornbread

My mom made this all the time when I was growing up, and it's *always* been one of my favorite comfort foods. I'm fairly certain I would not have survived my college years if she hadn't frozen individual portions for me to take back to my tiny dorm refrigerator. This is certainly not some cornbread at a buffet with just little pieces of pepper in it. It's a complete and balanced meal, and completely filling.

Ingredients

- 1 Tbsp canola oil
- 1 lb ground beef
- 1 large onion, diced small
- Kosher salt and pepper, to taste
- Garlic powder
- 2 tsp cumin
- 1 box corn muffin mix (I used Jiffy.)
- ⅓ cup milk
- 2 large eggs
- 1 can cream-style corn
- 2–3 cups extra-sharp cheddar cheese
- 1 4-oz can chopped chilies

For more heat, replace the chilies with ⅓ cup of diced jalapeños, *jarred or fresh*

Garnish

Sour cream and fresh-chopped cilantro

Notes:

How to…

Preheat oven to 350°F. Brown the ground beef, breaking it up into small pieces with spatula as you go. When about half done, add onions, salt, pepper, garlic powder, and cumin. Sauté until the beef is no longer pink in the middle and the onions are translucent.

In a large mixing bowl, prepare the cornbread with the milk and eggs. Mix in cream-style corn, half the cheese, and chilies (or jalapeños). Clean out the iron skillet and reuse it for this next step. To a hot skillet, add a bit of canola oil. When the oil is hot, add half the cornbread batter. Layer on the meat mixture and the remainder of cheese. To be perfectly honest, I add LOTS of extra cheese. Top the cheese with the remainder of cornbread batter. Bake in the oven for 50–55 minutes until golden brown and yummy! Serve with a dollop of sour cream and garnish with a little chopped cilantro if desired.

Tip» *If using fresh jalapenos, vary the amount of heat by leaving the seeds in (more spicy) or removing them (less spicy).*

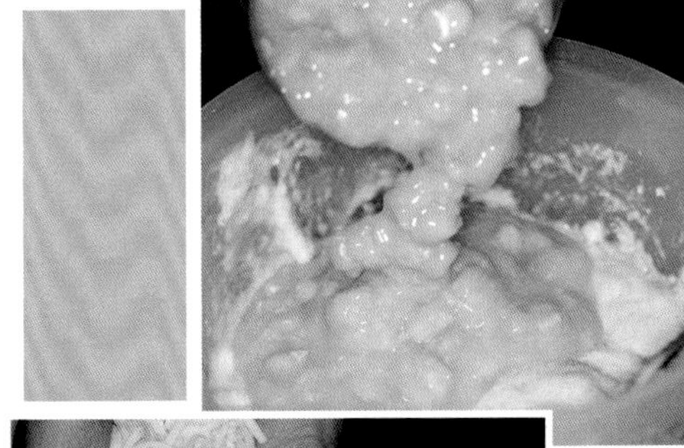

Meatballs Stroganoff

Beef Stroganoff is a Russian dish of sautéed pieces of beef served in a sauce with sour cream. From its origins in 19th-century Russia, it has become popular around the world, with considerable variations from the original recipe. Well, my kids like it with Italian-style meatballs. Yes, it usually has mushrooms, too, but I don't like them. So mine does not. But you could certainly add them.

This is such a quick and easy recipe! All the kids (plus a neighbor kid who always comes back for seconds) reaffirms this as one of our quick, easy, flavorful favorites. I'm giving you fair warning: this is NOT a "measure everything out" recipe. Instead, it's one of those things you throw together after work on a busy day because it works, it's delicious, your kids love it, and it's super fast.

Ingredients

Frozen Italian-style meatballs (½ oz each), *Make enough to cover the bottom of the pan, depending on who is home.*
1+ Tbsp Extra virgin olive oil, just enough to brown up the meatballs
2 cups beef broth
Use more for more meatballs... just go with this recipe. Don't overthink it.

Seasoning

Kosher salt and black pepper, to taste
Dried herbs (probably at least 1–1½ tsp each) parsley, oregano, and basil, *It will look like a lot of seasoning; but in the end, it will be great!*

1 cup sour cream
4 oz reduced-fat cream cheese, *optional*
1 cup heavy whipping cream or a slurry of whole milk plus a bit of corn starch
Wide egg noodles enough for whoever is there
Optional garnishes: fresh oregano leaves, Italian seasoning

Notes:

How to...

I start off with our favorite brand of frozen Italian-style meatballs. I brown them in a little olive oil in a black iron skillet. This is where you get all the good flavors—from the *fond* (brown bits) that gets stuck in the skillet. I don't think this would work as well in a non-stick skillet because it releases too much of that goodness.

After they are browned up nicely, deglaze the pan with about 2 cups of beef broth. Bring to a boil. Season them generously with salt, pepper, and dried herbs (parsley, oregano, basil). When it starts reducing, add about ⅔ cup sour cream, cream cheese if you are using it, and about a cup of heavy whipping cream. These will make the sauce creamy and silky and also act as a thickener.

Meanwhile, boil water in a separate pot and add the wide egg noodles. Boil until they are still just a bit al dente, then drain briefly and add to the simmering sauce. They will finish cooking in the sauce and also soak up a lot of that goodness.

The result is a nice, creamy sauce—slightly tangy from the sour cream, a little herbaceous from the nice green herbs, and a little beefy from the stock. ***Yum!***

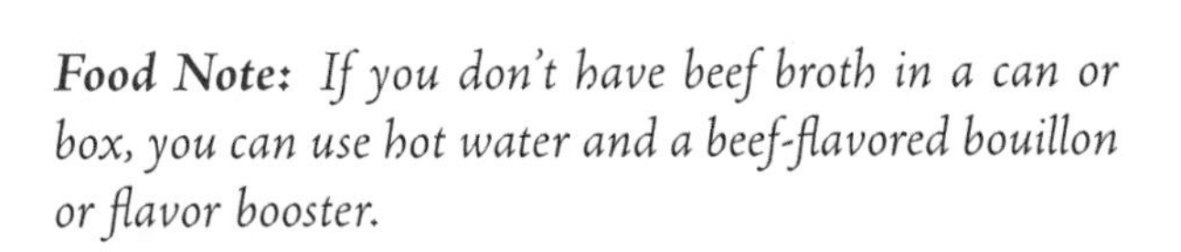

Food Note: *If you don't have beef broth in a can or box, you can use hot water and a beef-flavored bouillon or flavor booster.*

Caprese Burger

Well, well… I suppose we would have to call this a "fusion" recipe. I was making simple burgers for the kids, but what I was actually craving was something more Italian. I typically have all these things on hand in the fridge because caprese ingredients rank up there as some of my favorites. Bacon has nothing to do with it—I just wanted that extra texture and a little smoky flavor in there.

Ingredients

Your favorite blend of ground beef, *I use an 80/20 blend because I think the extra fat makes them juicy.*
Cooked, crumbled bacon, *or packaged real bacon bits*
Grape tomatoes
Fresh mozzarella
Fresh basil leaves
Steak seasoning, *or your favorite burger seasoning blend*
Your favorite buns and accompaniments

Food Nerd Notes: *Insalata Caprese (salad in the style of Capri) is a simple salad from the Italian region of Campania, made of sliced fresh buffalo mozzarella, tomatoes, and basil, and seasoned simply with salt and olive oil.*

Notes:

How to...

Form your ground beef into wide hamburger patties, making them quite a bit thinner in the middle sections (like a well) with a thicker border.

Fill with your… er… fillings of choice. Make a burger "sandwich" with another patty and grill them up! Oh, and make sure you have buns that are big enough! I had "junior-sized" buns and "king-sized" burgers. It was quite funny in the end. But cooking should be fun. The important part is that when I bit into it, warm, gooey mozzarella with tomatoes and basil oozed out. ***Yum!***

All said, you could add all sorts of "themed" fillings in there. Maybe Mexican with a stuffed poblano chili? Greek with feta and olives? French with ham and Gruyere?

Have fun. Do different and wacky things with your food. Cook with your kids. Eat at home. Love each other.

Prosciutto and Gruyere-Stuffed Chicken Breasts

One day, my coworker mentioned to me at a lunch meeting that he had stuffed some chicken breasts with prosciutto and Gruyere cheese. I think he may have mentioned a sauce or finishing them on the grill or something, but my brain never got past that initial sentence. I HAD to try that. My version is a flattened chicken breast covered in Italian seasonings, rolled up around the prosciutto and Gruyere, baked under a blanket of prepared vodka sauce, and then garnished with fresh basil ribbons. It's sort of an Italian version of Chicken Cordon Bleu, if you think about it.

Why should you try this? Well, good gracious, aren't we always looking for new ways to cook chicken? Something that's a little bit exciting? These may look a little bit fancy, but they were NOT complicated at all. And also, you could totally roll these up ahead of time and then cook them when you get home from work. I also have a sneaky suspicion that after browning them, you could throw them into a crock pot with the sauce to finish them. And we DO like options, right?

Notes:

Ingredients

1 package of skinless, boneless chicken breasts
Seasonings of your choice, *Kosher salt, black pepper, dried basil and oregano, Italian seasoning*
Thinly sliced prosciutto
1–2 slices per chicken breast
Gruyere cheese, cut into wide sticks about ½-inch wide, like a large French fry
garlic powder
2 Tbsp extra virgin olive oil
Pasta sauce of your choice (I used Jarred Vodka sauce.)
Fresh basil for garnish

How to...

Preheat the oven to 400°F.

Slice open the chicken breasts ALMOST to the other side. Lay them flat and pound them out flat as evenly as you can. Season the chicken with spices. Go easy on the salt, as the prosciutto and the cheese are fairly salty. Go heavier on the other seasonings. Roll the prosciutto around a piece of Gruyere, and then place it along one end of the breast. Roll the breast around the prosciutto and Gruyere, and secure with toothpicks. You may choose to also season the outside of the meat.

Add a couple of tablespoons of EVOO to a heavy skillet. Once the oil is really hot, carefully add the chicken breasts. It should immediately start sizzling if the oil is hot enough. Once you place the chicken, do NOT attempt to move them. They will release once they get a beautiful, golden-brown sear on them. Using long-handled kitchen tongs, turn the chicken to sear on all sides. Remove from heat.

Note» *The chicken is NOT cooked yet!*

Add some prepared sauce over the top of the chicken. I added about ½ jar of vodka sauce over mine. Insert a digital thermometer into the middle of the thickest breast you have, and then pop them into the oven until they reach 160°F. That took about 20 minutes for my chicken. I love using a digital thermometer that beeps when it reaches the correct temperature because that allows me to turn my focus to other things. It also ensures that my chicken is cooked properly without over baking it and drying it out.

Remove the pan from the oven and allow the chicken to rest (I would say for at least 5 minutes). Slice the chicken into thick pinwheels and garnish with freshly chopped basil ribbons. Serve with a little extra sauce from the pan it was baked in.

The meat is juicy and tender. You get the pop of unexpected flavor and texture in the middle and all that yummy sauce! Serve with veggies on the side or over pasta. YOU choose! ***Have fun!***

Crock Pot Beef and Broccoli

Well, in the aftermath of Hurricane Isaac, there was work to be done. My husband and I drove down to Cocodrie in South Louisiana to help my parents repair some of the damages to our beloved fishing camp. Nothing major, thank God, but enough roof, railing, and other small repairs that my mom called us for backup. What job did she give me? I was put in charge of figuring out a weekend menu, picking up groceries, and cooking so that everyone else could be up on the roof and doing hurricane cleanup out in the heat and humidity. ***Suited me fine!***

On our first night there, for everyone just driving in, I made the Creamy "Work Week" Chicken Enchiladas that everyone loves. By the time my parents got there, the enchiladas were coming out of the oven, the Black Bean and Corn Salsa was ready, Mexican rice was cooked, guacamole was ready, cold Dos Equis were appropriately outfitted with limes, and some Stevie Ray Vaughn was turned up loud. (Now THAT is the way to start off a work weekend!) For the second day, I wasn't sure how much of my help would actually be needed out in that humid inferno, so I planned a crock pot meal that I could put on early, freeing me up for other stuff. This Crock Pot Beef and Broccoli was a great choice! It's also perfect for throwing together in the mornings before you leave for work. Actually, I'm not sure how you could really mess it up, as the crock pot does all the work for you. Add, change, or delete the vegetables and the amount of heat you add in there to the preference of your family. Yes, it was a work weekend, but isn't it good to come together and work on something that brings our families so much joy?

Ingredients

1½–1¾ lbs stir fry beef (little strips) seasoned with salt and pepper.

Sauce

- 1 cup beef broth
- ½ cup soy sauce
- ½ cup brown sugar, packed
- 2 tsp sesame oil
- 1 tsp Sriracha hot chili sauce, *or hot sauce of your choice*
- 2–3 Tbsp rice wine vinegar
- 2–3 Tbsp fresh ginger, minced
- 3 large cloves garlic, minced
- 2 Tbsp corn starch
- Bag of fresh broccoli florets

Additional veggies I added

- A handful of baby carrots
- A can of water chestnuts, drained
- Half an onion, cut into thin strips
- Red and yellow pepper strips

How to...

Season the beef strips with salt and pepper and add to the crock pot. Mix the sauce ingredients and pour over beef. Mix the sauce with the beef so that each strip of meat is coated. Turn crock pot on low for 6–8 hours or high for 4 hours. After this cooking time, remove 2–3 Tbsp of sauce, let it cool slightly, and then mix it with 2 Tbsp corn starch to make a slurry. Add a bag of fresh broccoli florets and other vegetables of your choice to the beef. Add the cornstarch slurry back to the sauce and mix well. Cook on HIGH for an additional 30 minutes—lid on—no peeking! This will allow the sauce to come to a boil, for the cornstarch to thicken the sauce, and also for the broccoli and vegetables to cook. Adjust seasonings and serve over rice. Garnish with sliced green onions.

Tips

- *If you are making this in the morning for your "after work" meal, the last 30-minute cooking segment will give you enough time to put on a pot of rice. Not bad for pulling together a whole meal—and a delicious one at that—in record after-work time! And we all know that beef, cooked low and slow over all that time, practically falls apart on its own...* ***yum!***
- ***Even faster prep:*** *The night before, cut up beef and store the strips in a zip-top bag. Also, mix up the sauce and slice the onions. In the morning, take everything out of the fridge, combine the beef, sauce, onions, and carrots in the slow cooker, turn it on, and you are out the door.*
- *My mother noted that she would have enjoyed even more fresh ginger. If you are a ginger lover like she is, by all means, add more. If you don't have little kids sharing the meal, feel free to add more Sriracha chili sauce for a bigger kick. Just have fun with your meals. By all means, be guinea pigs for new recipes with some people that you love!*

Food Note: *If you are using a thin-cut sirloin, consider cutting it a little larger than you want the pieces to be at the end. The sirloin tends to shred more easily than the beef labeled "stir fry beef," which is likely to be skirt or flank steak. The "stir fry beef" holds together a little better.*

Notes:

Stuffed Pork Chops

I know you've all had those times when you wonder just what to make for dinner. You want something a little different, but you know that you really should be using all that frozen meat that you have in the freezer. Who's with me on this one? So this recipe came from the freezer, the pantry, and my little herb garden out back.

Besides all that, pork chops tend to get a bad rap. Like chicken, they can be a boring, blank slate. Did I mention that I wanted something out of the ordinary? I had been wanting to stuff some pork chops for a long time. We had purchased an entire huge pork tenderloin, cut it into individual servings of a generous thickness, and vacuum-sealed them in packs of two. I have to say, from an economical standpoint, that is definitely the way to go! It's much less expensive that way than buying individually cut pork loin chops. So on the way to work one morning, I was mentioning this to my best friend. I listed several stuffing ideas, and she immediately picked cornbread and Tasso out of the lineup! Sounded like a winner to me… so here we go!

Ingredients

The list may look a bit long, but aside from the Tasso, chances are these are mostly staple ingredients that you have in the house already. To find/order Tasso, see Food Nerd Notes *at the bottom of the recipe.*

- 1 skillet of cooked cornbread (about 2½ cups)
- ¼ cup kosher salt
- 3 Tbsp sugar
- 2 qts water
- 6 1½- to 2-inches pork loin chops, boneless
- ½ cup diced celery (about 2 stalks)
- ½ cup diced onion
- 1 Tbsp garlic, minced
- 1 tsp freshly chopped rosemary leaves
- 1 tsp freshly chopped sage leaves
- 2 Tbsp freshly chopped parsley leaves
- 1 Tbsp extra virgin olive oil
- ½ cup diced highly seasoned, thick-cut smoked ham (I used Tasso.)
- 1 Tbsp butter
- ⅔ cup diced apples
- ½ cup chicken broth for dressing
- ½ cup chicken broth for making pan gravy
- 1 Tbsp cold butter, *optional*

Kosher salt and black pepper, to taste

How to...

Steps you can prep ahead: Make the cornbread, brine the chops, and chop the veggies.

Cornbread: Begin your prep by making a skillet of your favorite cornbread. Or if you have cornbread left-over, this would be a perfect use for it! Then just set it aside and allow to cool.

Brine: Whisk salt and sugar together into 2 quarts of cold water. Add pork chops (thawed) and cover. Refrigerate for 1 hour. While brining the pork and allowing the cornbread to cook and cool, chop all the veggies and herbs. Remove the pork chops from the brine and dry them well!

Now let's cook! In a heavy-bottomed skillet, add about a tablespoon of the olive oil and begin to sauté the Tasso. Add in the chopped celery and onions, and after they start cooking down, add the garlic and butter. Cook until the onions and celery are soft and translucent. Add a teaspoon of kosher salt and some black pepper to taste to season up this vegetable mix. Add in the chopped herbs when the veggies are almost done and sauté until fragrant. Remove from heat and let them cool a bit.

In a large bowl, crumble the cornbread. Add chopped apples, the cooked vegetables, and ½ cup of chicken broth. It will probably still look dry to you, but trust me on this one. You don't want it overly soggy at the end! Mix well.

Notes:

With the pork, which you have removed from the brine and patted dry thoroughly, make a pocket in each, which extends deep into the meat. You want to leave the back and the edges intact to make an envelope. You also want all the borders to be uniform so they will all cook the same. Stuff each chop with ½ cup of stuffing. It will probably look like it won't fit... but it will compress! Use toothpicks to secure the openings so your stuffing won't come out. Season each stuffed chop with kosher salt and black pepper.

For this recipe, I grilled the pork chops on my trusty grill pan! On medium-high heat, I preheated about a tablespoon of olive oil in the pan first until the oil was really hot. I also inserted my digital thermometer into the meat portion of one of the thicker chops. You are going to want your internal temperature to be 145°F for the pork. Careful to not put the thermometer into just the dressing! I grilled them about 7 minutes per side and turned them on the cut side for a minute or so to get some nice color on the third side that I created with the pocket.

Remove the chops to a plate and allow them to rest for 5 minutes prior to serving them. This will allow the juices to redistribute rather than running out all over your plate and giving you dry meat. After removing the chops, deglaze the pan with about ½ cup of chicken broth. You could also add 1 Tbsp cold butter to make it silky. All those stuck-on bits of food in the bottom of the pan (called "fond") will release, combine with the broth, and make a great pan gravy. Season with a bit of salt and pepper. After you cook it down a couple of minutes (The chops are resting anyway, so why not?), pour that gravy over the chops. You have just elevated your chops from really nice to great! Garnish with extra herbs left over from making the dressing. I served these with a rice pilaf, stewed apples, and steamed broccoli.

Food Nerd Notes: *Tasso is a specialty of South Louisiana cuisine. It is a spicy, peppery version of smoked pork made from the shoulder butt. The butt, which will weigh 7 to 8 pounds, is sliced across the grain into thick pieces. These are dredged in a salt cure for a few hours, then rinsed, rubbed with a spice mixture containing Cayenne pepper and garlic, and hot-smoked until cooked through. Though Tasso may be eaten on its own, it is more often used as part of a flavor base for stews or braised vegetables. It is used in dishes ranging from pasta to crab cakes, soup to gravy. Appropriate to its roots, Tasso is most often found in recipes of southern or Cajun/Creole origin.*

The Tasso used in this recipe can be found at Day's Smokehouse in Watson, Louisiana. In case you are wondering, yes, they do ship their products! Visit their website at http://dayssmokehouse.com/. Other alternatives could be pancetta with extra spices added or Spanish chorizo or good old bacon! If you use another type of ham, use one that is very smoky and add extra spices.

Creamy Italian Sausage and Tortellini

Okay, let me be the first one to point this out: this is not a very *pretty* dish. It's okay; you can think that, too. On the flip side, however, my husband—a *big* fan of Italian food—boldly proclaimed, "This is one of the best things you've ever made!"

Moms out there will have several reasons to like this recipe:

1. It's fast—30 minutes.
2. It's super easy—brown the sausage and dump the rest together.
3. There are some very healthy veggies hiding in there!
4. It's delicious!

So if those are some criteria that you are looking for, BINGO! It will be perfect for the "after work/shuttle the kids to various events/practices/get out of the kitchen quickly so you can enjoy life" type of meal.

Ingredients

- 1 lb Italian sausage, *I used mild, but it typically comes in differing degrees of heat.*
- 2 cans of diced tomatoes with Italian seasoning
- 1 "family-sized" container of cheese tortellini
- 1 bag fresh baby spinach, stems removed and rough chopped (or one 10-oz pkg frozen spinach)
- 1 box (4 cups) chicken broth
- 1 8-oz block of reduced-fat cream cheese
- ¼ cup cold water plus 1 Tbsp cornstarch
- Dried basil and oregano, to taste

How to...

Remove the sausage casings and break apart the Italian sausage into bite-sized pieces as you brown it in a heavy pot. But don't brown it until it is dry and hard. Once it's no longer pink, dump everything else in. Add the seasoning last, so you can adjust as needed. Give it a nice stir to distribute the cream cheese. It's done when the tortellini are tender and the sauce has reduced and thickened, roughly about 10–12 minutes after dumping it all together. That's it, folks! You can't get much simpler than that!

Notes:

Cranberry Glazed Pork Tenderloin

When the cooler weather starts rolling in, there are cranberries aplenty in the grocery stores. They are sweet, tangy, pretty, and wildly healthy for you! This recipe may look fancy, but it is, in fact, very simple. The fresh, fragrant, slightly spicy cranberry glaze baked onto juicy pork tenderloin will definitely have your taste buds dancing. ***Yum!***

Ingredients

1 12-oz bag fresh (or frozen) cranberries
1¼ cup sugar
2 Tbsp orange zest (from 1 large orange)
⅓–¼ cup fresh ginger, minced
¼ cup orange juice
1¼ cup water
2–3 tsp fresh chopped rosemary
Pork tenderloin, *I actually cook two. One to eat, one to freeze for another time.*
Chicago steak seasoning, *or seasoning of your choice*
Canola or vegetable oil for searing meat

How to...

This is one of those sauces where all you have to do is combine all the ingredients in a saucepan and let it go! Really—that's it. Combine fresh cranberries, sugar, orange zest, minced ginger, orange juice, and water.

Note: *The easiest way to peel fresh ginger is with the edge of a spoon. Seriously. So easy. And the fragrance? Wow... somewhat like a spicy lemon. Really adds a note of "Wow!" to the dish. If you are cooking for small children, you may want to use a little less ginger. It can be a little spicy for them.*

Notes:

Allow the cranberries to come up to a boil, then cook for about 10–15 minutes on medium heat. At some point, the cranberries will start to pop. Then you can lower the temperature down to a simmer for a while until it gets to the desired consistency. Add the chopped rosemary last. You can keep the sauce on a low simmer or turn off completely. The sauce can easily be refrigerated if making ahead. Also, depending on the texture and appearance you desire, you can either leave it chunky or you can pass the sauce through a fine mesh sieve to get all the chunks out and have a smooth sauce. But either way, believe me… this cranberry sauce is MUCH MORE flavorful than the stuff in the can! Personally, I actually like the aesthetics of the chunkiness, so I do not strain my glaze.

Now for the pork. Season the pork liberally with the seasoning of your choice. Sear the pork on ALL sides in hot (canola or vegetable) oil. We want to sear in the juices and also have a beautiful crust on the outside. Be sure to pat the meat dry before you do this, or it will not develop that beautiful brown color. You can see here that one of my tenderloins had more moisture on it than the other, and did not brown as well.

After the meat is seared, insert a digital thermometer into the thickest end of the pork. I use the kind that has a coated wire that leads from the inside of the oven to the outside. You can set the desired temperature of the meat so there is no guesswork. Remember, the pork will continue to cook even after you remove it from the oven while it rests. You don't want it overdone or dried out. After getting the thermometer set, pour the cranberry glaze over the tenderloins. Bake uncovered at 375°F until internal meat temperature reaches 145–150°F. This will depend on the size and weight of the meat, most likely around 20–25 minutes. PLEASE allow the meat to rest for about 5–10 minutes before cutting into it. You must give it time to rest. This will redistribute the juices in the meat. If you do not, all the juices will run out all over the cutting board and out of the meat. This would result in a drier product. Dry meat is not good.

Slice the pork into ½-inch pieces and serve with some of the sauce on the side. Mmm… isn't it pretty?

So this is the final product. Fresh, fragrant, slightly spicy cranberry glaze baked onto a juicy pork tenderloin. ***Yum!***

Leftover Pot Roast Pot Pies

One night, we had a nice big beef pot roast with all the veggies. Today, we have leftovers! This afternoon after being abandoned by all my kiddos (one of those nights where they all go in different directions), I decided I should do something with that leftover roast. Now even if you aren't the abandoned-and-alone mom, I think you will love this! Pot pie is re-purposing at its best. The Marsala gravy gives it a completely different taste than the first dish, so it really does feel like you are eating something new. Now THAT's the way to stretch your dollars!

This is really one of those "what do I have around here" dishes... a pot roast pot pie with a flaky, golden, puff pastry topping! ***Yum!*** Of course you could put anything in here that you wanted. How easy is this? Everything is pretty much all cooked. Throw it all together and throw some pastry on top!

Ingredients

Right away, you'll notice that there aren't many measurements here. That's because the amount of leftovers varies! Just sort of eyeball it.

Puff pastry sheets
Canola oil
Flour
Beef broth
Fresh thyme
Marsala wine, *or regular red wine*
Salt, pepper, granulated garlic, or onion powder
Leftover beef roast and veggies
Frozen peas and corn
1 egg plus water
Garnish with fresh cracked pepper and a few fresh thyme leaves

Notes:

How to...

Take out a sheet of puff pastry first (about 40 minutes ahead of time) to thaw.

Make a simple roux with a couple of tablespoons canola oil and a couple tablespoons of flour. Cook until about the color of peanut butter and then start adding the liquids. I probably added up to about 2 cups of beef broth. Stir to incorporate until smooth and then add herbs. Something in here needs to be fresh and bright for a balanced flavor. Next add about ⅔ cup or so of Marsala wine to the gravy. The Marsala is a game changer here. It deepens the flavor and gives it a delicious complexity. Season well with kosher salt, black pepper, and granulated garlic. You need to keep cooking the gravy on low until it loses the floury taste.

To individual ramekins, add a cup or so of chopped leftover roast beef and then leftover chopped veggies (carrots, potatoes, onions, and peppers). I had a bit of gravy left in my roast, so I gave a nice spoon or so to each dish. Careful to not add TOO much of the original gravy or else it will still taste like last night's pot roast. Now in my head, pot pies always have peas and corn in them. As these didn't have a place in my original roast, I added some frozen ones. Layer the delicious Marsala gravy over the veggies and roast. It'll cook down and mix in on its own. But if you want to mix it, knock yourselves out.

Cover—Open up the thawed puff pastry on a lightly flowered cutting board so it won't stick. I made circles to follow with a bowl that was just a little larger than my ramekins. I wanted some of the pastry to hang over the sides a little bit. Then I cut the pastry with a paring knife. Fit the pastry over the ramekins. Prepare an egg wash with 1 egg and a tablespoon or so of water. Whisk to mix. Brush the egg wash over the pastry—this will give it a beautiful golden sheen.

Finish the pastry with a few sprinkles of fresh cracked pepper and a few fresh thyme leaves and then cut a few vents in the pastry to allow steam to escape. I put them on a cookie sheet in case anything boiled over. Bake at 400°F about 18 minutes or so. You'll see when they're done.

Tip » *Feel free to change this up by using pie crust or even biscuit dough on top!*

Black Iron Skillet Deep-Dish Pizza

One day, I got a craving for a good deep-dish pizza—the fork-and-knife kind, not the eat-out-of-your-hand sort. But I certainly did not feel like sitting in a restaurant while they cooked one for me. I also remembered that I had some amazing Italian sausage marinara in the freezer. BINGO! This thing was definitely going to happen!

If you have the time and inclination to make your own pizza dough, it's not hard at all, but it is somewhat time consuming. So on this busy work-week day, I grabbed some pre-made dough and thawed out my marinara… and this amazing pizza came together in a snap! I decided to make it in a cast iron skillet for a few reasons. They make a great crispy crust. They distribute and retain heat extremely well. And I bet more people have a black iron skillet than a pizza stone (much less a deep-dish pizza stone cooker). So let's use what we have and make it awesome!

How to…

The Crust

Preheat the oven to 350°F. I picked up some pre-made pizza dough on the way home so that dinner would come together quickly. This was enough dough to make a standard large pizza. If you prefer, you can make your own dough. We are also going to go for the stuffed crust concept, so let's get our cheese sticks ready by cutting a block of cheese into little logs. Then get your dough rolled out. Roll out the dough on a floured surface and then sprinkle the rested dough with more flour. Don't forget to flour your rolling pin also, so it won't stick. Roll out the dough in a nice wide circle.

Now prepare your black iron skillet. Add a tablespoon or so of canola oil to the bottom. We want a crunchy crust on the bottom. Transfer the dough to the pan. Let it drape loosely. Gently press the dough all the way into the pan. Add some logs of mozzarella string cheese to the edges of the crust. I've also used Vermont white cheddar. Add what you have. Roll the edges of the crust around the cheese. Then you are all ready to put in the filling.

Notes:

Ingredients

Okay, here's fair warning. I didn't measure a thing! This is more of a concept recipe. People vary widely in their preference for amounts of sauce, cheese, meats, veggies, etc. So do what feels right for your family.

Premade Pizza Dough

Bench flour for rolling out dough
1 Tbsp canola oil for skillet

Mozzarella string cheese
Pepperoni or deli meats of your choice
Green bell peppers, chopped
Fresh tomatoes, some diced, some sliced
3–4 cups shredded or chopped mozzarella cheese

Dried Seasonings of your Choice

Dried basil
Dried oregano
Garlic powder

2–3 cups Italian sausage marinara
Garlic butter sauce

My blog, Menu Musings, *has a recipe and step-by-step tutorial to make* Italian Sausage Marinara. *Do you have to make the Italian sausage marinara? I personally think it will taste better, but if you are pressed for time, grab a jar of marinara, crumble and brown some Italian sausage, and add them together with some extra spices! Just reduce the sauce down so it isn't too runny.*

You can also visit the blog for a recipe and step-by-step tutorial to make your own pizza dough. *But if you are making this after work, where can you find premade dough? Try your local wholesale club or even ask your local pizza place to sell you some! In a pinch, you can even find it in a can (next to the canned biscuits) at the grocery store.*

The Filling

For the deep-dish pizza concept, we are NOT going to add the sauce first. We are actually going to create a barrier between the dough and the sauce with the other fillings. First, cover the whole bottom with pepperoni. Feel free to use turkey pepperoni or your choice of deli meats (ham, turkey, salami, etc.). There should be no spaces left. Follow the pepperoni with a handful of green bell peppers. Of course you should feel free to add whatever fillings suit your fancy!

Next, add a chopped up fresh tomato and then a layer of cheese. In the photos, it appears as if Lily is casting a spell on the Pizza Spirits for good luck! But then again, she's always working her magic in in the kitchen!

Add about half of the chopped mozzarella for this first cheese layer. Season it up well with some dried basil. Finally, here comes the sauce. *If you purchased the marinara,* promise me you'll make your own one day because this made the whole pizza wonderful!

Add the other half of the diced up mozzarella cheese to the top, and then add thin slices of a large juicy tomato. Season it up with some freshly ground Italian seasoning. Lastly, sprinkle some fresh oregano leaves, stripped from the stems, over the top.

Cooking Directions

Now let's do some magic! To get that crunchy crust, let's do a little trick. Before we throw the whole thing in the oven, *cook it on the stovetop for a few minutes* on high/medium-high so that oil in the bottom can get super hot and start cooking the bottom of the crust.

Next, put it into the oven for about 10 minutes on 350°F and then kick the temperature up to 450°F for the next 10–12 minutes. After you remove it from the oven, brush the crust with some melted garlic butter. Why? Because it tastes great that way! When we do get pizza delivery, I LOVE the garlic butter that comes with it, so I incorporated that idea into this recipe as well.

Brushing on the garlic butter gives your pizza several minutes to rest. After all, you don't want the whole thing to collapse when you cut into it. Haven't we ALL had that happen with layered dishes—like a too-hot lasagna? Not pretty!

I can tell you that from this end, it was fabulous: rich and satisfying thanks to the homemade marinara, melted cheese, crunchy crust, and meaty filling with fresh flavors from the tomatoes, herbs, and peppers! I bet you wish YOU had a fork and knife to dig in! So all in all, a great afternoon project! We had a good time making this and had a great meal in the end. I hope you'll try it as well!

Roasted Vegetable Chicken Pot Pie

Chicken pot pie is such a classic comfort dish! When I have a crazy day that makes me crave comfort, this is often my therapy of choice. If I am really pressed for time, I use a quick recipe of a bag of mixed frozen veggies, but if I have a bit more time, this is definitely my preference. Part of the therapeutic process for me is the peeling, chopping, and dicing. Besides that, roasting brings out the sweetness of vegetables that *no* other method can and gives you a whole additional textural element that works beautifully in this dish. They get that crusty caramelization on the edges that is delectable. This is also a great way for you to use up extra roasted chicken that you may have.

So all in all, this dish is chock-full of healthy roasted vegetables, lean roasted chicken, a creamy sauce, and a flaky puffy crust. ***Mmmm****. . . .*

Ingredients

for 4 generous servings

4 carrots, sliced into equal-sized coins
4 small red potatoes, cut into about 8 pieces
6 fresh pearl onions, cut into halves
A big handful of fresh green beans
About 2 Tbsp extra virgin olive oil
Kosher salt and cracked black pepper, to taste
Garlic powder, to taste
4 Tbsp butter
4 Tbsp flour
1–1½ cups chicken stock
⅔ cup half-and-half
About ½ tsp poultry seasoning
1 Tbsp cooking sherry
1 tsp fresh dill, plus more for garnish
2 roasted chicken breasts, chopped roughly
Frozen sweet corn
Frozen sweet peas
1 sheet of puff pastry, thawed for about 30 minutes

How to...

Roasted Vegetables

Preheat the oven to 425°F. Get the vegetables roasting first. Wash, trim, peel, and chop your veggies. Drizzle them with olive oil and sprinkle with salt, pepper, and garlic powder. The potatoes need a bit more salt than the other vegetables. Spread them out on a baking sheet (or two) so that they are in a single layer and, if possible, not touching each other. I separated the green beans out from the vegetables and roasted them separately as it occurred to me that they would roast much more quickly than the others. The green beans will only take about 15 minutes (shake them around halfway through). I roasted the other vegetables for 35 minutes, shaking these halfway through as well.

Notes:

Sherry Cream Sauce

In a saucepan, melt the butter and whisk in the flour to essentially make a roux. Let these cook together for a couple of minutes until just a faint bit of color develops. Add in the chicken stock gradually and stir in until smooth. Don't be frightened when it becomes a big blob. Ha ha! Next, add in the half-and-half (or milk if you prefer). Stir until smooth. Cook over medium-low until it's all nice and thick and bubbly (about 5 minutes). Season the sauce with salt, pepper, and poultry seasoning to taste and stir in the sherry. Whisk until smooth again and then turn off the heat. Add in the fresh dill and stir.

Assembly

After the vegetables have roasted, let them cool for a couple of minutes while you rough chop the roasted chicken. I like to have sizable chunks of chicken in my pot pies, as I don't want the chicken to break down too much when I stir it all together. Add the chicken, frozen corn and peas, and roasted vegetables to the cream sauce. Stir together gently to avoid breaking up the chicken.

Add the mixture into individual ovenproof ramekins. Sprinkle the partially thawed puff pastry with a little flour and roll it a bit to sort of erase the creases. Cut the sheet into quarters. Place each of the pieces on top of the filled ramekins, allowing the edges to drape gently over the sides. Brush the tops of the pastry with melted butter and sprinkle with kosher salt, cracked black pepper, and a little chopped fresh dill. Bake at 425°F for 15 minutes or until golden brown.

Prep Ahead . . .

You could prepare this ahead of time for a hot dinner later. Prepare recipe through the point of filling the ramekins. Cover the filled ramekins with plastic wrap and keep in the refrigerator. Later, pop them in the oven for about 20 minutes on 350°F. Then turn up the heat to 425°F and top each with the pastry, salt, pepper, and dill. Bake an additional 15 minutes with the pastry until the top is fluffy and golden brown.

Feel free to substitute a "roll out" pie crust for the puff pastry if you prefer. Bake as directed on package. If I use pie crust, I like to have one crust on the bottom and a second one on top. It's nice to have options!

Grilled Tilapia with Lemon Basil Vinaigrette

As the weather heats up and the summer months begin to approach, we often find ourselves outside grilling more. These tilapia filets are brushed with a bright and flavorful lemon basil vinaigrette and treated to a dusting with bold citrus spices before hitting the grill for a light and healthy meal. This vinaigrette would be suitable for the fish of your choice or even grilled chicken or shrimp.

Ingredients

for about 8 filets of tilapia

Garnish Preperation

Roasted grape tomatoes
1 cup grape tomatoes, EVOO, kosher salt, black pepper, and dried basil

Vinaigrette

2 Tbsp extra virgin olive oil
1 tsp lemon zest (from 2 lemons)
3 Tbsp freshly squeezed lemon juice (about 1½ lemons)
2 tsp capers, drained
2 cloves of minced garlic (about 1 rounded tsp)
2 Tbsp fresh minced basil
½ tsp kosher salt
¼ tsp black pepper

Fish

8 tilapia filets
Citrus seasoning blend of your choice, *I used two different kinds to try them out (separately, not mixed).*
Mojito lime marinade (I used McCormick.)
Citrus BBQ rub (I used Feiny's Rubs, see www.feintastingfoods.com.)

Garnish

Fresh lemon slices
2 Tbsp fresh basil, minced

Notes:

How to...

Roasted Tomatoes (for garnish)

Start these first, as this takes the longest. Slice the grape tomatoes in half. With the cut side up, drizzle them with a little EVOO. Sprinkle with kosher salt, black pepper, and dried basil. I never measure. Just sprinkle a bit. Roast them in a shallow baking pan at 400°F for about 25 minutes. They will start dehydrating a bit as they roast. Cover to keep warm and set aside when they are done. When you get them in the oven, start on the vinaigrette.

Vinaigrette

Mix together the EVOO, lemon zest, lemon juice, capers, garlic, basil, salt, and pepper. Set aside about ⅓ of this vinaigrette to use on the cooked fish. Use the bulk of it to season the raw filets.

Please note » *If you have a little one helping you, YOU will probably want to handle the microplane zester to zest your lemon yourself. For those of you who have never "zested" before, be careful to ONLY get the colored portion of the fruit. Do NOT get any of the white pith underneath, as it is bitter. The zest contains all the fragrance and oils of the peeling.*

Fish

If using frozen filets, thaw first. Spray aluminum foil with a bit of cooking spray and set the fish on them. Brush the fish with the vinaigrette designated for the raw filets. Season the fish filets generously with seasoning blend of your choice. Grill the fish on the foil trays at about 325–350°F for around 10–12 minutes. It's hard to say exactly since each batch of fish you get will be different thicknesses. The fish will start to flake easily with a fork when they are cooked. At the end, brush the fish with the reserved vinaigrette prior to serving. Garnish with the roasted tomatoes, a slice of lemon, and some fresh basil ribbons.

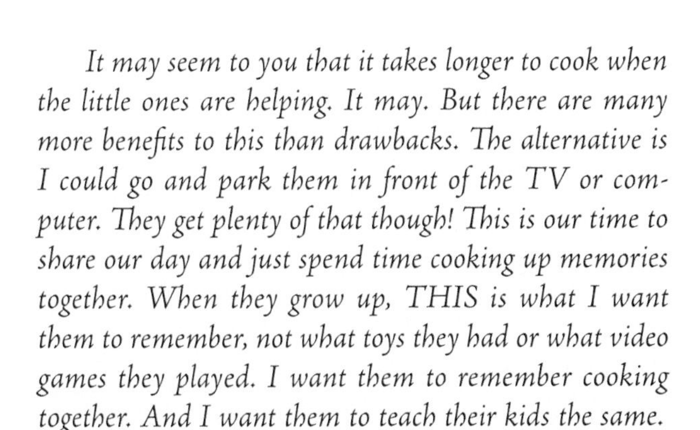

Behind the scenes: *With our fish, we had grilled sweet corn and Balsamic Roasted Brussels Sprouts with Parmesan. In case you are wondering, yes, I do let my kids use knives. Big ones. Sharp ones. It's the way my mom always taught us. The sharp knives require much less pressure and are less dangerous than dull ones. They learn knife skills under my supervision. That way, the "almighty knife" is much less of a mystery that they will be tempted to play with when my back is turned.*

It may seem to you that it takes longer to cook when the little ones are helping. It may. But there are many more benefits to this than drawbacks. The alternative is I could go and park them in front of the TV or computer. They get plenty of that though! This is our time to share our day and just spend time cooking up memories together. When they grow up, THIS is what I want them to remember, not what toys they had or what video games they played. I want them to remember cooking together. And I want them to teach their kids the same.

Pickle Brined Fried Chicken

So somehow, I went to bed and dreamed I was making fried chicken. Seriously?! Yes. As I sat there in the morning trying to plan the menu for the evening, I wondered what angle I wanted to take. Then there was Mr. Picky Palate (who shall remain nameless), who came down for breakfast. We apparently purchased the "wrong" kosher pickles, and yes, he noticed that the ones in his lunch weren't the same as usual. Sigh… so it hit me. I have chicken in the freezer. I am going to marinate these in a pickle juice brine. (*Thank you, Mr. Picky Palate!*) Think about it: it has all those flavors in it—the salt, the acid, the slight sweetness. ***Yes!***

Okay, I'll admit that you have every right to be a bit circumspect, but this was definitely going to happen. Every other time I've brined my poultry, I've been very pleased with the results. Why should this be different, right? OH MY WORD! Can I just tell you that the kids went nuts over this chicken! It was so tender and juicy… and that very faint pickle flavor in the background was very similar to the chicken that we get from that our favorite fast food chicken chain! SCORE! I actually did a little happy dance in the kitchen. Yes, really. Scout's honor.

You MUST try it! My two teens even took the leftovers for their lunch the next day. And the best part, for all you busy people out there, is that the technique I used actually cut OUT a few steps!

Ingredients

- 2 lbs boneless, skinless chicken tenders
- Pickle juice from 1 jar of kosher pickles
- 16 oz container of plain, non-fat Greek yogurt
- 1 box seasoned flour (I used Kentucky Kernel.)

Plus my OWN seasonings!

- ½ tsp kosher salt
- ½ tsp black pepper
- ¼ tsp cayenne pepper
- 1 tsp garlic powder
- ½ tsp onion powder
- 1 tsp dried oregano
- 1 Tbsp parsley flakes
- 1 tsp baking powder

Canola or peanut oil for frying

How to...

I threw my chicken into a gallon-sized zip-top bag and poured a whole jar of pickle juice over them. I allowed them to brine in the pickle juice for 2½ hours in the fridge. I took them out to take some of the chill off while I got the rest of the stuff ready.

I wanted moist, tender chicken with a slight tangy flavor. Rather than do a typical egg wash, I decided to go with a plain, non-fat Greek yogurt. It's thick and creamy, has no fat but lots of protein, and has a great tangy flavor.

I wanted a very flavorful coating. What is fried chicken without a great flavorful coating, right? Just combine all the stuff and remove the chicken from the brine. Coat the chicken first in the Greek yogurt and then in the seasoned flour (includes my seasonings). Make sure you get lots of that great flour coating on it! Fry at about 350–360°F until golden brown and crispy... and, of course, cooked inside! I found out that when I fried about 3 strips at a time, it took about 6 minutes. When I fried only 2 at a time, it took a couple of minutes less. You may have to figure out what works best for your fryer or pot.

They were SO juicy and tender and wonderful! And let's see—what did we cut out? I did NOT season the chicken before battering because the brine had lots of flavor, including salt, already. I did not have to make up an egg wash. And I did not have to salt the chicken when it came out of the fryer. These were a homerun with my kids!

Notes:

Creole Red Snapper

Recently, we were on a Father's Day trip with my husband's extended family. They took a deep-sea fishing trip and limited out on red snapper, so you bet we were going to cook them up! The thing is, after getting up so early and fishing all day in the heat, most of the fishermen promptly fell asleep. So what do we do with these beautiful, HUGE filets? It had to be something fairly simple, since we were staying in condos with limited cookware, etc. I wasn't sure of the palates of some of the family members, so I was shooting for a balance between "regular enough to feel safe for someone to try it without hesitation," but "exciting enough" to feel special.

So this is what came out of the equation! Oh my goodness… this may be one of my favorite fish preparations ever, and so easy! Very moist and flavorful too!

When I say 3 filets, that's because each filet was so large that they took up a whole casserole dish! If you are using smaller fish filets, adjust accordingly.

Ingredients — for 8 servings

- 2 sticks of butter
- 4 cloves of garlic, minced
- 1 tsp Worcestershire sauce
- 2 tsp Creole seasoning
- Juice of 1 large lemon
- 2 Tbsp chopped chives
- 2 Tbsp chopped parsley
- 3 large filets of red snapper, *Each one takes up a whole dish.*
- Enough sliced onions or carrots to make a "bed" for the fish, *optional*
- 1 cup bread crumbs
- ⅔ cup freshly grated Parmigiano Reggiano

Notes:

How to...

Begin by preparing your sauce. In a medium-sized sauce pan, melt butter and add the next six ingredients together. These things will then magically transform into a fabulous sauce! Brush this sauce liberally over both sides of the fish filets. I like to first do one side, then flip that side down onto a bed of sliced onions or carrots, then brush the other side. Why on a bed? Well, the vegetables impart some additional flavor to the fish while it bakes, AND they do a very important job—which is to keep the fish up off of the bottom of the dish so it won't stick!! Nothing is worse than making a beautiful piece of fish that you can't get off of the dish, or that tears apart when you try to unstick it! My preference is sliced onions (round, like onion steaks); but on this particular day, I didn't have any.

So now let's make the breadcrumbs. If you have some Panko breadcrumbs, these would be fine to use, but I didn't, so we made breadcrumbs. Some dried out French bread works great, too. (The drier, the better!) But like I said, if you don't have any, just make them. Throw a few pieces of bread in the blender, and let it go! Mix the breadcrumbs and Parmesan cheese into the remainder of the sauce. We are going to turn this into a wonderfully seasoned paste that will bake on the top of the fish and create a crust!

Now, spoon that awesome cheesy breadcrumb paste onto the top of the filets, distributing it evenly among the fish. For these big filets, I baked them at 400°F for 30 minutes. The fish should be opaque and flake easily in the center with a fork. For smaller fish filets, adjust your cooking time. Garnish with a few extra-fresh chives and thin lemon slices. Each person can squeeze a little lemon over their own portion. Each of these large filets is probably enough for 3 adult portions.

Seared Marinated Tuna Steaks

Yes, we love grilled tuna steaks! Tuna is one of the best sources of lean protein out there, and it can essentially be a blank slate for flavors. For this recipe, we marinated the steaks in an Asian-inspired sauce that will both flavor and further tenderize the meat. The key to a great tuna steak is to cook it as a medium-rare steak, as overcooking will produce a tough, dry fish.

Ingredients

- ½ cup soy sauce
- ⅓ cup rice wine vinegar
- 1 tsp Sriracha chili sauce, *or hot sauce of your choice*
- 4 green onions, chopped
- 2 large cloves garlic, finely chopped
- 1½ inches of peeled ginger, finely chopped or grated
- 1 Tbsp brown sugar
- 4 dinner-sized sushi-grade tuna steaks
- White and black sesame seeds, mixed

How to...

In a bowl or measuring cup, combine the soy sauce, rice wine vinegar, Sriracha sauce, green scallions, garlic, ginger, and brown sugar. Add the marinade over the tuna steaks in a shallow dish. Cover and let sit in the fridge for up to 2 hours, spooning the marinade over the tuna periodically.

Remove the tuna from the fridge and let sit in the marinade outside of the fridge for 20 to 30 minutes so the steaks can come up to room temperature. When the tuna has come to room temperature, remove it from the marinade. Gently scrape off some of the marinade when ready to sear the tuna. Sprinkle the top surface with the mixture of sesame seeds.

Notes:

Bring your grill pan (or grill) to very high heat. When the pan is VERY hot (but not quite smoking), add the tuna steaks, sesame seed side DOWN, and sear for about 4–5 minutes on the first side. Don't try to move them during this time. While searing, sprinkle the top (naked) side of the tuna with additional sesame seeds. Flip the steaks and sear on the second side for about 3 minutes. The second side will not take as long to cook, as the tuna will have begun to heat up by this point.

Remove the tuna from the pan and let it rest for 4 to 5 minutes. Garnish with additional green onions if you'd like.

If you desire a sauce for the tuna, you could bring the marinade to a boil for 2–3 minutes in a small saucepan and serve on the side. For a thinner dipping sauce, boil as is. For a thicker sauce, add a tiny bit of cornstarch (¼ tsp) before heating, then bring to a boil. By boiling for a few minutes, you will kill any bacteria from the raw tuna and render the sauce safe to eat. If this makes you too nervous, you could just double the marinade recipe and separate it prior to adding the tuna.

Mardi Gras Pasta

The month of February always ushers in carnival season! And Mardi Gras is celebrated with great enthusiasm down here in the South. The name of this dish comes from the bright variation of colors and textures—purple from the sausage and purple onions; green from the green bell peppers, basil, and oregano; and gold from the yellow bell peppers, carrot doubloons, and long ribbons of pasta… ***yummy!***

What we end up with is a super-creamy, smoky sauce with both chicken and smoked sausage, the sweetness of the peppers and onions, and the saltiness of the grated cheese… ***yum!*** And the best part is how easy this is! It's a great way to incorporate more veggies into everyone's favorite thing—pasta! Unless you are using spicy sausage, this recipe is super family friendly!

Ingredients

½ green bell pepper, julienned
½ yellow bell pepper, julienned
½ red bell pepper, julienned
1 large garlic clove, minced
½ large purple onion, julienned
3 large carrots, peeled and cut into coins
1–1½ lbs chicken breast tenderloins cut into chunks, about 1 inch each
½ lb smoked pork sausage or Andouille sausage, cut on the bias
Dried seasonings: *salt, pepper, garlic powder, dried basil, dried oregano, all to taste*
1–2 Tbsp extra virgin olive oil
2 cups chicken broth/stock
1 jar Alfredo sauce
Fettuccine noodles (I usually use 1 lb.)
Freshly grated Parmigiano Reggiano cheese for garnish

Notes:

How to...

Gather up your team players... julienne slices of various peppers, a large clove of garlic, part of a red onion, and some carrots. Next, cut up your chicken and Andouille sausage. Season the chicken LIBERALLY! This seasoning will carry the whole sauce! Use salt, pepper, garlic powder, basil, and oregano (or whatever strikes your fancy!).

Heat a large (12-inch) skillet and add olive oil. Add the seasoned chicken pieces to HOT oil—you want the outside to sear! Add the sausage pieces to the chicken. Once the fat starts coming out of the sausage, and the chicken is starting to brown nicely, add the veggies, stirring to sauté. The flavors need to "marry" for a while. When chicken is almost done, add chicken broth to deglaze. Stir together.

TIP» *I leave my veggies sliced or in a large dice so the "picky eaters" can pick them out. Plus, they look really pretty like that. Cut them however you most enjoy them.*

Add the jar of Alfredo sauce and stir together. Simmer for a while.

Boil water for fettuccine in medium/large pot, and boil noodles according to directions on package. Drain and immediately add the noodles to the sauce. Garnish as desired with freshly grated Parmigiano Reggiano cheese, chopped parsley, or chopped, fresh basil if desired. Serve with fresh French bread.

TIP» *You will want to leave your sauce "soupier" than you would think. It will thicken as it sits; and once you add the pasta in, the noodles will absorb a lot of the juice as well.*

Oven Baked Fajitas

Sizzling-hot fajitas right off of the grill are amazing, but there are times when you just don't care to be standing outside grilling them (hello, Old Man Winter!). I also hear from a lot of you who (a) don't own a grill, (b) aren't comfortable with the grill, or (c) are just super busy and need something you can throw in the oven while you are tending to other things like helping kids with homework, etc. So for times like those, a dish like this may totally be up your alley! You could even have the whole thing prepped and ready to go in the fridge so that you can pop it into the oven when you get home. How's that for a busy mom/dad recipe?

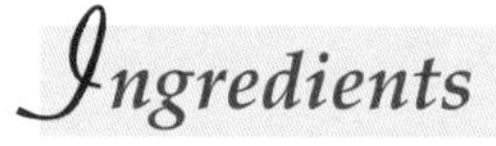

Ingredients

- 2 lbs chicken strips
- 1 medium onion, sliced into strips
- 1 cup mixed sliced bell pepper strips, *I used green, red, orange, and yellow.*
- 2 Tbsp vegetable oil
- 2 tsp chili powder
- 2 tsp cumin
- ½ tsp garlic powder
- ½ tsp dried oregano
- ½ tsp salt
- ¼ cup chicken broth, *or ¼ cup water and ¼ tsp chicken broth granules*
- 1 4-oz can diced green chilies
- 1 15-oz can diced tomatoes, *with chipotle, optional*
- Flour tortillas
- Your favorite fajita "fixings": *grated cheese, sour cream, guacamole, etc.*

Notes:

How to...

Preheat oven to 400°F. Prepare a 9 × 13 casserole dish with nonstick spray, and then add the trimmed chicken strips. Top the chicken with the sliced onions and pepper strips.

> **TIP »** *If you want the veggies tender-crisp, use fresh onions and peppers. If you want them softer, use frozen onions and peppers as they break down faster.*

For the sauce, combine vegetable oil, chili powder, cumin, garlic powder, dried oregano, and salt. Add the chicken broth and pour the diced chilies over the vegetables. Add a can of diced tomatoes on top as well. Pour your lovely sauce over everything. Give it a good stir and throw it in the 400°F oven for about 35 minutes. Every 10 minutes or so, give it a stir.

When you are ready to serve, heat your tortillas. You can microwave them with a damp paper towel over them, or if you have a gas stove, blister them a little with tongs. Now put it all together with your favorite toppings: avocado, a fresh squeeze of lime, cheese, sour cream, fresh cilantro... the list is endless!

Mediterranean Chicken Pasta

They always say that you eat with your eyes first, right? Well this colorful pasta dish is an excellent way to get more healthful veggies into your family with a big pop of flavor, colors, and textures!

It's true. I DO cook a lot of chicken, so I like to find ways to make it different. This flavor profile is reminiscent of the Mediterranean coast with spinach, sun-dried tomatoes, pine nuts, feta, and olives. If there is something else you think you'd like in here, add it. If there's something you don't care for, leave it out. Just have fun with this beautiful dish!

Ingredients

4–6 servings

Olive oil to sauté the garlic and shallots
- 4 tsp chopped garlic (about 4 large cloves)
- 2 Tbsp shallots, chopped
- 1 cup dry white wine (I used Pinot Grigio.)
- 2 cups chicken stock
- 1 Tbsp corn starch
- 6 Tbsp butter
- 4 Tbsp extra virgin olive oil
- 6 Tbsp jarred sun-dried tomato bruschetta, *or sun-dried tomatoes in oil*
- 4 oz package crumbled feta cheese
- 2 cups fresh baby spinach, stems removed
- 1 lb cooked penne noodles, al dente, drained and rinsed

Kosher salt and black pepper, to taste
- 1 lb chicken breast tenderloins

Greek seasoning, *I used the no-salt version.*

Veggie rub seasoning (I used Feiny's.), *optional*
- ½ cup toasted pine nuts

Additional sun-dried tomatoes

Sliced black olives to garnish

Notes:

How to...

Garlic Wine Sauce

To a sauce pan, add olive oil, half the garlic, and half the shallots. Sauté them until golden brown, then add the white wine. Allow it to come up to a boil, then reduce by half, stirring frequently. In a measuring cup or bowl, stir together the cold chicken stock and corn starch to make a slurry. Add the slurry to the reduced wine sauce. Bring to a boil, then simmer for about 10 minutes until it has thickened up a bit. Strain the sauce and discard the garlic and shallots. *The sauce can be stored in the refrigerator until you need it if you are making it ahead of time.*

Put It All Together

Season the trimmed chicken breast tenderloins liberally with Greek seasoning and veggie rub seasoning if you like. Sauté until golden on both sides in butter and olive oil over medium-high heat. They will probably not be cooked all the way through yet; however, they will be by the time we are finished. *If they ARE cooked all the way through, remove them to a plate and cover to keep warm so they won't overcook and dry out.*

Add in the other half of the chopped garlic and shallots. Add in the sun-dried tomato bruschetta (or sun-dried tomatoes that were packed in oil). Add in about half of the garlic wine sauce. Add in the butter and half of the feta cheese. *The butter will make the sauce really silky. The feta will melt into the sauce and give us a tangy flavor characteristic of the Mediterranean flavor profile.* Stir in the chopped spinach and drained noodles. Season to taste with kosher salt and black pepper.

By this time, the chicken breast tenders should be cooked through. Please don't overcook them. To finish, add in the remainder of the garlic wine sauce and garnish with the remaining feta, toasted pine nuts, tomatoes, and sliced olives. The garnishes can be added to the whole pot or to each bowl as you serve it.

Tip » *To dry toast the pine nuts, just add a nice handful to a small skillet and toast them on the stove top until they are nice and golden, moving them around as you go.*

Make-Ahead Time Savers

You can make, drain, and rinse the pasta ahead of time. Then when you want to cook dinner, all you need to do is cook the chicken and throw it all together.

Also, get all of your veggies chopped before beginning. I have a great helper for this type of thing! Remember, there's always some aspect of a recipe that the kids can help with! My spinach didn't necessarily NEED to be chopped, but it gave Lily a sense of being needed and involved. And this is just as important as any of the rest of the things you do!

Creamy "Work Week" Chicken Enchiladas

There are endless combinations for individualizing your chicken enchiladas, depending on your time constraints and the palates of your table. In my opinion, that's pretty cool.

Today, I had the "super picky" crowd (who all want to see zero veggies inside), and limited time, so I cheated my way through this, which is what a lot of moms do during the busy workweek. And that is TOTALLY fine, as it still puts a hot, home-cooked meal on the table, costs less, and is healthier than eating out! Also, these enchiladas freeze wonderfully. (If they make it that far- they usually end up on the "bring lunch to the office" list.) This recipe is very special to me, as this was the first dish I cooked for my husband back when we were dating. I guess that means they are *that* good!

Notes:

How to...

For Those Starting with Raw Chicken

Lightly season the chicken. Cook the chicken first. I usually either poach them (season the water with salt, pepper, a little poultry seasoning, then boil the chicken until just done, no longer pink and clear in middle) or pan sauté them in a little butter/olive oil. But please don't overdo the chicken because it will be dry.

For Everyone

Separate chicken from the skin and bones, cut into bite-sized chunks, and set aside. In a saucepan, melt butter, then add onion and sauté until translucent. Add the green chilies and cook along with the softened onions a few minutes. At this point, if you have really picky people, you can blend the onions and chilies in a

Ingredients

1 rotisserie chicken, skinned and boned; otherwise, use:
4 skinless, boneless chicken breasts, cooked and cut into 1-inch cubes.
1 Tbsp butter
2 Tbsp finely chopped onion
1 4-oz can chopped green chilies
1 cup prepared, jarred salsa, *mild to hot, your choice*
4 oz softened, reduced-fat cream cheese
1 cup grated cheddar cheese*
1 cup grated Monterey Jack cheese with jalapeno peppers, *You can also use the mixed "Mexican cheese blend" cheese instead of two separate cheeses.*
Salt and pepper, to taste
Cumin, to taste (about 1 tsp)
8–10 flour tortillas, *or corn tortillas if you prefer them*
1 cup whipping cream

Optional: red enchilada sauce and green salsa verde for extra color and flavor if you like; sour cream, tomatoes and cilantro for garnish

- If you prefer an all-red sauce, add about half of a 14-oz can of mild red enchilada sauce on top of the cream and then top with cheese. Left up to me, there would be a whole bag of cheese on the top, but that's just me. You can change these up any way you see fit!
- In my "make them for me, not the kids" fantasy, I would add some corn niblets and some rinsed/drained black beans to the mixture just before rolling them up. This would add additional flavor, texture, fiber, and the *Yum Factor!* But I don't think it would go over that well with this tough crowd.

mini-food processor until smooth. For an adult audience, leave it chunky. Add the salsa and cream cheese to the onions and chilies, and stir constantly over medium-low until blended. Add the chicken (either rotisserie chicken or home-cooked). Add half of the cheeses. Stir to blend. Adjust seasoning with salt and pepper, and then season with cumin. This will amp up the Mexican flavor. Remove from heat or turn down to very low. Soften tortillas if needed according to package directions. I usually put them between two damp paper towels on a plate and microwave for about 10 seconds—makes them nice and soft and pliable so they won't crack and tear. But if they are soft and pliable, skip this step. If you choose to use corn tortillas, you will definitely need to steam them first to avoid them cracking.

Place about 3 Tbsp of filling in the center of each tortilla. Roll up tortillas and place seam-side down in a greased 2-quart casserole dish; (You can also use 9 × 13 × 2 dish). Pour whipping cream over enchiladas. It will cook down, thicken, and get all bubbly. You can go directly to the cheese step or add some different sauces on top. This time, I added red enchilada sauce on some of them (yep—out of the can), then some salsa verde on others. You can totally leave it white if you want. Top with remaining cheese. Bake uncovered at 350°F for 25 minutes or until hot and bubbly. Top with your favorite garnishes and dig in!

Did I mention that these freeze great? So if you are cooking for two (or even one), just put them in smaller ovenproof dishes and bake only what you need, freezing the rest. I would freeze them before they go into the oven. Great for sending your kid off to college with a "heat-n-eat" meal, or even for yourself later in the busy workweek. Take them out of the freezer the night before and thaw in the fridge. Then when you get home, pop them into the oven. I find that Mexican food, Italian food, and gumbo always improve the next day anyway!

And yes! I'm THAT serious about cooking for your family! While it *does* take longer, it's important: time together, skill building, conversation, teaching opportunities, health factors, financial factors, you name it!

Italian Sausage Calzones with Homemade Marinara

Have extra kiddos over? Have a calzone party! This is a recipe that is sure to please everyone because you can add just about any ingredients you fancy in them. I bought this little calzone maker from Williams-Sonoma a few years ago, and it has been a really fun kitchen toy. Most of this can be made ahead of time (the dough and marinara) and assembled before baking. Let the kids make their own—it's lots of fun! In this recipe, everything is made from scratch: the dough, the marinara, and the filling! But feel free to use convenience items if you wish. The whole point of it is to get the kids involved and have a good time (And you can hide veggies in the marinara!).

Ingredients

Marinara

1 Tbsp extra virgin olive oil
3 cloves garlic, finely chopped
½ cup diced onion
⅓ cup diced carrot
1 cup red wine (I used a Shiraz.)
1 28-oz can crushed tomatoes with basil
1 tsp sugar
1½ tsp pizza seasoning, *a blend of dried herbs*
1½ tsp salt
¼ tsp red pepper flakes
Handful fresh herbs
¼ cup freshly grated Parmesan cheese

Dough

1 cup warm water
1 pkg yeast
2 tsp sugar
2–3 cups all-purpose flour
1 tsp salt
⅓ cup freshly grated Parmesan
1 tsp each dried herbs: *oregano, basil, Italian seasoning*
1 Tbsp canola or olive oil

Filling

Italian sausage
Cheese, tomatoes, herbs, any others of your choice

Marinara

I had been dying to make a made-from-scratch marinara. For the longest time, I felt that it needed to be made from fresh tomatoes; but after doing some research, it appears that the Italians are not ashamed at all to use good quality canned tomatoes, as they are picked and canned at the height of freshness. So now, I just go with that. It definitely extends the "growing season" for me!

Sauté the garlic, onion, and carrots in the olive oil in a pot for several minutes until they start to soften. De-glaze with red wine. Add crushed tomatoes, sugar, and rest of the dry seasonings to the pot and simmer for 30 minutes or so until you develop the flavor you like. Add a handful of mixed, fresh herbs in for the last few minutes and then remove from heat.

Notes:

Dough

Get the pizza stone preheated to 500°F from the very beginning!

Mix warm water and yeast, then add sugar. Start adding flour (at least one cup) before adding salt, then add cheese and herbs, then more flour. I just love putting some fresh herbs into the dough because it has such a prettier finish with all the specks of color in it... and putting the Parmesan cheese into the dough gives it a little more saltiness and changes the texture of the finished product. Knead the dough for 5–8 minutes, stretching and turning each time. It will get nice and elastic, with a silky feel. Put the oil in a large bowl, and turn the dough ball over a couple of times in the oil to coat. Cover the dough with a damp kitchen towel and microwave at Power 1 for 2 minutes, then let rest 10 minutes. Repeat until dough doubles. Punch down, divide into 6 pieces, and roll out just before ready.

Filling

I would say here to knock yourself out and go crazy with whatever kind of filling you desire. I hardly EVER recommend pre-grated cheese, because it has much less flavor than cheese you grate yourself, but a "pizza blend" of cheeses would work really well here (Yes—the kind in the bag!). If I had one criticism of my final dish, it was that it needed to be gooier with cheese... so add more cheese!

Remove the sausage from the casings and break apart in a skillet. Cook until the sausage is browned

Food Note: *As an option for the filling, I'm really thinking that chicken, artichoke, and spinach in a béchamel sauce would be delicious.*

through, but still soft. Mix the sausage with a cup of the marinara that you have simmering in that pot and smelling up the house. Have other filling ingredients ready—cheese, tomatoes, herbs, etc.

The Building Process

This is really the fun part—and the part where you bring in the kids and let everyone participate in the assembly! Roll out a piece of dough on a floured surface until it's approximately an 8-inch circle. Don't forget to flour your rolling pin as well! You can use the open calzone mold as a guide if this is the method you are using. Sprinkle the mold with just a tiny bit of flour. Lay the dough over the open mold and add your filling of choice—I added ⅓ cup of the filling as above, then layered it with thinly sliced tomatoes, chunks of mozzarella cheese, and a sprinkling of more herbs. If you don't have a calzone mold, just add your filling to one side, being careful not to get any filling on the edges. Flip the dough over and close the mold, pressing to seal and crimp. If no mold, use your finger to dampen the edges of the dough with water and close the dough, then crimp with a fork to seal. Brush the top of the calzone with extra virgin olive oil and sprinkle the top with herbs and grated Parmesan.

Transfer calzones two at a time to a pizza peel that has been sprinkled with cornmeal. This will keep them from sticking and allow them to slide off onto the pizza stone. This is the stuff you feel under the bottom of your pizza when you go to a brick oven pizza place. Bake at 500°F for 10–12 minutes (I baked all of mine for 10 minutes). Remove from oven with the peel and allow to sit about 5 minutes before eating. They are like pockets of molten lava at this point, so I don't advise biting into one right out of the oven. Serve calzones with a little dish of the marinara that you made for "dipping" and a little grating of Parmesan.

Notes:

» *These dough balls freeze really well and can be thawed and rolled out at a later time.*

» *The marinara will just improve in flavor if you make it in advance, and it also freezes well.*

» *So... this recipe lends itself well to making the components ahead of time and having a "make your own calzone" party; or for most of us, prepping the components on the weekend and putting them together for dinner during the busy week.*

» *FYI–the Williams-Sonoma Calzone Mold was $12. That was a lot of entertainment for the money! You can also use them to make sweet fruit-filled pies, so you can get even more use out of these! ☺*

» *In a time crunch, I don't see why you couldn't just get the pre-made pizza dough from the can or freezer section. I'm certainly not going to frown on you!*

Roasted Red Pepper and Basil Pesto Penne

If you're looking for a quick and super-tasty pasta dish, this is definitely one to try. You can make this pesto in the time it takes to boil the noodles! I'm a huge fan of the roasted red bell peppers that come in the jar. They are healthy, beautiful, super delicious, and a very versatile pantry item. For a side dish, the pasta is perfect. To make this a main dish, I add some rotisserie chicken—an ingredient you just about can't beat to stretch a dollar.

Ingredients

- 4 cloves garlic
- ⅓ cup extra virgin olive oil
- ⅓ cup pine nuts
- ⅓ cup freshly grated Parmesan
- 1 cup of jarred roasted red bell peppers, drained
- 1 cup fresh basil leaves
- Salt and pepper, to taste
- 1 lb penne pasta
- ½ cup heavy cream
- Roasted rotisserie chicken, *optional*

Note » *For Roasted Grape Tomatoes, see bottom of recipe.*

How to...

Throw the garlic cloves in a small pan and add the cold olive oil. I slowly pan-roasted the garlic a while to mellow it out. When you heat the garlic with the cold oil, the oil becomes flavored. Add the pine nuts to the warm oil and let them simmer just a minute or two.

Add the garlic, pine nuts, and oil to the food processor and pulse until they are a fine paste. Add the Parmesan cheese and pulse. Add the red pepper, basil leaves, salt, and pepper. Pulse to combine into a paste. Set aside.

Notes:

Cook pasta according to package directions. Drain and return to the pot. Add the pesto to the pasta and stir to combine. If desired, stir in heavy cream for a creamier sauce. Heat until warmed through. *If you are trying to avoid cream (or dairy in general), feel free to add a little chicken broth in the place of the cream. I've also done this with canned evaporated milk, and that works great as well!*

Stir in roasted rotisserie chicken if you want or serve plain. Garnish with extra pine nuts (dry toast them in a pan), chopped basil, and grated Parmesan (and roasted grape tomatoes). Serve immediately.

Note: *Make it a little soupier than you think you will need it. The pasta will soak up a lot of the sauce.*

Roasted Grape Tomatoes

I had to go back and edit this recipe because many readers wrote and asked me about the tomatoes garnishing the top. No, they are not part of the original recipe, but I threw them on top for their beautiful color and the textural difference. HOWEVER, I MUST admit to you now that since then, I find myself putting more and more of them on there. Fast forward from the origination of the dish—because now I am roasting the tomatoes each time I make this recipe. The grape tomatoes are super sweet, and I roast them in the oven, which makes them even sweeter! Now I couldn't think of having this dish without them.

Grape tomatoes—maybe half a pint—cut in half
A drizzle of extra virgin olive oil
Kosher salt and black pepper
Dried basil

Cut tomatoes in half. Drizzle with EVOO and sprinkle with salt, pepper, and dried basil. Roast in oven for about 20–25 minutes at 400°F. The edges will start getting dried and shriveled. Let them cool a bit and add them either on top or mix them in. The acidity in the tomatoes really brings a whole new dimension to balance out the creaminess of this dish.

Sun-Dried Tomato Chicken

This is a very simple and fast weeknight dinner for the chicken that you probably already have in the fridge! Chicken tenders cook up so quickly that dinner is a snap. You could have this with a side salad or even over some pasta. Start the water for the pasta when you start the chicken because this cooks fast! The sauce is super silky with a pop of flavor from the tangy sun-dried tomatoes and the fresh basil.

Ingredients

A large pack of chicken tenderloins (1½–2 lbs)
Salt and pepper, to taste
2 Tbsp extra virgin olive oil
½ cup onion, diced
2 tsp garlic, minced
⅓ cup sun-dried tomatoes, chopped small
2 Tbsp all-purpose flour
1½ cups chicken broth
½ cup white wine
1 Tbsp butter
¼–½ cup heavy cream
¼ cup fresh basil, chopped

How to...

Trim away any extra fat and those rubbery tendons that extend from the ends of the chicken tenderloins and season simply with salt and pepper. Cook the chicken in the hot oil until cooked through (maybe 6–7 minutes).

When you add the chicken to the oil, it should immediately start sizzling. If not, it is NOT hot enough. I used a black iron skillet because it gives me the best sear. Once you put the chicken down, do NOT move them until cooked on that side. They will release easily from the pan when ready, but if you try to pick them up and move them around while still uncooked, they will stick. Just put them in and let them cook!

Notes:

Remove the cooked tenders to a plate and cover to keep warm. To the same hot oil, add the chopped onions and garlic and cook a couple of minutes until softened. Add in the chopped tomatoes next and stir to incorporate. Add in the flour and stir until smooth, cooking a couple of minutes. Add in the chicken broth and wine and stir until smooth. Allow it to reduce a bit. Add in the cold butter and cream and cook until sauce is thickened. Adjust seasonings of the sauce, and then add the cooked chicken and chopped basil to the sauce. Turn off the heat. Serve alone or over pasta.

Food Nerd Notes: *What ARE sun-dried tomatoes? Sun-dried tomatoes are ripe tomatoes that are placed in the sun to remove most of the water content from the tomatoes. Cherry types of tomatoes will lose 88% of their initial (fresh) weight while larger tomatoes can lose up to 93% during the process. As a result, it takes anywhere from 8 to 14 kilos of fresh tomatoes to make a single kilo of sun-dried tomatoes. After the procedure, the tomato fruits retain their nutritional values, being very high in lycopene, antioxidants, and vitamin C and low in sodium, fat, and calories. Sun-dried tomatoes can be used in a wide range of recipes and come in different varieties, shapes, and colors. Traditionally, they were made from dried red plum (Roma) tomatoes, but they can also be purchased in yellow varieties of tomatoes as well. Sun-dried tomatoes may also be preserved in olive oil, along with other ingredients such as rosemary, basil, dried paprika, and garlic.*

Mongolian Beef

Trust me on this one: make more of this than you think you will need! Each time I've made this, I ended up with more folks at my house than I originally started with. It's like some strange math equation that I just can't quite grasp. Who knew that the smell would extend past your house, into the neighborhood, and bring teenagers to the table? Even some who don't belong to you!

Asian food may seem mysterious, but it's easy to make. Chop, drop, sizzle, and stir! I'll take you through it step-by-step. We will end up with a silky sauce that has an awesome balance of sweet, sour, tangy, and just a tad bit of heat.

Notes:

Ingredients

- 1 lb beef flank steak
- ½ cup soy sauce
- ¼ cup hoisin sauce
- 1 tsp sesame oil
- 3 Tbsp corn starch
- 1½ cups Jasmine rice
- 1 Tbsp minced garlic
- 1 Tbsp minced ginger
- 4 green onions
- 1–2 Tbsp canola oil
- 2 Tbsp rice wine vinegar
- ⅓ cup brown sugar
- Handful of snow peas
- ½ cup water
- 1 tsp Sriracha sauce, *or hot sauce of your choice*

How to...

Here's the game plan: Prep everything, then put on the rice, and then start cooking. First, slice the flank steak across the grain with your knife at an angle (not straight down). This exposes more of the meat, resulting in a more tender cut. It may also help if you put the meat in the freezer for about 10 minutes to firm it up. To the sliced beef, add the soy sauce, hoisin sauce, sesame oil, and cornstarch. It won't be very pretty after this, but trust me here. Marinate all of this together at room temperature for around 30 minutes. Get the Jasmine rice going now.

Next, prep the veggies. Peel and mince the garlic and ginger, chop the green onions, and then dig everything else out of the fridge. Now let's cook! Get the oil in the wok really hot first. Add the beef strips (I sort of drain them a little first). Sauté them around until they brown on the outside, then start adding the other stuff: minced garlic, minced ginger, and rice wine vinegar. Sauté these for about a minute until fragrant. Next, add the rest of the marinating sauce. To this, add the brown sugar, snow peas, green onions, some water, and a little Sriracha for a bit of a kick. Let all this cook for about 5 minutes, at about medium/medium-high, and it's done! You don't want to overcook the beef. The sauce is super silky!

Serve hot over the jasmine rice. ***And watch 'em come running!***

Pumpkin Ravioli with Brown Butter and Crispy Sage

On our very first trip to New York together, my husband and I shared the most amazing pumpkin ravioli! That dish haunted me so much that I was absolutely compelled to come home and develop a version of it for my family.

Homemade pasta is SO simple (and inexpensive) to make that you are almost in disbelief when you consider the make-at-home price compared to the prices in fancy restaurants. In addition, any extra raviolis that you make can be stored in a zip-top freezer bag and frozen for later. Fresh pasta is wonderfully tender, and without all the preservatives of dried (store-bought) pasta, it cooks in about 2–3 minutes! So really, you could make these in advance, store them in the freezer for later, pop them in boiling water when you get home, and toss them with a sauce, and dinner is ready! You can also flavor the pasta dough with just about any herb you can dream up!

If you are that super intimidated by making the pasta, or just pressed for time, feel free to make this recipe using store-bought wonton wrappers. They work great as well. Then maybe next time, I can talk you into making the dough!

Notes:

Ingredients

Fresh Pasta Dough–*(for about 2 dozen raviolis)*

1⅔ cups all-purpose flour
2 large eggs
1 Tbsp extra virgin olive oil
Pinch of salt
Maybe a few drops of water

Filling

½ small can of pumpkin, *NOT pumpkin pie mix*
4 oz light cream cheese
¼ cup freshly grated Parmigiano Reggiano
6 leaves of fresh sage, chopped small
Salt and pepper, to taste

Brown Butter Sauce with Crispy Sage Leaves

Half stick of butter
Fresh sage leaves
Salt and pepper, to taste
Chopped walnuts, lightly toasted
Parmigiano Reggiano for topping, *optional*

Food Nerd Notes: *The bright orange color of pumpkin is a dead giveaway that pumpkin is loaded with an important antioxidant, beta-carotene. Beta-carotene is one of the plant carotenoids converted to vitamin A in the body. In the conversion to vitamin A, beta-carotene performs many important functions in overall health. Current research indicates that a diet rich in foods containing beta-carotene may reduce the risk of developing certain types of cancer and offers protection against heart disease as well as some other degenerative aspects of aging.*

How to...

Make the Basic Pasta Dough.

Sift the flour onto a clean work surface and make a well in the center with your fist. Break the eggs into the well and add the oil and a pinch of salt to the well. Gradually mix the egg mixture into the flour using the fingers of one hand and bringing the ingredients together into a firm dough. If the dough feels too dry, add a few drops of water (maybe 1 teaspoon max); if it's too wet, add a little more flour. Knead the pasta until smooth, about 5 minutes. Lightly massage it with a hint of olive oil, pop the dough into a plastic zip-top bag, and allow it to rest at room temperature for at least 30 minutes. The pasta will be much more elastic after resting.

The dough must not be too soft—it should require some serious effort when kneading! However, too much extra flour will make the pasta too tough to handle or put through the pasta machine, and when cooked, it will taste floury. You could opt to roll the pasta by hand using a long wooden rolling pin, but using a pasta machine makes for far less work and faster prep. You can also make a large batch and freeze it once it's been cut and shaped.

Pass the Dough Through the Pasta Machine.

Cut your dough in half or even thirds before beginning. Start to feed a blob of it through the widest setting of a pasta machine (I still use my manual Atlas Pasta Machine). As the sheet of dough comes out of the machine, fold it into thirds and then feed it through the rollers again, still on the widest setting. Pass the dough through this setting a total of 4 or 5 times. This effectively kneads the dough, ensuring the resulting pasta is silky smooth.

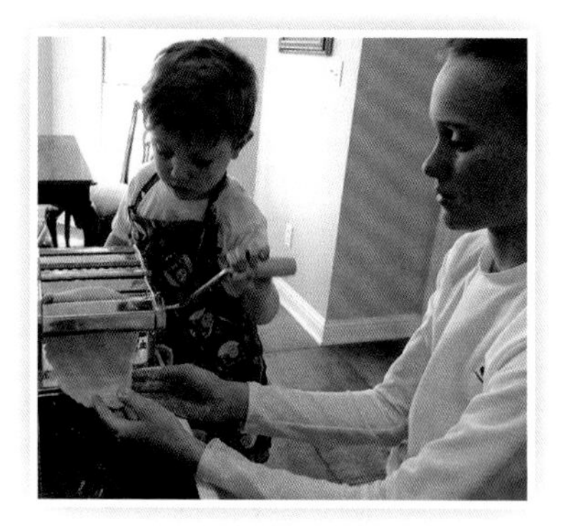

Pass the pasta through the machine again, starting at the widest setting and gradually reducing the settings one pass at a time until the pasta achieves the required thickness. The pasta sheet will become very long. If you are having trouble keeping the dough from folding onto itself, or if you are are making ravioli, cut the sheet of dough in half and feed each half through separately. Generally, the second-from-last setting is best for ravioli and any other shapes that are to be filled, as you don't want it so thin that it tears after adding the filling.

Make the Filling.

In a mixing bowl, combine the pumpkin with the reduced-fat cream cheese, ¼ cup of Parmesan, and chopped sage leaves. Season to taste with salt and white pepper.

Fill the Pasta.

Place thinly rolled out pasta sheets on a ravioli maker mold. Or place them on a clean work surface and drop filling by the tablespoonful along one of the long edges

about 2 inches apart and about 2 inches from the edge. Brush around the filling lightly with some water so that you can "seal" the ravioli together. *Alternatively, you can just brush the whole "upper" pasta sheet with water and then place it over the bottom one—wet side touching the bottom sheet.* Cover with another sheet of dough and cut the ravioli apart with a knife or pizza wheel (if not using a ravioli mold) or rolling pin (if you ARE using a ravioli mold). Then, press the edges carefully to seal. It's important to make sure you pay attention to getting out all the air bubbles! These can expand when boiling and burst the ravioli. Repeat with the remaining filling and pasta sheets until you have used all of the filling.

Place the ravioli in the boiling water and cook, in batches if necessary, until pasta is al dente, maybe around 2 minutes. They will all be floating at the top by that point. Remove from the water and drain. Please handle them gently so they won't tear or burst. They are more delicate than a big pot of noodles that you would dump into a colander in the sink. Season the ravioli with salt and pepper if desired and cover lightly to keep warm while you make the sauce. Store any extra uncooked ravioli in a resealable plastic food storage bag in the freezer for later use, stacking them between wax paper or parchment paper to prevent sticking. But make sure they are dry and not still sticky to the touch when you put them up.

Make the Sauce.

Heat a sauté pan over medium-high heat, and when hot, add the butter and let it melt in one spot. Do not move the pan. When the butter has begun to brown around the edges, pick up the pan and swirl it around to keep the melted butter from burning and to melt the remaining butter. Add the sage leaves and reduce the heat to medium. Continue to cook until the leaves are crispy, 1 to 2 minutes. Season with salt and pepper. Carefully remove the crispy sage leaves to drain and dry on a paper towel. A fork works great for this job.

To serve, simply lay the ravioli in a shallow bowl and spoon the brown butter over the top. Garnish with the crispy sage leaves. Sprinkle with toasted, chopped walnut pieces and Parmigiano Reggiano. Serve immediately.

Spicy Garlic Shrimp

I have been craving pasta... again! This recipe is super easy and fast! You could definitely do the whole thing in less than 30 minutes (for all you busy moms and dads). This is fabulous for a quick, light summer evening meal that won't leave you feeling weighed down. It is spicy, garlicky, tangy, and then balanced by the sweetness of the sugar snap peas and roasted tomatoes. ***Yummmm!***

Ingredients

- ½–⅔ pint grape tomatoes, roasted with olive oil, coarse salt, and pepper
- ½ bag of fresh sugar snap peas (about 4 oz)
- ½ pack of linguine
- 1 large lemon, zested and juiced
- 2 Tbsp extra virgin olive oil
- 1 Tbsp butter
- 5 cloves garlic, diced medium
- Handful of chopped, frozen red and yellow bell peppers
- 24–30 medium-large shrimp, de-veined and peeled (41–60 count)
- ¼–½ tsp crushed red pepper flakes (See the caution below.)
- 2 tsp steak seasoning (I used McCormick Montreal steak seasoning.)
- ½ cup white wine, *Or you could use chicken stock/broth.*

Notes:

How to...

Turn on the broiler to high in your oven. Cut grape tomatoes in half, drizzle with olive oil, coarse salt, and freshly cracked pepper. Roast for about 20 minutes. *Note: line pan with aluminum foil for easy clean up. After roasting, the tomatoes will be slightly charred and wilted but will taste super sweet.* Start cooking the linguine, wait 3–5 minutes, and add the sugar snap peas (vary the time you wait based on how tender or firm you want them). Continue cooking another 4–5 minutes. Zest the lemon first with the microplane or grater of your choice. Be very careful not to remove any of the pith (the white part) of the lemon, as this is bitter. You JUST want the yellow part. Then you can cut the lemon in half and get the juice out.

Tip» *Microwave the lemon for about 15 seconds and roll it on the back and forth under firm pressure before cutting it. This will give you more juice than from a cold lemon.*

Add 2 Tbsp olive oil and 1 Tbsp butter to the pan. Add chopped garlic and diced red and yellow bell peppers to the hot butter/oil. Cook for about 2 minutes on medium-high. You want the peppers to wilt down, but you don't want the garlic to get too brown. Have the shrimp rinsed and patted dry waiting for the vegetables to cook down. Add the shrimp to the pan. Add crushed red pepper flakes. ***Caution***—control your heat at this step! Use anywhere from a pinch to a half teaspoon. Add the Montreal steak seasoning.

Tip» *If you use steak seasoning, you do NOT need to add salt or pepper.*

Cook for about 2 minutes. Add the lemon juice and wine. Cook until shrimp are opaque and pink. Do NOT overcook the shrimp. They only need to cook a few minutes.

Remove from heat. Add in the lemon zest. Toss the shrimp and sauce with drained linguine, sugar snap peas, and top with the oven-roasted tomatoes. ***Enjoy!***

Maple-Mustard Glazed Chicken

Are you a fan of spicy, tangy, and sweet all wrapped up together? The tangy and sweet flavor combo of this maple-mustard sauce will have you licking the plate! This recipe, adapted from *Cooking Light,* gets so much flavor from these low-fat ingredients that you will swear that you should be feeling guilty. ***But don't!***

Ingredients

1 Tbsp extra virgin olive oil
3–4 skinless, boneless chicken breasts, *Mine came 3 to a pack.*
Kosher salt and cracked black pepper, to taste
⅓ cup low-sodium chicken broth
⅓ cup maple syrup
2 tsp fresh thyme leaves, stripped from stems
4 medium garlic cloves, thinly sliced
1 Tbsp apple cider vinegar
1 Tbsp stone-ground Creole mustard

Options:

» *Some red pepper flakes would be great in here too!*
» *This recipe would also be great using center-cut pork loin chops!*

Notes:

How to...

Preheat oven to 400°F. Heat a large black iron skillet (or heavy, ovenproof skillet) over medium-high heat. Add oil and swirl to coat. Sprinkle chicken liberally with cracked black pepper and kosher salt. Add chicken to pan and sauté for 3–4 minutes on each side, or until golden brown. The meat should release easily from the pan when ready. Remove the chicken from the pan.

Add chicken broth to the pan to deglaze. Then add syrup, thyme, and garlic to the pan. Bring this all to a boil, scraping up the browned bits at the bottom of the skillet. Cook 2–3 minutes, stirring frequently. Add vinegar and mustard to the sauce. Cook for 1 minute, stirring constantly.

Return the chicken to the sauce and spoon the maple-mustard glaze over the breasts. Bake uncovered at 400°F until internal thermometer reads 160°F (about 11 minutes). Remove chicken from the pan and let it sit for 5 minutes. Meanwhile, place the pan back over medium heat and cook the maple-mustard sauce another 2 minutes or until it is syrupy, stirring frequently. Serve the sauce over the chicken. Garnish with a sprig of thyme.

This is one low-fat and healthy recipe that you are sure to come back for! Man, oh, man… this sure is good!

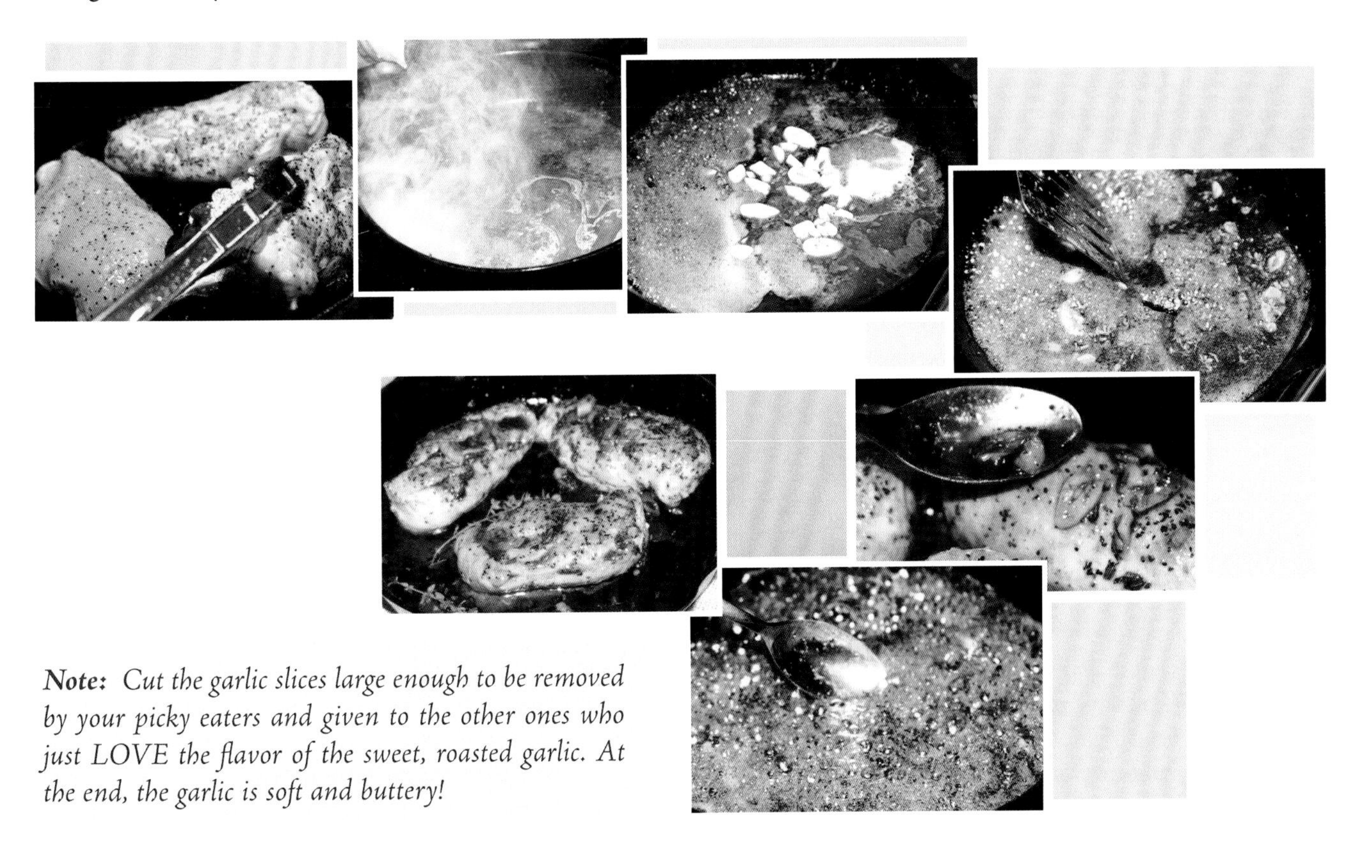

Note: *Cut the garlic slices large enough to be removed by your picky eaters and given to the other ones who just LOVE the flavor of the sweet, roasted garlic. At the end, the garlic is soft and buttery!*

Thai Chicken with Peanut Curry Sauce and Coconut Rice

This recipe is very easy and very tasty. This taste-of-the-Orient recipe gives us a whole range of flavors and textures, from creamy, spicy, and sweet from the sauce to the brightness of lime, cilantro, crunchy nuts, water chestnuts, and chewy raisins—not to mention a whole rainbow of great colors. What's not to love? It's important that you use the thawed frozen peppers as they really do break down and cook a lot more quickly than fresh peppers. I'm not a huge raisin fan, but they work really well in this dish. I think it could also use a finely sliced green onion over the top, but please don't forget the cilantro and lime juice at the end. They totally brighten the dish!

Ingredients

8 oz thawed frozen cut green beans
8 oz thawed frozen pepper strips (red, yellow, green)
1 ½-lb chicken breast in 1-inch pieces, seasoned with salt and pepper, to taste
2 Tbsp canola oil

Sauce

1½ cups light coconut milk
½ cup low-sodium chicken broth
1 Tbsp red curry paste
⅓ cup creamy or chunky peanut butter
2 Tbsp brown sugar
2 Tbsp fresh lime juice and wedges for garnish
½ cup cashews, rough-chopped
Handful dark raisins
1 small can drained water chestnuts

Coconut Rice

¾ cup light coconut milk
1 cup low-sodium chicken broth
½ lime, juiced
2 cups instant rice
½ cup shredded sweetened coconut, toasted in oven
For garnish: *lime wedges, a bit more toasted coconut, and chopped cilantro*

How to...

Initial Prep

Remove frozen vegetables from the freezer and allow them to start thawing. Trim, cut, and season your chicken with salt and pepper.

Tip » *This can be done ahead of time. Heat oil in large frying pan over medium-high heat. Add the seasoned, cut-up chicken and sauté until cooked through, about 5 minutes.*

Tip » *To get this on the table faster, make the sauce up ahead of time and store in the refrigerator.*

Notes:

Start the Sauce.

While chicken cooks, start the peanut curry sauce. In a medium mixing bowl, whisk together all ingredients for the sauce.

Busy Mom Tip » *If you are a busy parent in the evenings, feel free to prep your chicken, sauce, and toasted coconut ahead of time, storing each separately in the refrigerator. When you get home from work, take out the frozen vegetables, remove the prepped ingredients, and you can have this meal on the table in way less than 30 minutes! But it sure will taste like something you have worked really hard on!*

Start building.

To the chicken that is just cooked through (PLEASE don't overcook it!), add the green beans and pepper strips and continue cooking for another 3–5 minutes (It will take longer if you use fresh peppers). Pour sauce into the pan over the chicken and vegetables and stir. Turn heat up to high and bring to a boil, stirring occasionally. Reduce heat and simmer until sauce thickens slightly, about 6–8 minutes. Serve over coconut rice or plain steamed rice.

Rice: In a medium saucepan, combine coconut milk, chicken broth, and lime juice. Add instant rice when it comes to a boil. Remove from heat and cover for 7–9 minutes. While waiting for the rice to absorb all the liquid, make the toasted coconut.

I put my coconut in a cake pan and put it under the broiler for about 5 minutes. Shake it around every minute or so and watch it CAREFULLY! It is fabulous toasted but will burn in an instant if you neglect it! Stir toasted coconut into the cooked rice. Fluff with a fork.

Tip » *The coconut can be toasted ahead of time. Store in a zip-top bag until you are ready for it.*

Plate: Serve chicken over coconut rice with lime wedges, a bit more toasted coconut, and chopped cilantro for garnish. You definitely need the acid from the lime and brightness of cilantro to bring out these flavors and make them all come alive!

Notes:

- » *I typically choose a low-sodium broth that comes in a box. The leftovers can just be refrigerated.*
- » *Curry paste can be found in larger markets or specialty markets. I use Neera's Spicy Vindaloo Red Indian Curry Paste in 4-oz jar.*
- » *I use Peter Pan Honey Roast peanut butter, as that is the one my family enjoys. Feel free to use any type.*
- » *I like the Taste of Thai coconut milk in a can. If all you have on hand is coconut milk beverage, you may need to add a teaspoon or so of cornstarch to the cold sauce so that it will thicken properly when cooked.*

Chicken Cordon Bleu

This may be more of a "you have some time on the weekend to make a special meal for some special people" kind of dish… but it is OH SO WORTH the effort! Effort may not be the right word, because there's nothing hard about this dish. It's just multi-step. Just imagine… we have a gorgeous, juicy, tender chicken, with a creamy and cheesy filling, saltiness from the ham, and this gorgeous crunchy golden crust speckled with fresh thyme! ***Yum!***

"Cordon Bleu" is a French term, literally translated as "blue ribbon," that originally referred to an award for culinary excellence given to women cooks! The term can now apply to any superior cook (yes, men too), and also to this dish (chicken, ham, and Swiss cheese slices, breaded and sautéed).

Notes:

Ingredients

- 3 double chicken breasts (about 7 oz each), skinless and boneless
- 1–2 Tbsp Dijon mustard
- 6 thin slices deli ham
- 4 large slices (Baby) Swiss cheese, *Many recipes call for Gruyere cheese, but Swiss is more economical.*
- Kosher salt and freshly ground black pepper, to taste
- 1 cup Panko bread crumbs
- 2 tsp fresh thyme leaves, coarsely chopped
- 1 tsp olive oil
- 2 eggs
- 2 tsp water
- Flour
- 6 Tbsp butter
- ½ cup dry white wine
- 1 tsp chicken bouillon granules
- 1 tsp cornstarch
- 1 cup heavy whipping cream

How to...

Preheat oven to 350°F. Cut the chicken open (butterfly the breasts), turning as you go to make a large "sheet" of chicken. Lay the chicken between 2 pieces of plastic wrap. Using the flat side of a meat mallet, gently pound the chicken to ¼-inch thickness. Take care not to pound too hard because the meat may tear or develop holes. Paint a layer of Dijon mustard on each breast. *I like to use a paint brush to do stuff like this. It is totally dedicated to food use and washes well in the dishwasher.* Lay 2 slices of ham followed by a slice of cheese (2 slices if small) on each breast, leaving a ½-inch margin on all sides to help seal the roll. Tuck in the sides of the breast and roll up tight like a jellyroll. Squeeze the log gently to seal and secure with toothpicks or kitchen twine. Season with salt and pepper.

Mix the breadcrumbs with thyme, kosher salt, pepper, and oil. The addition of the oil will help the crust brown. Prepare an egg wash with the beaten eggs and water. The mixture will be really fluid. Prepare a breading "station" with the flour, egg wash, then breadcrumbs. Lightly dust the chicken with flour, then dip in the egg mixture. Gently roll to coat in the bread crumbs, pressing to get them to stick. These are now ready to be browned. Allow about 4 Tbsp butter to come to a high heat. You want the chicken to really sizzle when it hits the butter. The butter will JUST start turning a bit of a color. Allow the color to develop richly on the bottom before you turn them. Don't move them around once you have them set in there. This is important to "setting" that beautiful crust. Turn and brown each side. Carefully transfer the chicken to a baking pan and bake for 20 minutes until browned and cooked through or until meat thermometer inserted into the center reaches 160°F. Allow the breasts to rest several minutes so all the cheese doesn't run out. *Remove the toothpicks if you used them!* Cut into pinwheels and serve with wine sauce. Garnish with fresh parsley.

The Wine Sauce

Melt 2–3 Tbsp of butter in a pan. Add the white wine and allow to reduce slightly. Add the secret ingredient—a crushed chicken bouillon cube or bouillon granules. Mix/whisk the cornstarch in with cream and add to the sauce. Allow to come to a full boil, then reduce heat. Cook until it reaches the desired consistency and coats a spoon nicely. Season with fresh cracked black pepper. Taste and adjust seasoning, adding a bit of salt if needed.

Notes:

- *Be careful about the amount of salt you add. The ham and cheese both have a lot of salt already.*
- *Choose side dishes that are NOT rich. You actually want something with some acid in it to cleanse your palate in between bites of all this richness.*
- *This dish could easily be broken into multiple steps. You could prepare the chicken bundles and freeze or put in the fridge to just pop into the oven after work. The wine sauce could be made ahead of time and reheated before serving.*

Pronunciation» (Fr. kôr-dôn blœ´)

1. *The sky-blue ribbon worn as a badge by knights of the highest order of French knighthood under the Bourbons.*
2. *Some similar high distinction.*
3. *One entitled to wear the cordon bleu.*
4. *Any person of great distinction in a specific field, esp. a distinguished chef.*
5. *A dish made with thin slices of veal, chicken, etc., interlaid or stuffed with ham and cheese and then sautéed: chicken cordon bleu.*

Fireworks Roast
(aka Beef Pot Roast)

I don't even know how, but years ago, when they were little, my older kids named this dish "Fireworks Roast." They were just kidlets back then, and they said it smelled like fireworks (Ewww!). That sounds terrible, and they laugh about it now, but they still say, "Well, that's what we thought… but it tastes great!" I still don't know how to take that as a compliment: but since it's one of their favorites, I'm not complaining.

The secret to this roast is to cook it low and slow for a *long* time. All of the connective tissues in the meat just melt, and the meat starts to fall apart. I know many people who feel roast should be sliceable, but my kids like it where it's so tender that you can't possibly cut it. A fork is all you need!

Ingredients

- 4–5 lb beef chuck roast
- Creole seasoning, to taste, *available in low-sodium as well*
- 2 Tbsp canola oil
- 3–4 large carrots, peeled and chopped into large pieces
- Half a large onion, cut into large chunks
- 3–4 large cloves of garlic, cut into a medium chop
- 3–4 small/medium red potatoes, cut in half
- ⅓ each of a red, yellow, and orange bell pepper, cut into large pieces
- 2–3 stalks of celery, cut into large pieces
- 1 packet of onion soup mix (I used Lipton's Recipe Secrets.)
- 1 can condensed soup (I used Golden Mushroom.)
- 1 can fire-roasted diced tomatoes
- 1 box reduced-sodium beef broth

Notes:

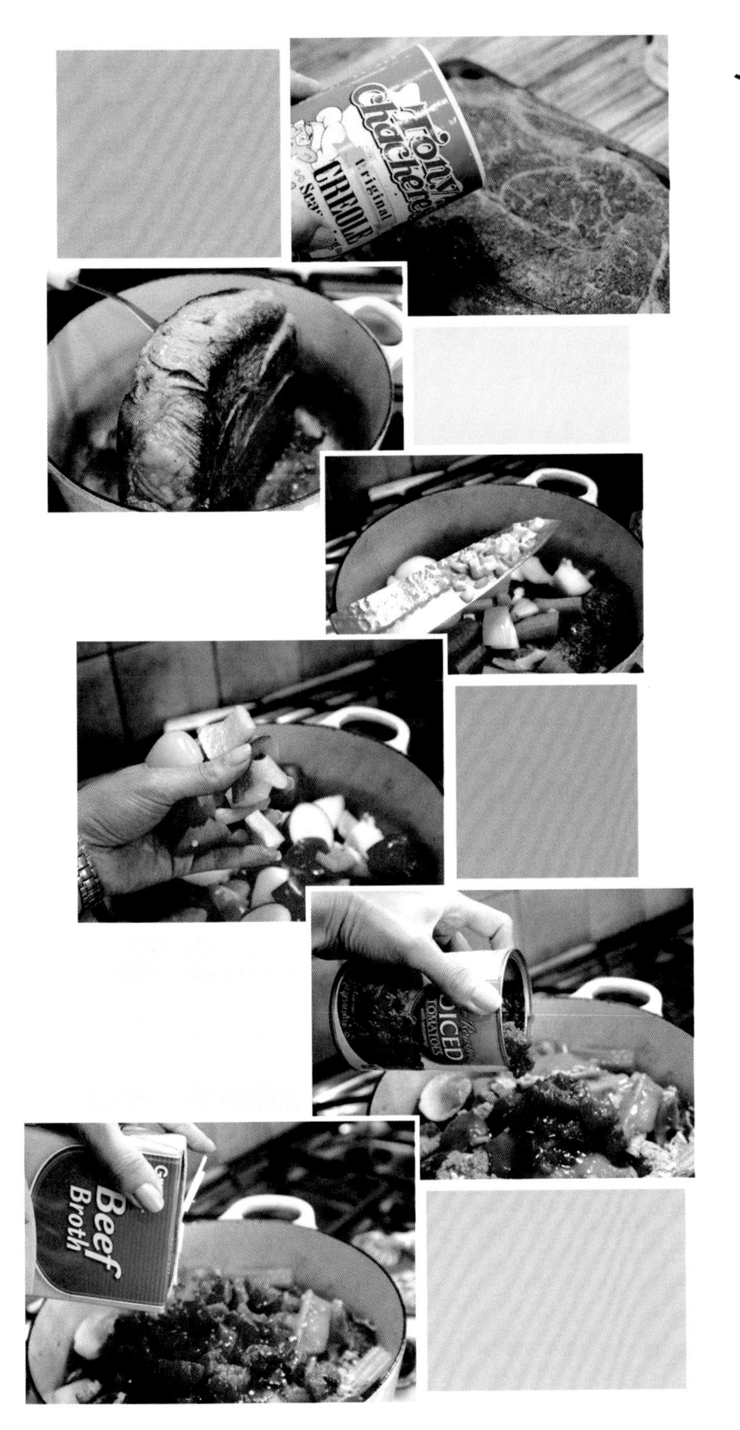

How to...

Season the roast fairly liberally with the Creole seasoning. I like using a chuck roast for this dish. In a heavy pot or Dutch oven, get your oil really hot and sear the roast. Just put it in there and LEAVE IT ALONE until a nice brown color has developed. Keep turning it and browning EACH SIDE of the roast, including the edges. Once all the edges are seared, turn off the heat. Now, just add all the other stuff. Leave all your veggies in large pieces because we are going to cook them for a long time. If your roast isn't totally covered after the veggies and broth are all added, add enough water to completely cover the meat. Throw it in the oven, uncovered, at 350°F, set the timer for 4 hours, and walk away. I usually turn the meat over after the first two hours. You can't rush this, or it won't be the same. Your 4 hours may be 4½ hours if you have a larger roast, so be flexible with the time, and look for the end result to be super tender, falling apart meat as the indicator of "doneness."

After 4 hours, this is what you get. The veggies on top get a bit of roasted char on them that I LOVE, the gravy we made has condensed down into this silky texture, and the meat is falling apart. Don't expect to stick a meat fork in there and pull the roast out. It will fall apart. Oh my gosh, it's so tender! And since we left all the veggies large, they have the perfect amount of doneness now. So promise me you'll give this a shot. Yes, it's sort of an old-fashioned recipe, but it's comfort food at its finest!

Beef Wellington with Green Peppercorn Sauce

If you've never had Beef Wellington, you are absolutely in for a treat! This amazing recipe is for a beef tenderloin filet that has been seasoned and seared, covered with wild mushroom duxelles and prosciutto, and all wrapped up and baked inside a puff pastry. Can you get more decadent than that? Well, yes you can. Because then you serve it with this green peppercorn sauce that is creamy and beefy with a hint of brandy and the ever-so-slight bite of the peppercorns.

My husband and I had a rare weekend with no kids around, so it was a treat to plan something special and spend the evening cooking together. Please don't be intimidated by any perceived technical difficulty here. While this is a multi-step dish that does honestly take some time, absolutely none of the steps are difficult at all. That said, you could certainly prepare the dish ahead of time and have it refrigerated until you are ready for it to go into the oven.

Most recipes call for a large beef tenderloin (maybe 3 pounds). If you are making this for a crowd, I would certainly seek one out; however, for just the two of us, I knew that would be way too much meat. Also, it is MUCH easier to find a couple of beautiful 6–8-oz filets from your local grocer, than to seek out an entire 3-pound tenderloin.

According to Julia Child, the most frequent issues with this dish seem to be overcooked meat and soggy pastry. She described it as a "damply dumpling under its handsome exterior." You can guard against overcooking by inserting a digital thermometer into one of the filets during the baking process. The one I have allows me to set a target temperature (130–135°F), and there is an alarm that goes off when it reaches that temp. That is about as foolproof as you are going to get, folks! As far as the soggy pastry goes, the step where you wrap the beef and duxelles tightly with the prosciutto will help hold in the juices to prevent soggy pastry.

Notes:

Ingredients

For the Duxelles

1 package (4–8-oz) wild mushroom medley
2 shallots, peeled and roughly chopped
4 cloves garlic, peeled and roughly chopped
2 sprigs fresh thyme, leaves only
2 Tbsp butter
2 Tbsp extra virgin olive oil
Kosher salt and freshly ground black pepper, to taste

For the Beef

2 nice-sized (6–8-oz) beef filet mignons, trimmed
Extra virgin olive oil
Kosher salt and freshly ground black pepper, to taste
12 thin slices prosciutto
6 sprigs of fresh thyme, leaves only
2 Tbsp Dijon mustard
Flour, for rolling out puff pastry
1 lb puff pastry, thawed if using frozen
2 large eggs, lightly beaten
½ tsp coarse sea salt
Minced chives, for garnish

Green Peppercorn Sauce

2 Tbsp extra virgin olive oil
2 shallots, sliced
2 cloves of garlic, peeled and smashed
3 sprigs fresh thyme, leaves only
1 cup brandy
1 box beef stock
2 cups cream
2 Tbsp grainy mustard
½ cup green peppercorns in brine, drained

How to...

To Make the Duxelles

Add mushrooms, shallots, garlic, and thyme to a food processor and pulse until finely chopped. Add butter and olive oil to a large sauté pan and set over medium heat. Add the shallot and mushroom mixture and sauté for 8–10 minutes until most of the liquid has evaporated. Season with salt and pepper and set aside to cool.

To Prepare the Beef

Drizzle each filet with olive oil, season with salt and pepper, and sear all over, including the ends, in a hot, heavy-based skillet lightly coated with olive oil, about

2–3 minutes. Meanwhile, set out your prosciutto on a sheet of plastic wrap (plastic needs to be about a foot and a half in length so you can wrap and tie the filet up in it) on top of your cutting board.

Tip» *Buy more prosciutto than you think you will need. The amount I bought did not quite make it all the way around the beef filets.*

Shingle the prosciutto so it forms two large rectangles that are big enough to encompass each filet entirely. Using a rubber spatula, cover the prosciutto evenly with a thin layer of duxelles. Season the surface of the duxelles; top with coarse salt, black pepper, and thyme leaves. When the beef is seared, remove from heat and smear lightly all over with Dijon mustard. Allow to cool slightly, then roll up in the duxelles-covered prosciutto using the plastic wrap to tie it up nice and tight. Tuck in the ends of the prosciutto as you roll to completely encompass the beef. Roll it up tightly in plastic wrap and twist the ends to seal it completely and hold it in a nice log shape. Set in the refrigerator for 30 minutes to ensure it maintains its shape.

Preheat oven to 425°F.

On a lightly floured surface, roll the puff pastry out into two large squares, about ¼-inch thickness each. Remove beef from refrigerator and cut off plastic. Set the beef in the center of the pastry and fold over the longer sides, brushing with egg wash to seal. Trim ends if necessary, then brush with egg wash and fold over to completely seal the beef—saving ends to use as a decoration on top if desired. Top with coarse sea salt. Place the beef seam-side down on a baking sheet.

Brush the top of the pastry with egg wash, and then make a couple of slits in the top of the pastry using the tip of a paring knife—this creates vents that will allow the steam to escape when cooking. Bake for 25–30 minutes (depending on the size of the filets and the temperature you desire) until pastry is golden brown and beef registers 125°F (medium rare) to 135°F (medium) on an instant-read thermometer. I covered mine with aluminum foil about

20 minutes into the oven so that the crust wouldn't over-brown. Remove from oven and rest 10 minutes before cutting into thick slices. Remember, the beef will continue to cook (probably an extra 5 degrees) after you remove it from the oven. But if you cut into it right away without allowing it to rest, all of the juices will run out and your meat will be dry. Garnish with minced chives and serve with green peppercorn sauce.

Green Peppercorn Sauce

Add olive oil to pan after removing beef. Add shallots, garlic, and thyme; sauté for 1–2 minutes. Next, add brandy and beef stock and reduce by about half. Strain out solids and then add 2 cups cream and mustard. Reduce by half again, adjusting seasoning with salt and pepper, then shut off heat and add green peppercorns.

Food Nerd Notes: *The origin of this dish seems to be quite muddled, as various cultures seem to lay claim to it. The French had a dish called "filet de boeuf en croûte" which seems pretty similar. But Wellington is an English name. Some sources say it was named after the guy (the Duke of Wellington) who defeated Napoleon. He apparently was NOT a foodie, and his chefs kept leaving his employment as he had no appreciation for their food… until one of the chefs made this dish for him. So I guess this dish finally won him over with its decadence (as originally the beef would have been smothered in pate before being wrapped in the pastry).*

Duxelles is a finely chopped (minced) mixture of mushrooms, onions, shallots, and herbs sautéed in butter, and reduced to a paste (sometimes cream is used, as well). It is a basic preparation used in stuffings and sauces (notably, beef Wellington) or as a garnish. Duxelles can also be filled into a pocket of raw pastry and baked as a savory tart (similar to a hand-held pie). Duxelles is made with any cultivated or wild mushroom, depending on the recipe. Duxelles made with wild porcini mushrooms will be much stronger flavored than that made with white or brown mushrooms. Fresh mushrooms are usually used; however, reconstituted dried varieties are used, as well. Duxelles is said to have been created by the 17th-century French chef François Pierre La Varenne (1615–1678) and to have been named after his employer, Nicolas Chalon du Blé, marquis d'Uxelles, maréchal de France.

Skinny Mexican Pizza

I only consent to going to Taco Bell about twice a year. But back when I was a teenager, this was my favorite menu item there. Now, my teens love this! My version is much heartier than the one at the fast food chain, and I'm making some substitutions that will make me feel better serving it. No one will guess this is turkey!

Ingredients — enough to feed 3–6 people

- 6 whole wheat flour tortillas, medium-sized
- Canola oil to brush tortillas
- 1 lb lean ground turkey
- Seasonings: *½ tsp salt, 1½ tsp pepper, 1½ tsp cumin, 1 tsp chili powder, 1 tsp oregano*
- 1 packet of beef-flavored "flavor boost" (concentrated stock)
- 1 pkg taco seasoning (I used Taco Bell brand; low-sodium seasoning is available.)
- ¾ cup water
- 1 can fat-free refried beans (I used Taco Bell brand.)
- ½ cup low-sodium chicken stock
- Salsas of choice (I used Herdez red salsa and green salsa verde.)
- Mexican blend grated cheese
- Medium taco sauce (I used Taco Bell brand.)
- 1 diced tomato
- 1 small can sliced black olives
- 2 fresh green onions, thinly sliced on the diagonal

Serve with reduced-fat sour cream and spicy guacamole.

How to...

Brush whole wheat tortillas with canola oil and broil in the oven about 4–5 minutes per side until puffy and golden. *They look so cool when they puff! Very rustic.* Break up and brown the ground turkey in a nonstick skillet, adding salt, pepper, cumin, chili powder, and oregano as the ground turkey is browning. Once it's cooked through, add one packet of beef "flavor boost" stock (goes a long way to dress up our turkey in a cow suit), taco seasoning, and water. Let it cook until this makes a thick-ish sauce, and then turn off the heat. To the refried beans, add a little chicken stock to thin it out. We want to be able to spread it.

Assembly: Paint the bottom tortilla with red salsa, and then add meat and a layer of cheese. To the second tortilla, add beans, and then flip it over so that the beans are on the bottom next to the cheese. On the top of the second tortilla, paint green salsa and add cheese, taco sauce, tomatoes, olives, and green onions (or whatever you choose).

Bake at 400°F until all is melted, or put it back under the broiler in the oven. Cut into wedges with a long knife and serve with condiments of choice. I like spicy guacamole and some reduced-fat sour cream. Yumm! This is perfect for summer with a tall, ice-cold bottled Mexican beverage of your choice—like one with a lime stuck in the top of it.

These baked tortillas are a not as crunchy as the fried ones. If you desire a really crunchy, "fall apart when you eat it" bite, you can buy them already fried crispy. But the point of the recipe is to make it a little healthier.

Pancetta Wrapped Stuffed Pork Tenderloin

Pork wrapped in pork? Yep! Can I get an Amen?! And to top that off, it's filled with a delicious caramelized onion, apple, and toasted walnut filling. Yum! The pancetta helps to keep the pork moist, as do the juices from the apples, and the flavors are just huge in your mouth!

My family really enjoys pork tenderloins, which are super lean these days. But they are also a blank slate, just waiting for you to add some pizzazz. Well this, my friends, is pizzazz!

This recipe is a bit more labor intensive (in terms of number of steps) than some other recipes. But rest assured, each step is simple; and I will walk you through it one step at a time. You could easily assemble the whole thing ahead of time and have it "oven ready" and waiting in the fridge for you to walk in from work. Your regular pork chops will be so jealous! Can you say "dinner party worthy"? You could also use the filling as a delicious topping for your pork chops as a time-saving alternative.

Ingredients

Filling

- ⅓ cup toasted walnuts, chopped
- 3 Tbsp butter
- ½ onion, chopped
- 2 medium apples, chopped
- 1 tsp fresh thyme

Kosher salt and black pepper, to taste

- ⅓ cup freshly grated Parmigiano Reggiano cheese

Pork

- 1½–2 lbs pork tenderloin
- 6 oz pancetta

Dressing

- 2 Tbsp chopped fresh herbs: *rosemary, sage, chives*
- 2 Tbsp garlic, minced
- 1 tsp kosher salt
- 2 Tbsp extra virgin olive oil
- 1 tsp mustard powder
- 1 Tbsp white wine vinegar

Notes:

How to...

Here's the general plan of attack:

Prepare the filling, stuff the pork, prepare the dressing, wrap the pork, and cook.

Step 1. *Let's start with the filling.* This can also be made ahead of time and refrigerated.

Start by toasting the nuts. I put them in a dry pan and toasted them in the oven at 400°F for 7 minutes, shaking them around about halfway. Remove the toasted nuts from the oven and let them cool. Then chop them.

Now let's get this filling going! Sauté together butter, onions, apples, thyme, salt, pepper, and the chopped nuts. I want everything to really cook down and start to caramelize. Let that all cook down a while. The onions and apples should get nice and soft (but not mushy). It will be pretty fragrant. When they seem done, give them the master treatment with some freshly grated Parmigiano Reggiano cheese. Of course, you MUST taste this. You need to check your seasonings anyway, right? Sweet, crunchy, salty, herbaceous... ***yum!***

VARIATION » *If you are short on time or do not need an entire pork tenderloin, this would be a great topping by itself for some thick, center-cut pork loin chops! Just let it cook down a bit more.*

Step 2. *Let's stuff the pork.* Take your beautiful, lean pork tenderloin and trim it of any exterior fat. Then remove the silver skin. Next, butterfly the pork, going *almost* to the end, but not quite. Err on the side of leaving more thickness than you think. You can always cut deeper later. Cover the butterflied pork with a sheet of plastic wrap and pound away. We want to achieve a uniform thickness.

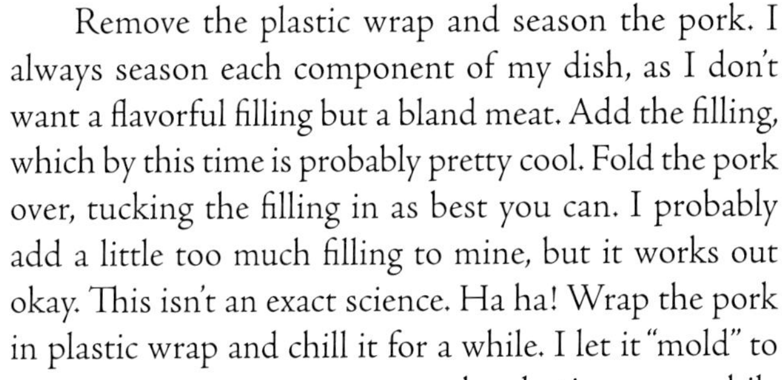

Remove the plastic wrap and season the pork. I always season each component of my dish, as I don't want a flavorful filling but a bland meat. Add the filling, which by this time is probably pretty cool. Fold the pork over, tucking the filling in as best you can. I probably add a little too much filling to mine, but it works out okay. This isn't an exact science. Ha ha! Wrap the pork in plastic wrap and chill it for a while. I let it "mold" to the plastic wrap a while so that I can make my dressing and get my pancetta ready.

Step 3. ***Let's make the outside dressing.*** Simply add all the ingredients together. I went out and gathered some herbs from my garden, but use what you have. I had rosemary, chives, and sage. Chop them finely and add to the dressing. I was going to add some Dijon mustard, but I couldn't find any, so I added some dry mustard powder and a bit of white wine vinegar. Now just mix it all together. It will probably make your mouth pucker, but it will season the whole outside of the pork.

Step 4. ***Wrap the pork.*** Here's where it really gets fun! Set out a large sheet of plastic wrap. On top of the plastic wrap, arrange your pancetta, slightly overlapping each other, until the rectangle is large enough to completely cover the pork. I pretty much just used my chopping board as a guide. Add the pork slightly to the side. Cover the pork with the herb-seasoned dressing. Give it a nice massage. This will be another layer of flavor for the pork that we will wrap inside the pancetta blanket.

Now starting from one side, use the plastic wrap to help you roll the pancetta up and around that awesome pork. Wrap it tightly, using the plastic wrap. Pull the wrap back before it would start rolling over onto itself. Twist the ends of the plastic wrap tightly and let the whole thing rest in the refrigerator about 30 minutes so the pancetta will sort of mold itself to the pork.

When you are ready to cook the pork, tie up the pancetta with kitchen twine. I roasted the meat on a cooling rack set into a cookie sheet so that the hot air could circulate underneath it since I didn't want the bottom to be soggy. Bake at 400°F until it reaches an internal temperature of 150°F (per digital thermometer). This took about 43 minutes for my pork.

Recommended Cooking Tip » *A wise investment is a thermometer that you can set at the temperature you want: one that will alert you when that temperature is reached. This takes a LOT of the guesswork out of cooking any meat, especially pork. You want it cooked, but not overdone. And you definitely want it to be juicy.*

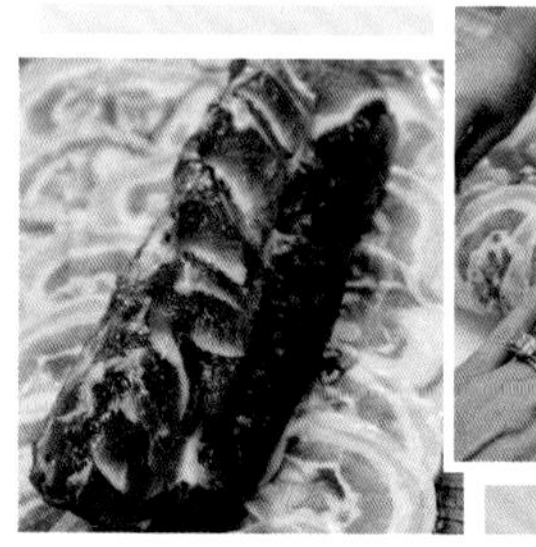

And ta-da! Here we have it! Beautiful, right? The pancetta gets all crispy, but our pork is still juicy. But PLEASE, do NOT cut into it yet. Tent the pork with aluminum foil and let it rest about 10 minutes so the juices won't all run out of it.

The main photo is a shot of the inside of the pork. Tender, juicy, and very flavorful. Sweet and crunchy filling inside, tangy dressing on the outside. And crispy Italian bacon surrounding the whole thing? All you need are some great sides, and you have the makings of a beautiful meal, whether this is for Sunday supper with the family, date night with your sweetheart, or a dinner party.

Cornbread Cowboy Chili

This is comfort food at its finest. I have no idea what real cowboys actually ate; but in my head, they are out under the stars with a giant pot of chili over an open fire, with a big hunk of sweet cornbread on the side. This recipe puts these two favorite dishes together!

This one-pot recipe gives you the big, bold flavor of chili toned down by the sweet, homey cornbread—made perfect with a cool scoop of sour cream and the brightness of cilantro. It's also a great way to "repurpose" leftover chili that you may have, if you made a big pot to start with!

Ingredients

- 1 small pot of your favorite chili recipe, prepared
- 1–2 cups shredded cheddar cheese, *or a shredded cheese blend*
- 1 box of your favorite cornbread batter recipe (I used Jiffy.)
- 1 egg
- ⅓ cup milk

For garnish: *sour cream and cilantro*

How to...

Pour the chili in the bottom of a black iron skillet, to about ⅓–½ of the way to the top. Add cheese on top of meat to form a barrier. Top chili and cheese with uncooked cornbread batter. Bake per cornbread instructions until golden brown, about 400°F for about 20 minutes. Spoon it out with a great big spoon! Top with sour cream, grated cheddar cheese, and a little cilantro for garnish. Enjoy out under the stars... or on the couch in front of the fireplace!

Cook's Notes: *This would also be great in individual ramekins. If you anticipate having leftovers, consider putting more chili in the bottom, as the cornbread will start soaking up the chili after it sits a while, even with the waxy layer of cheese.*

Notes:

Smoky Sweet Pulled Pork

The traditional method of making pulled pork is to smoke the pork for hours and hours, which gives the meat a deep smoky flavor and a fall-off-the-bone, unbelievable tenderness. The long smoking time also creates a beautiful bark crust on the outside. This style of cooking is typically equated to lazy days in the South where you can smell the meat literally melting in the smoker while you go about your business. ***HA!*** Little did I know, in my inexperience, that smoking meat is a real babysitting job! That said, when it was all said and done, the boys and I stood there pulling thick strips off of it saying, "Oh. My. God!" In my family, that is pretty much a good indicator that you've made something amazing!

There are four major components to this pulled pork recipe—a pork butt (which is really a pork shoulder), a smoky, sweet, and spicy rub, LOTS of time out there in the smoker, and a spicy vinegar barbecue sauce. I slow smoked this pork butt with hickory and apple wood.

Ingredients

6–7 lbs bone-in Boston butt pork roast
Smoky-sweet dry rub
¼ cup kosher salt
¼ cup firmly packed brown sugar
2 Tbsp + 2 tsp paprika
2 Tbsp granulated sugar
2 tsp garlic powder
2 tsp freshly ground pepper
1 tsp dry ground mustard
1 tsp ground cumin
1 tsp ground ginger
Apple and hickory wood chips
A couple cups of apple cider vinegar
BBQ sauce of your choice (I used the Dr. Pepper "Sweet and Kickin' BBQ Sauce.")
Fluffy white bread buns
Cole slaw mix of your choice

Food Nerd Notes: *Why is it called a pork butt if it's really the shoulder?*

As stated by the National Pork Board, "in pre-revolutionary New England and into the Revolutionary War, some pork cuts (not those highly valued, or 'high on the hog' like loin and ham) were packed into casks or barrels (also known as 'butts') for storage and shipment. The way the hog shoulder was cut in the Boston area became known in other regions as 'Boston Butt.' This name stuck, and today, Boston Butt is called that almost everywhere in the US… except in Boston."

How to...

This rub is something that you can throw together in about 5 minutes. You probably have all the stuff in the cabinet already. **The night before,** trim the pork of the majority of the fat (I have super picky kids who do NOT like fat), and then smother it with the entire batch of rub. Rub and pat those spices into the pork like it's getting an expensive massage! Cover the pork and let it sleep with that blanket of spices overnight in the fridge. Also, get your wood chips soaking.

The next morning, add the soaked wood chips to the charcoal coals in your smoker. You are going to smoke the pork butt with the hickory and applewood for basically the whole day–going out about every hour to add more coals and more soaked wood chips. Ideally, you want the smoker to maintain a temperature between 225–250°F. After about 5 hours, turn the pork over for the duration of the day. I keep a digital, internal thermometer stuck into the biggest part of the pork to keep an eye on the actual internal meat temp. Once it gets to about 130°F, take it out of the smoker, cover it, and put it in the fridge.

The next day, pop it in the oven on 300°F (covered) with about 2 cups of apple cider vinegar in the bottom of the pan and about a cup of BBQ sauce slathered over the top. We want that acidic vinegar to steam into the pork, adding back moisture. Keep it in the oven until the digital thermometer reads 195°F. At that point, the meat will have begun to pull away from the bone, the collagenous tissues will have all been broken down and gelatinized, and the fat will have liquefied.

Notes:

You can see the level of smoke penetration when you pull off a strip of the bark. All that outer pink color is smoke. And don't let the black part fool you... it is NOT burned. That is the BEST part. All of those smoked spices create this caramelized outer crust that is SO good!

Allow it to rest for about 20 minutes, then start shredding it. After shredding it, I take some of the apple cider vinegar from the bottom of the pan, which at this point has become its own sauce of sorts, and pour about half of it over the shredded pork. Serve on those fluffy white buns with your choice of BBQ sauce and cole slaw.

Coconut Lime Chicken

This Indonesian-inspired chicken dish gets a definite "thumbs up" from my teens! It is super easy to make, which is great for those nights when you are playing taxicab driver back and forth across town, bringing kids to practices. You just throw the marinade together and shove the chicken into it, then grill it up when you get your brood all back together under the same roof.

Anything with coconut, lime, and cilantro is automatically going to get my vote, because that flavor profile just rocks! And then with the addition of a spicy kick? Yes, please! This dish is adapted from a recipe found in *Fine Cooking*, Winter 2006.

Ingredients

- 1 pkg of skinless, boneless chicken breasts
- 3 Tbsp canola oil
- Zest of 1 large lime
- 1 tsp cumin
- 2 Tbsp soy sauce
- 1–1½ tsp kosher salt
- 3 Tbsp sugar
- 2 tsp curry powder
- ¾ cup canned coconut milk
- Juice of 1 lime
- 1 Serrano pepper, finely minced or cut into thin slivers, *optional*
- ¼ cup chopped fresh cilantro
- Lime wedges

How to...

The prep for this dish takes all of about 10 minutes. Slice chicken breasts completely in half, as if you were butterflying them. Place them in a gallon zip-top bag and flatten them uniformly with a meat pounder (or heavy pan, wine bottle, etc).

In a bowl, add all of the marinade ingredients together: oil, lime zest, cumin, soy sauce, salt, sugar, curry powder, coconut milk, lime juice, and Serrano pepper if you are using one. This marinade may taste pretty salty to you right now; but once we put it over the chicken and bland rice, it will balance out. Pour the marinade over the chicken in the zip-top bag, squeeze the air out, and allow to marinate at least 30 minutes, or preferably up to 2 hours in the fridge.

After marinating, grill the chicken over moderately high heat in a pan prepared with a bit of cooking spray or canola oil. Get the pan really hot before you add the meat. You want it to sear. Allow the meat to sit without moving it for several minutes on each side until just cooked. The time will depend on the thickness of the meat. While cooking the meat, add the marinade to a small saucepan and bring to a full boil for at least 2–3 minutes. This is sufficient to kill all of the bacteria in it. *Or you could double the marinade, divide in two, and just toss out the part that you used for the chicken.*

Serve the chicken and a drizzle of the sauce over rice with chopped cilantro and fresh lime wedges. This is a very important part, as these flavors bring balance and brightness to the dish.

Notes:

Spinach and Apricot Stuffed Pork Tenderloin

Since I was a small girl, my mother has always ENCOURAGED me to write in my cookbooks. Yep. You heard me. Browsing through her cookbooks (and now mine) becomes a walk down memory lane. As I looked back at this recipe, I was a little taken aback that I've been making this since my oldest children were just toddlers! Wow! The inspiration for this recipe comes from the cookbook *Come On In!: Recipes from the Junior League of Jackson, MS.*

Looking at the title and remembering that I have picky eaters may have you scratching your head. Well, I can explain. One of the great things about pork tenderloins, aside from being really lean but still tender and juicy, is that they usually come 2-to-a-pack. That's fortunate because I can stuff one and leave the other one plain. Doesn't that work out nicely?

In my opinion, the stuffing of this pork really brings it to life. It's sweet and savory at the same time and beautiful to look at and gives you a wonderful textural component to the bite.

Ingredients

- ½ lb fresh baby spinach, washed and chopped
- 3 cloves garlic, minced
- 3 Tbsp butter
- 1 cup dried apricots, sliced
- 2 Tbsp chopped fresh rosemary plus 2 tsp dried
- Kosher salt and black pepper, to taste
- 1 pork tenderloin (2 lbs), pounded out to ¾-inch thickness

Notes:

How to...

Filling: Sauté spinach and garlic briefly in butter. Mix in the sliced apricots and chopped rosemary and season with salt and pepper. Set aside.

Meat Prep: Starting on one edge of the pork, slice down, leaving a border on the side and at the bottom of the meat. When you get about an inch or so from the bottom, turn the knife and continue to cut to the side. You can essentially make a border the whole way around. Pull the meat open as you go. I'm not that great at making it perfectly uniform, so I pound it out to a uniform thickness. Be careful to not tear the meat or make it too thin. Season generously with salt and pepper.

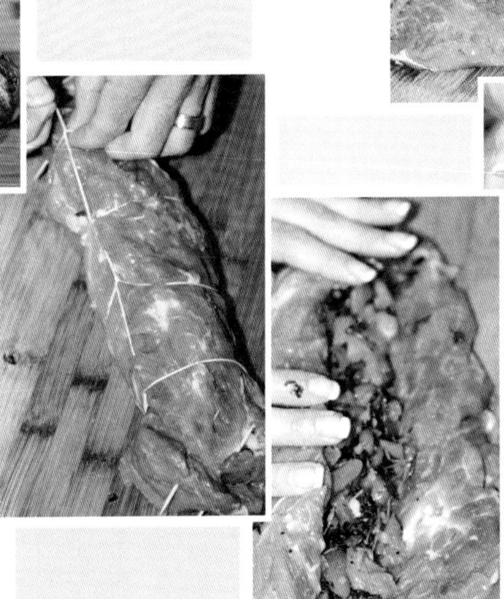

Assembly: Spread the apricot stuffing over the flattened tenderloin. Roll up the pork and secure with kitchen twine (I usually add a few toothpicks as well). Grill on each side until internal meat temperature reaches 150°F. Tent the grilled meat and allow to rest for 10 minutes. If you don't let it rest, all the juices will run out of the meat, leaving it dry. So just don't! *Don't forget to remove the toothpicks and string!* Slice tenderloin, serve, and enjoy!

Chicken Molcajete

Well, this dish has a great story to it! This Mexican-style meat and vegetable stew has become one of our favorite Mexican dishes. While on vacation one year, we found ourselves stopping for lunch at a little roadside restaurant, complete with dirt floors and open-air seating, in the foothills of the Sierra Madre Mountains in Northwestern Mexico. We had just visited the little town of La Noria (the restaurant being named the same). The town of La Noria has been around since the late 1500s, and I dare say has changed very little since then. It's a quaint, little place where you can watch craftsmen making leather goods, ceramics, and the like, about 20 miles east of Mazatlan. Only a couple of the roads are paved in cobblestones, and the rest are dirt and rocks. Nope—it's not glamorous, but it's the kind of place that your heart falls in love with when you are there—smiling babies, little old ladies and leathered old men going about their work, and shy young boys running about handing you flowers.

So, back to the restaurant and this dish. A **molcajete** (mohl-kah-HEH-tay) is a stone tool, often carved from volcanic rock, and is among the world's oldest kitchen tools. It is the Mexican version of a mortar and pestle that is used for grinding food products. The molcajete was used by pre-Hispanic Mesoamerican cultures (such as the Aztec and Mayans), stretching back several thousand years. The rough surface of the stone is ideal for crushing and grinding spices and in the preparation of salsas and guacamole. Molcajetes are also used as serving vessels in restaurants and homes. While recipes are usually not cooked in them, the molcajete stays hot for a **very** long time, and it is not unusual for a dish to still be bubbling a half hour after serving.

The dish that was served to us in the molcajete that lazy afternoon in La Noria was similar to fajitas but served in a rich, tomato-based soup/stew. Similar seasonings and meats (chicken, flank steak, shrimp, etc.), similar vegetables (onions, peppers, etc.), all bathed in a bubbling stew of beefy, tomato-based broth, topped off with a Mexican crumbly cheese and slices of cool, creamy avocado. It was served with tortillas that had been slightly charred over an open fire. To wash it down? Big handmade ceramic mugs of fresh-squeezed and slightly frozen slushy limeade. All the while, colorful roosters are walking around like they own the place, checking you out, daring you to speak out against this humble little family-run establishment. Hey roosters—keep your spurs on! The food was AMAZING, and I'm sure we'll be back there at some point in our lives.

Please don't be intimidated by the long list of ingredients. This dish is one of those chop, prep, and dump-it-all-together recipes—very easy. If you are not lucky enough to own an "*authentico*" molcajete, perhaps because TSA wouldn't let you carry it through security, you can just serve it from a black iron skillet or maybe a cast enamel Dutch oven. Both of those would hold the heat very well.

Ingredients for 2–3 adults

1 large head of garlic (still in the paper skin)
1½ Tbsp extra virgin olive oil
1 lb chicken tenders, *or boneless skinless chicken breasts trimmed and cut into strips*
Salt, pepper, Ancho chili powder, and cumin, all to taste
2 slices of bacon, cut into 1-inch pieces
1½ Tbsp vegetable or canola oil
½ large onion, *a sweet variety*, sliced into strips
A handful of colored bell pepper slices, *green, red, orange, yellow—your choice*
1 large tomato, cut into about 8 wedges
8 oz can of tomato sauce
½ can (about 1 cup) of mild red enchilada sauce
2–3 cups chicken stock/beef broth
Oregano
1–2 limes, juiced
1 ripe avocado
Queso fresco Mexican crumbling cheese
Shredded Mexican "quesadilla" cheese, *could substitute mozzarella*
Flour tortillas, *Corn tortillas are more authentic to this recipe, but we prefer the flour tortillas.*
Optional additions for garnishing and serving: *chopped cilantro and sour cream, with added lime zest*

How to...

Start by getting the garlic roasting, as this step takes the longest. You can have this going the whole time you are chopping, trimming, and doing all the other prep. Preheat the oven to 400°F. Chop only the top of the garlic off, exposing all the little "cells" of garlic cloves. Line a small pan with aluminum foil and place the garlic clove in the middle. Pour the olive oil over the garlic, allowing it to go down into the cloves. Close up the aluminum foil, and bake for about 45 minutes in the oven. The garlic will become almost as creamy as butter, and the flavor will mellow out tremendously. No longer will the caramelized roasted garlic have the bite associated with raw garlic. After baking and cooling, you can just take the whole garlic head, turn it over and squeeze out the soft roasted garlic.

Notes:

While the garlic is in the oven, start on chicken and veggie prep. Trim the chicken of any fat and cut into strips if using whole breasts. Season the chicken with salt, pepper, ancho chili powder, and lots of cumin. Watch that ancho chili powder—it's hot! Cut the veggies into strips, the tomatoes into wedges.

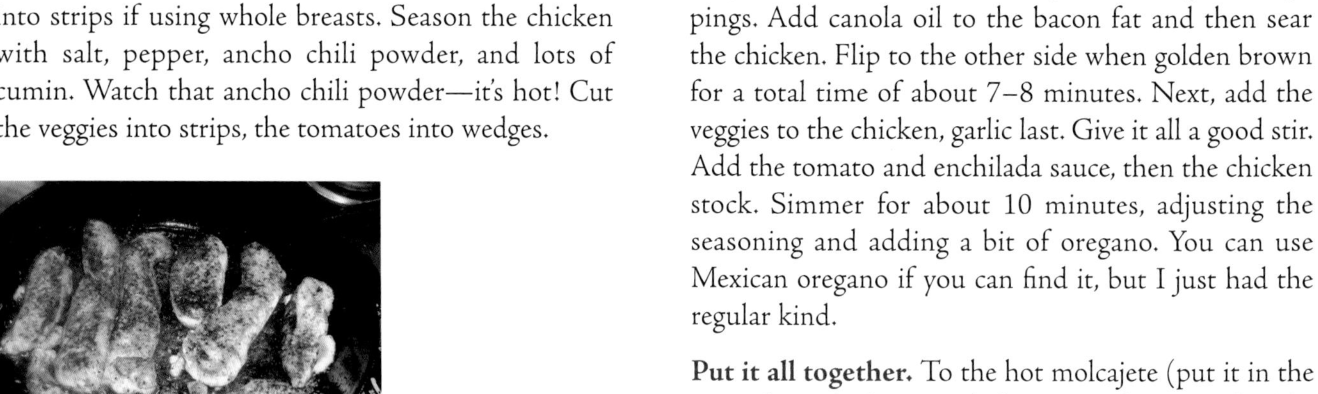

Start the cooking. Cook bacon pieces until brown and crisp, then remove to another plate, leaving the drippings. Add canola oil to the bacon fat and then sear the chicken. Flip to the other side when golden brown for a total time of about 7–8 minutes. Next, add the veggies to the chicken, garlic last. Give it all a good stir. Add the tomato and enchilada sauce, then the chicken stock. Simmer for about 10 minutes, adjusting the seasoning and adding a bit of oregano. You can use Mexican oregano if you can find it, but I just had the regular kind.

Put it all together. To the hot molcajete (put it in the oven if you don't routinely have use of an open fire like in Mexico), add the broth, chicken, vegetables, and lime juice (you need the acid to brighten it up). Garnish with a ripe avocado that has been sliced and drizzle with lemon juice, fresh cilantro if desired, queso fresco crumbling cheese, and some quesadilla melting cheese.

Serve. Serve on slightly charred tortillas, with some added crème fraiche or plain old sour cream with a little lime zest, some chopped cilantro, and maybe an extra little squeeze of lime juice.

Chicken Tamale Casserole

One of my oldest son's favorite things to order when we are on the Northwestern, Pacific side of Mexico would be handmade tamales that you can pick up as you walk through the market. Tamales are seasoned meat and cheese wrapped in that soft masa cornmeal dough and steamed inside the familiar corn husks. Making those can be a pretty time-consuming operation, and not something I am going to be starting after a day at work. This, on the other hand, is very simple to assemble, and I will be making use of some convenience items to speed things along. This is an "after your work day" meal, not a "work all day at it" meal. We have included ***Food Nerd Notes*** at the bottom of this recipe.

Cornbread, on the other hand, is fast and easy. So what about a cornbread crust seasoned up with cheese, corn, cumin, chilies, and the shredded meat on top? And what if we added some great color and texture with black beans and corn, melted cheese, chips, avocados and tomatoes, with cilantro and lime and sour cream… oh, my! I get excited thinking about all those flavors put together in a simple-to-assemble casserole.

Ingredients

- 1 box of your favorite cornbread mix
- ⅓ cup milk
- 1 large egg
- 1 cup shredded Monterey Jack/cheddar cheese
- ½ 15-oz can cream-style corn
- 1 tsp cumin
- 2 oz canned, chopped green chilies
- 1 Tbsp vegetable oil
- 2–3 cups cooked chicken, shredded, *I often use a rotisserie chicken to save time.*
- 1½ cups red enchilada sauce, divided, *mild to hot, your choice*
- 1 packet taco seasoning, *You can choose regular or a low-salt variety.*
- ¾ 15-oz can drained and rinsed black beans
- 1 10-oz can drained corn niblets, *I use a "Mexican-style."*
- 2 cups shredded mozzarella cheese
- Crumbled tortilla chips, *enough to cover the top. I don't measure.*

Garnish

- Chopped tomatoes
- Chopped avocado
- Fresh lime juice
- Kosher salt and black pepper
- Chopped purple onion
- Sour cream to serve it with

How to...

Preheat the oven to 400°F. Prepare a box of your favorite cornbread mix. If that means you like to make it from scratch, do so. But if you are making it from a box, make it according to the directions with the milk and egg called for. Add in the yellow cheese blend, cream-style corn, cumin, and green chilies. Add about a tablespoon of vegetable oil to your iron skillet and let it get really hot. Pour in the cornbread batter. The hot oil will help it form a crispy crust on the bottom and sides. Then pop the skillet into the oven for about 25 minutes.

While cornbread is baking, combine shredded, cooked chicken with a cup of red enchilada sauce and the taco seasoning. This may seem really salty, but we are balancing out the sweetness from the cornbread.

Food Nerd Notes: *First, let's talk about tamales–A tamale is a traditional Mesoamerican dish made of masa (a starchy corn-based dough), which is steamed or boiled in a leaf wrapper. The wrapping is discarded before eating. Tamales can be filled with meats, cheeses, fruits, vegetables, chilies or any preparation according to taste, and both the filling and the cooking liquid may be seasoned. Tamales have been traced back to the Ancient Maya people, who prepared them for feasts as early as the Preclassic period (1200–250 BC). Some sources say tamales originated in Mesoamerica as early as 8000 to 5000 BC. Aztec and Mayan civilizations, as well as the Olmeca and Tolteca before them, used tamales not only as portable food, often to support their armies, but also for hunters and travelers. Tamale use in the Inca Empire had been reported long before the Spanish visited the New World.*

Notes:

Remove cornbread from the oven and add all the toppings: rinsed black beans, corn niblets, chicken and sauce, crumbled tortilla chips, then *lots* of mozzarella cheese. Drizzle about another ½ cup of enchilada sauce over the top, then put it back into the oven for 15 minutes.

Garnish with chopped cilantro and a little salad of chopped tomatoes, avocado, definitely some fresh lime juice, salt and pepper, and some purple onion. Serve hot with a big dollop of sour cream.

Are you hungry yet? Sweet corn flavor throughout, the color and texture of the beans and corn, spicy-ish chicken, gooey cheese, the bright flavors of fresh tomatoes and purple onion, the creamy avocado, bold cilantro, creamy sour cream, and a pop of sunshine from the fresh lime!

Yes! Score!

Food Nerd Notes » *For sure, food trends come and go. Casseroles were all the rage in the 1950s, then fell out of favor in the 1970s. Now we can't get enough of them! We are busy. They are comforting, easy, and flavorful. But what is a casserole really?*

A casserole, from the French word for "saucepan," is a large, deep dish used both in the oven and as a serving vessel. The word casserole is also used for the food cooked and served in such a vessel, with the cookware itself. In British English, this type of dish is frequently also called a "bake," coinciding with the cooking technique used to cook casseroles. In Minnesota, this type of dish is sometimes called "hot dish."

Casseroles usually consist of pieces of meat, various chopped vegetables, a starchy binder such as flour, potato, or pasta, and, often, a crunchy or cheesy topping. Liquids are released from the meat and vegetables during cooking, and further liquid in the form of stock, wine, vegetable juice, etc. may be added when the dish is assembled. Casseroles are usually cooked slowly in the oven, often uncovered. They may be served as a main course or a side dish, and may be served in the vessel in which they were cooked.

In 1866, Elmire Jolicoeur, a French-Canadian immigrant, invented the precursor of the modern casserole in New Hampshire. The casseroles we know today are a relatively modern invention. Early casserole recipes consisted of rice that was pounded, pressed, and filled with a savory mixture of meats such as chicken or sweetbreads. Sometime around the 1870s, this sense of casserole seems to have slipped into its current sense. Cooking in earthenware containers has always been common in most nations, but the idea of casserole cooking as a one-dish meal became popular in America in the twentieth century, especially in the 1950s when new forms of lightweight metal and glassware appeared on the market.

Tomato Basil Chicken

No need to grab that jar of premade pasta sauce! This light and fresh sauce comes together in MINUTES from ingredients that you probably have right this minute! I've always been told that the key to great Italian food is fresh ingredients made simply. Now if you've ever labored over a big casserole of lasagna, you may be scratching your head on that one, but that's another story!

This Tomato Basil Chicken will have you grabbing your fork at the 30-minute mark, which is great news when you need to have a nice, hot meal on the table quickly.

Ingredients

4 servings

2 chicken breasts
Kosher salt, black pepper, dried basil, all to taste
2 Tbsp extra virgin olive oil
2 cups chopped fresh tomatoes
½ cup fresh basil, chopped
4 Tbsp cold butter
2 tsp minced fresh garlic
Freshly grated Parmigiano Reggiano cheese, for garnish

Notes:

How to...

Season chicken breasts with kosher salt, fresh cracked black pepper, and dried basil. Add a couple of tablespoons of extra virgin olive oil to your skillet. This may seem like quite a bit, but it will form the base for the sauce. While waiting for the oil to heat up, go ahead and get your water going for the pasta. When the oil

Cook's Note: *The granules of kosher salt are larger than table salt, which makes it harder to over salt your food. The freshly cracked black pepper tastes much fresher than the stuff in the can. If you want the chicken to cook a little faster, consider pounding them out just a little so they are more of a uniform thickness.*

is HOT, add the chicken breasts. After about 4–5 minutes, the chicken breasts should be ready to turn. By the way, when did chicken breasts get SO HUGE? You'll want to cook them on the second side another 4–5 minutes or until the juices run clear when you pierce them with a small, sharp knife. If you pounded yours out thinner, they will cook faster than this.

After the second side has been cooking for about 4 minutes, go ahead and add in the fresh tomatoes that you have chopped up. Next, add the fresh basil that you have chopped into ribbons, the cold butter (makes the sauce silky), and the minced garlic, and you will probably want to add some more kosher salt and black pepper to season the sauce. Now give it all a good stir so all those flavors will marry together.

When your chicken is cooked, turn the sauce down on the lowest setting to keep it all warm until the pasta is cooked, which should be any minute now. At this point, if still waiting for the pasta, you can remove the cooked chicken to a cutting board, and after letting it rest just a couple of minutes, cut the chicken into slices on the bias. Divide the pasta among individual bowls, and top each with half of a chicken breast, sliced into pieces, and equal portions of the tomato basil sauce. Top with more fresh basil and freshly grated Parmigiana Reggiano cheese.

Love this recipe and want another great option? My best friend uses shrimp in this recipe sometimes... totally awesome! We decided this would be amazing as a dinner party option. Just think: tomato basil shrimp over grits!

For this option, you will want to cook the shrimp only at the end for about 3–4 minutes after the sauce has reduced. She seasons the shrimp with salt, pepper, and some seafood seasoning. These shrimp are tails only and peeled before adding to the sauce. She uses 1½ lbs of shrimp. For this, consider adding in some additional white and red pepper.

Shrimp and Grits with Tasso Cream Sauce

Oh, my! Why did it take me so long to make this?! Delicious, fast, easy, tons of flavor… woo hoo! It's simple enough to make any evening, but definitely fancy enough for guests. Serve in a martini glass for a gorgeous appetizer!

Ingredients — for 2 servings

- 2 servings cooked grits, plus milk and shredded cheddar cheese
- Salt and pepper, to taste
- 2 Tbsp diced onion
- 2 Tbsp diced peppers, *I used red, orange, and yellow.*
- Green onion tops, chopped
- 1 large garlic clove, finely diced
- ½ cup diced, highly seasoned smoked ham (I used Tasso.)
- 20 medium-to-large shrimp, peeled and de-veined, with tails on
- 1 Tbsp extra virgin olive oil
- 1 Tbsp butter
- ¼ cup white wine
- ½ cup heavy cream

First » *I should give you the analysis I got from my 12 year old. The flavor was awesome, but the tails on the shrimp were pretty, but annoying. He methodically went through and took all of the tails off so he could "just enjoy them." If this is your preference, hey—knock yourselves out! That's what is great about cooking.*

Notes:

How to...

Tip » *Get the grits going and prep all the veggies, meat, etc. first before starting, because this goes really quickly!*

Prep: Dice the Tasso into small cubes. It is so wonderfully smoky! You could use a highly smoked, seasoned ham to substitute for tasso.

Cook grits according to package directions, but rather than using all water, use half milk, half water. Season with salt and pepper, and stir the grits a lot to make them creamy. Grate the cheese into the grits, stir, and set aside (but keep warm).

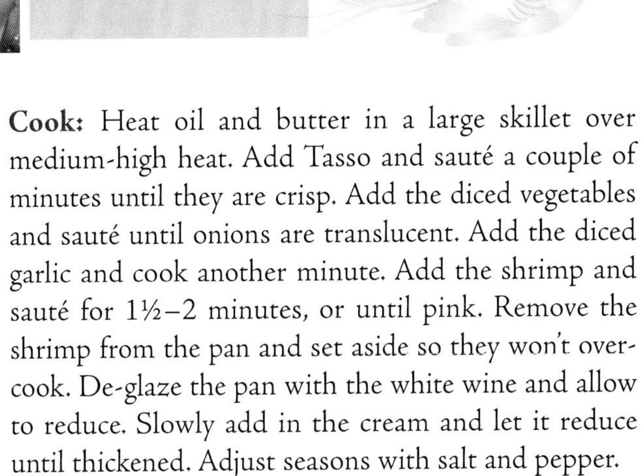

Cook: Heat oil and butter in a large skillet over medium-high heat. Add Tasso and sauté a couple of minutes until they are crisp. Add the diced vegetables and sauté until onions are translucent. Add the diced garlic and cook another minute. Add the shrimp and sauté for 1½–2 minutes, or until pink. Remove the shrimp from the pan and set aside so they won't overcook. De-glaze the pan with the white wine and allow to reduce. Slowly add in the cream and let it reduce until thickened. Adjust seasons with salt and pepper.

Serve: Add the grits first to each serving dish. Add half the shrimp to each dish (10 shrimp per serving). Pour sauce over grits and garnish with fresh green onions.

Southwestern Taco Pie

I've had this recipe for years, and occasionally it comes out of the stack of old standbys. This taco pie is a mix of comfort (which often comes wrapped in a flaky pie crust) and excitement (which epitomizes big, bold Mexican flavors in your mouth). I realize that it's not easy to make a "brown in the middle" pie look pretty, but it sure is tasty!

This recipe can totally be made ahead of time, refrigerated, and popped into the oven to bake when you get home from work. It's really as easy as (1) combine, (2) layer, (3) bake! You don't even have to make the pie crust!

Notes:

Ingredients

- 1 lb package frozen green, red, and yellow peppers and onions*
- 1 lb lean ground beef
- 1 Tbsp vegetable oil (if the beef is very lean)
- 1 1¼-oz pkg taco seasoning mix
- ⅓ cup water
- 1 tsp garlic powder
- 1 tsp onion powder
- ¼ tsp salt
- ⅛ tsp pepper
- ½ cup salsa of your choice
- 1 11-oz can sweet whole kernel corn, drained
- 1 can chopped green chiles
- 1 15-oz pkg refrigerated pie crusts, softened as directed on package
- 2 cups shredded cheese, *Colby/Monterey blend or Mexican blend*

Garnish: *sour cream, taco sauce*

Note: *If using fresh peppers and onions, use 1½ cups chopped onions and 2½ cups chopped peppers and increase prep time and stovetop cooking time.*

How to...

Preheat the oven to 400°F. Chop the onions and peppers as you desire. Brown ground beef in large skillet over medium-high heat. When the beef is about halfway cooked, add the peppers and onions, cooking until beef is thoroughly cooked and vegetables are tender, stirring frequently. At this point, you may choose to drain any excess fat. If you used very lean beef, there may not be any to drain. Add taco seasoning mix and water; mix until ground beef is well coated. Add garlic, onion powders, salt, and pepper. Combine salsa, drained corn, and green chilies with the ground beef mixture; mix well.

Prepare pie crusts as directed on package for 2-crust pie using 9-inch glass or metal pie pan.

Sprinkle ½ cup of cheese evenly in bottom of crust-lined pan. Spread ½ of beef mixture evenly in pan over cheese and pat down. Sprinkle ¾ cup cheese in pan and spread evenly with remaining beef mixture. Pat down and top with remaining ¾ cup cheese. Top with second crust and flute; slit in several places. If you are making this in advance, cover with plastic wrap and refrigerate it at this point.* If you're making this now, bake for 35–40 minutes or until crust is golden brown.

Cover edge of crust with aluminum foil or a pie crust shield after 15 minutes of baking. Let stand at least 5 minutes before serving. Garnish as you like. Some suggestions: a dollop of sour cream, guacamole, fresh cilantro, and some green onions. ***Endless possibilities!***

**So after a long day at work, you remove the plastic wrap, pop this into the oven, make some good old Mexican-flavored rice, and there you have dinner! Flaky crust, bold taco flavors, sweet corn nibblets, some crunchy toppings, and the smooth, creamy sour cream and guacamole! Can you taste it?*

Crawfish Crepes with Creole Cream Sauce

My best friend was visiting her family in South Louisiana over the holidays and wrote to me bragging about the great deal she got on frozen crawfish tails. Not only was I jealous, but it also gave me a craving for a great crawfish dish. As I browsed through the pantry to prepare my grocery list, my eyes landed on the crepe maker that my brother gave me several years ago. That's all it took for my mind to formulate a grand scheme for that evening's meal. I knew it would just be my husband and me, so this would be the perfect opportunity to break out an elegant meal that did not include juice pouches or homework projects.

These crepes are delicate and delicious, and whomever you cook them for will definitely be feeling loved! It's really a shame that you would only typically get this in a fine dining restaurant because it's a simple dish. You could easily make this ahead of time and pop it into the oven for a dinner party or some such celebration. And if you live in an area where you can buy ready-made crepes, then you are home free! Crawfish are in season here in the South in the spring, but you can purchase the frozen tails all year round, which is super great.

Don't be intimidated to make this! Firstly, it's less expensive and way cooler for you to go buy the ingredients to make this yourself than to drive down to New Orleans. Secondly, you are going to impress the heck out of someone with this! Thirdly, I'll walk you through this step-by-step! Deal? Now I know that you looked at this long list and said, "No way." But seriously, there are just a bunch of seasonings here… nothing hard! If there is one thing you learn about cooking when you grow up in Louisiana, it's that food should be well seasoned!

If I can't talk you into making the crepes, try the filling and the creole cream sauce over crostini as a FABULOUS appetizer!

Ingredients

for 4 servings

Crepes

2 large eggs
¾ cup milk
½ cup water
1 cup all-purpose flour
3 Tbsp melted butter
1 tsp finely chopped chives
Pinch of kosher salt

Filling

3½ oz herbed goat cheese, *You can use Boursin cheese, if goat cheese not available.*
2 oz cream cheese
1 tsp finely chopped shallots
1 tsp finely chopped chives
¼ tsp kosher salt
¼ tsp black pepper
¼ cup rinsed, chopped crawfish tails
2 tsp finely chopped parsley

Notes:

Creole Cream Sauce

2 Tbsp butter
3 Tbsp finely diced onion
2 Tbsp diced bell peppers, *mixed red and green*
¼ cup chopped crimini mushrooms (baby bellas)
¼ cup diced tomato
1 Tbsp finely minced garlic
1 Tbsp finely chopped parsley
1 tsp Creole seasoning
1 tsp flour
1 cup dry white wine
1 cup heavy cream
1 cup rinsed crawfish tails
2 Tbsp butter to finish
Kosher salt and black pepper, to taste

Garnish

Finely diced tomatoes
Chopped parsley

Menu Options! *If you don't have crawfish available to you, you could certainly use shrimp, scallops, or lobster. Even lump crabmeat would be delicious. I'm thinking the sauce would also be amazing over a nice bed of linguine or angel hair pasta.*

Plan of Attack! *You can make this ahead of time for your dinner party (even a couple of days in advance). The crepes can be made and filled and just refrigerated. Same goes for the sauce.*

How to...

For making on the same evening: Make the crepe batter first. Make the filling second. Make the sauce last. It doesn't take long at all, and you can do it while the crepes bake if you have everything prepped.

Crepes

Combine all the ingredients, whisking them together. It should be the consistency of a heavy cream, not as thick as a pancake batter. If you have time, refrigerate it for a while (30+ minutes) to allow the bubbles to dissipate.

Cook about 1 oz of batter at a time. If cooking in a skillet, swirl the batter until you get a thin circle. They only need to cook about 1 minute until the slightest brown. Flip and cook about 15 seconds on the second side. Set out on cooling racks. I'm using a crepe maker, so my method was a little different, in that you just dip it and the batter cooks directly on the machine.

Filling

Combine all ingredients and set aside. *I've also made this filling with herbed Boursin cheese when I couldn't find goat cheese, and it worked really well.*

Fill the Crepes.

Prepare pan with nonstick cooking spray. Divide the filling equally among the crepes. It comes out to about 1 Tbsp each. Roll them up and place them seam side down in a casserole dish prepared with nonstick cooking spray. It won't look like much, but it's a rich filling, so the proportions work well with the amount of crepe you get per bite. If you think you'd like more filling, the recipe is easily doubled.

Sauce

In a skillet, sauté diced onions and bell peppers in the butter. Cook a few minutes until they start to soften. Add the chopped mushrooms and allow them to cook down a minute. Add in the diced tomatoes, chopped garlic, and parsley. Cook another minute or so until fragrant. Season with Creole seasoning. Add in the flour and stir it around to form the basis for our roux. Deglaze pan with white wine and heavy cream. Bring to a boil and cook until the sauce thickens and coats the back of a spoon. Then add in the crawfish tails and pats of butter. Cook only 1 minute or so *more* to warm the tails through. They are already cooked, and you don't want them to be tough. Turn off the heat. Adjust seasoning with salt and pepper.

Assemble

Okay, here we are back at the crepes that we rolled. When you are ready, bake the room temperature crepes uncovered at 350°F for about 10–15 minutes until heated through. Arrange a couple of crepes on a plate and spoon some of the crawfish sauce over the top. Garnish with a bit of chopped tomatoes and fresh chopped parsley.

Stuffed Peppers

Stuffed peppers are super simple to make. They freeze well, can be made ahead of time, and carry not only a big flavor explosion, but a hefty nutritional punch as well! You could stuff them with just about anything and have them made up and ready to pop into the oven to warm once you get home. I grew up eating these, so I associate them with comfort food. Additionally, the meat "dressing" or filling is also a clever vehicle for hiding miniscule chopped veggies for your picky eaters.

Ingredients

This is such a touchy-feely recipe that the measurements may be a tad sketchy. I usually season freely and adjust as desired. For an even lower-fat version, feel free to substitute ground turkey in this recipe or even add some different vegetables (squash, zucchini, carrots, parsnips, etc) and mushrooms with seasoned breadcrumbs for a vegetarian version.

1 lb lean ground beef, *I used 94% lean.*
1 medium onion, minced
Salt, pepper, garlic powder, all to taste
2–3 tsp dried basil
2 tsp dried oregano
Handful of chopped peppers
1 can Italian-style diced tomatoes
A few Tbsps Worcestershire sauce
About 1 cup red wine
1 cup rice
Mixed bell peppers, *or color of your choice*
About 1½–2 cups beef broth
Grated cheese, *optional*
Seasoned breadcrumbs, *optional*

Variation: *You could change this recipe from an Italian flavor profile to a Mexican profile really easily. Rather than basil and oregano, use ground cumin and/or chili powder and maybe some cilantro; substitute tomatoes seasoned with typical Mexican flavors. Rather than the grated cheddar on top, use cotija or Queso Chihuahua. Serve with a dollop of sour cream.*

Tip: *CANNED tomatoes provide even higher levels of accessible lycopene (a powerful antioxidant) for you than fresh tomatoes! This is your family that you are in charge of keeping healthy!*

How to...

Brown lean ground beef or turkey in a pan. For very lean versions, use a nonstick pan to avoid sticking or scorching. When ground meat is about half cooked, I add the chopped onions, salt, pepper, garlic powder, dried basil, and oregano and let them cook down with the meat. After the onions have cooked a few minutes, add in a nice handful of chopped peppers. I just used leftover pieces from the pepper pack. If you have frozen peppers, these would even be better as they break down even faster. Allow the peppers to cook down for a while until meat is basically cooked through and vegetables are soft. Then add a can of diced tomatoes. I use the seasoned ones as they bring even more flavor to the party. Season to your taste with the Worcestershire. I am pretty liberal with it. Do at least several good shakes. Add about a cup of red wine. Add in a cup of rice.

Allow everything to come to a boil, then cover, lower the heat, and simmer for about 20 minutes or until the rice is soft and cooked. You want it to initially be really soupy, as the rice will soak up a LOT of the liquid. While the rice is cooking, we will blanch the peppers that have been halved and seeded. I cut them straight through the stem, as I think they look prettier like that. Don't forget to add some salt to the water. We want each component of the dish seasoned. Cook them until they are about halfway softened—maybe 10–15 minutes. I just keep checking them.

Food Note: *The red wine adds a lot of depth to the dish that beef broth alone does not. Here again, red wine contains resveratrol that is heart healthy. Don't worry about the alcohol, as it will cook out; and when divided amongst all the peppers, each person is not getting very much.*

Notes:

If you notice that your rice has absorbed all the liquid and is still not soft, feel free to just add more liquid—like beef broth. We don't want our filling to be dry and hard in the end. When the peppers are mostly cooked, but not mushy, remove them from the water, drain them, and lightly season the cavity with salt. Turn them over on paper towels to dry out.

If you are going to add seasoned breadcrumbs to your filling, add it now before filling the peppers. Add the cooked filling to the peppers in an oven-safe casserole dish. If you want to, sprinkle some shredded cheese on the top (This is a cheddar/Monterey Jack blend). Finish them with a little more dried basil and pop them into the oven, uncovered. Bake for about 20–25 minutes until peppers are soft, the filling is hot, and the cheese is all melty.

Food Nerd Notes: *Let's talk briefly about the health benefits of these colored bell peppers, especially the red ones. Red bell peppers are an impressive source of vitamin A and vitamin C with nearly double the vitamin C of citrus fruits! In addition to being a powerful antioxidant, vitamin C is important in wound healing and enhances the absorption of iron and calcium. In addition, these red peppers are also great sources of lycopene and beta-carotene, both of which have antioxidant properties. These peppers are also a good source of tryptophan. L-Tryptophan is a precursor to serotonin, which can help combat the symptoms of depression with improved mood, appetite, sleep, and impulse control. Finally, there are a lot of folks out there who don't care for green bell peppers because they can have a bitterness to them. Well if this is you, give the red and yellow peppers a try. They are very sweet without that characteristic bitterness and definitely give you a healthy boost!*

Vietnamese-Style Lettuce Cups

For our last meal of 2012, I chose these gorgeous Vietnamese-Style Lettuce Cups. There were football bowl games to be watched, a fire to be snuggled up to, and the sounds of all the neighbor kids popping fireworks to listen to. So something we could sit in front of the television and eat while we cheered on our favorite team seemed to fit the bill. Not to mention these are full of veggies and create a flavor explosion in your mouth!

My husband's opinion? "I'm very impressed." That's quite an accomplishment because we all know that this is not the typical football-watching fare!

This would easily serve four as an appetizer, but two adults watching football ate all of it!

Ingredients

- 2 cloves garlic, finely minced
- 1½ Tbsp ginger, peeled and finely chopped
- 1 jalapeño pepper, finely minced
- 1 large carrot, peeled and grated
- 1 shallot, finely chopped
- 2–3 radishes, washed and sliced super thin
- 2 green onions, thinly sliced for sauce
- 1 Tbsp canola oil
- 1 lb ground pork
- Zest of 2 limes
- ¼ cup fish sauce
- ½ cup fresh-squeezed lime juice
- 1–2 tsp granulated sugar
- 1 tsp toasted sesame oil

Sauce

- ⅓ cup soy sauce
- ⅓ cup rice wine vinegar
- 2 Tbsp brown sugar

Serve

- Head of Butter or Bibb lettuce leaves
- 1 fresh cilantro for garnish
- Fresh lime wedges for garnish

Notes:

How to…

I recommend you have everything prepped and ready because this dish goes really quickly once you start. So begin by peeling, chopping, grating, squeezing, etc., as indicated above.

In a small bowl, combine the garlic, ginger, and jalapeño pepper. In a large wok (or large skillet), heat the oil over fairly high heat. Add the garlic mixture and stir-fry about a minute. Add the pork, carrots, and shallots and cook, stirring constantly for about 4 minutes until the pork begins to brown and is no longer pink. To the meat mixture, add the lime zest, fish sauce, lime juice, sugar, and sesame oil and cook for another 3–4 minutes. Remove from heat; taste and adjust the seasonings as necessary.

Mix all ingredients for the dipping sauce (green onions, soy sauce, rice wine vinegar, and brown sugar).

Spoon the warm pork mixture into lettuce cups; sprinkle with radishes and cilantro. Serve with lime wedges and dipping sauce.

Food Note: *You should just about see your fingers through the radishes! Don't be afraid of the radishes. Left large, they can be strong, but sliced this thinly, they give you a beautiful color contrast, some crunch, and just a hint of spicy. They help create the balance of the dish. To get them this thin, slice then on a mandoline.*

Ritzy Cheddar Baked Chicken

Here's a fun recipe that is different but so easy for a weeknight. This gorgeous chicken is baked with a cheesy, crunchy, buttery crust and topped with a yummy sauce that couldn't be simpler. It's sure to beat your regular old oven-baked chicken with its lively cheddar flavor, crispy exterior coating, and that juicy interior that you will love. One of my children is a cheese-o-phobe (Umm… is that a thing?), and even HE polished his off! You know what you call that? Winner, winner, chicken dinner! As a matter of fact, just look at the ingredient list. These are things you probably have on hand in the fridge or pantry right now!

Ingredients

Chicken

2 full sleeves Ritz crackers
1 cup reduced-fat sour cream, *or nonfat, plain Greek yogurt*
4 cups sharp cheddar cheese, freshly grated
2 Tbsp dried parsley
6 boneless, skinless chicken breasts

Seasoning

Kosher salt, black pepper, and Italian seasoning, all to taste

Sauce

¼ tsp dried dill
2 tsp parsley
1 tsp dill pickle juice (yep–from the jar)
1 can cream of chicken soup
2 Tbsp sour cream
3 Tbsp butter

Notes:

How to...

Crush your Ritz crackers in a large zip-top bag. This is a great job to let the kids help you with. Make yourself a breading station of sorts: (1) low-fat sour cream or Greek yogurt (If you feel it's a little too thick, thin it with a bit of milk.), (2) freshly shredded sharp cheddar cheese, (3) crushed-up Ritz crackers with the added dried parsley.

Trim your chicken breasts of fat and season well. I used kosher salt, black pepper, and Italian seasoning. Use whatever you prefer.

Coat your chicken in the sour cream or yogurt, then the cheese, and finally the crackers. Set them on your baking sheet. Here are some options. I used this silicone mat that has all of these little ridges. It kept the chicken raised up, allowing fats, etc. to run away from the meat while allowing the hot air to circulate underneath. You could also put your chicken on a cooling rack set into a sheet pan. Other options? Line your pan with parchment paper or aluminum foil. OR spray your sheet pan with nonstick spray.

Bake at 400°F for about 35 minutes or until internal digital thermometer reaches 160°F. It will continue to rise to 165°F when you remove from the oven. Allow the chicken to rest 5 minutes. Do yourself a favor and buy one of these instant-read thermometers. They take all the guesswork out of it so you can have juicy cooked chicken that is not under or overcooked!

Now for a super-quick sauce:

Combine all the sauce ingredients and stir until hot. Serve a spoon of this silky sauce over that crunchy chicken! It's that simple! Okay, so I know you may be skeptical. But give it a shot! It's creamy and tangy, and dill goes extremely well with chicken. Even my little kids loved it!

Crawfish Fettuccine

This is a recipe that was passed along to me from one of my kids' kindergarten teacher down in South Louisiana many years ago, with some minor alterations. The quantities will definitely serve a crowd if you are looking for something to bring to one of your school/work/church/family functions! Otherwise, you can just have a spare casserole tucked away in your freezer for another meal with zero prep work. How is THAT for efficient?!

As far as price goes, yes, crawfish can get a little pricey. BUT, when you consider that this recipe will serve a crowd—probably at least 12–15 people—it actually comes out as a bargain in the end. And we all like bargains, right? Especially when you consider the cost of just ONE of those menu items in the restaurant! But if you prefer, you could always substitute some leftover cooked chicken in the place of the crawfish.

Ingredients

- 3 lbs crawfish tails, cleaned and rinsed, no fat left on them
- 1 medium onion, chopped
- ½ green bell pepper, chopped
- ½ red bell pepper, chopped
- 1½ cups unsalted butter
- 1 cup flour
- 1 qt half and half
- 1 lb jalapeño cheese (I used Velveeta.)
- 3 cloves garlic, chopped fine
- Salt, pepper, and Creole seasoning, all to taste (I used Tony Chachere's.)
- 6 Tbsp fresh parsley, divided
- 8 oz sliced mushrooms, fresh or canned
- 1–2 cups chicken broth
- Add evaporated milk, *optional*
- 2 Tbsp Worcestershire sauce
- 1 lb fettuccine noodles
- ½ cup freshly grated Parmigiano Reggiano cheese

Notes:

How to...

Chop the vegetables and sauté in melted butter. When wilted and softened, add the flour. Cook over low, stirring frequently until vegetables are nice and soft. You don't really want to cook it so long that your flour starts browning. We're just making a very light roux. Add half and half, Velveeta cheese, garlic, salt, pepper, creole seasoning, parsley, and mushrooms. You could probably use evaporated milk here if you have some on hand in the pantry.

Cook for 20 minutes or so over low, stirring frequently. It will become really silky after a bit. See all the delicious spices? If your sauce becomes too thick, thin it out a bit with chicken broth. I like somewhat of a soupier sauce at the end. Remember that you will be baking it, which will further thicken it; and also the noodles will suck up some of the sauce. So I would recommend making it a little looser than you feel you will need it in the end.

Note: *This is when you want to start boiling the water for the noodles. Ideally, you want these 20 minutes to correspond with the noodles being cooked and drained so neither the noodles nor the sauce has to sit and wait on the other one.*

Finish off the sauce with a couple tablespoons of Worcestershire sauce. And maybe a couple of shakes of hot sauce would be excellent, too! This adds another level of depth to the sauce. You don't want it to be too one-dimensional.

Cook and drain the fettuccine noodles according to package directions (about 11 minutes), then add them immediately to the sauce mixture. Add the crawfish tails to the sauce, then stir in the grated Parmigiano Reggiano cheese.

Bake uncovered in a greased, low Pyrex casserole dish for about 15–20 minutes in a 350°F oven.

Now you may be wondering where we were to add the parsley? The original recipe never said. I add it directly to my sauce because I think it's so pretty. I also like to use extra fresh parsley as garnish.

Food Nerd Notes: *What is the difference between Cajun and Creole seasoning?*

Well two of the biggest distinctions are origin, and to some extent a socioeconomic and lifestyle difference in the two groups of people. The Creole foods were largely "city" cooking that was based certainly in the traditions of the French, but with far-reaching influences from Spain, Africa, Germany, Italy, the West Indies, and the Indians of the region, all of whom came to settle in the New Orleans area and imparted their culinary marks. Cajun cooking, on the other hand, was typically peasant food from the swampy Acadiana area of Louisiana (people who came to be known as the Cajuns). These people settled, and learned to live off of, the Louisiana swamps; and they developed a certain style of cooking that is more pungent and more highly spiced than the more refined food of the Creole people.

Both styles of food were heavily dependent upon improvisation, but in different amounts. Cajun food is well seasoned, with a predictable blend of fresh onions, celery, bell pepper, garlic, green onions, and parsley. These seasonings along with a dark brown Cajun roux are the basis of flavor. Creole dishes were more tomato-based. However, to complicate matters, this distinction switches for some dishes. For example, a Cajun jambalaya is roux-based and a Creole jambalaya is tomato-based. On the other hand, a Cajun étouffée is tomato-based, while a Creole étouffée is roux-based. Go figure.

Both Creole and Cajun cuisines and a fusion of the two forms of cuisines can be found in the southern part of Louisiana. So to all you Northern people (and folks from other places in the world), when you see statistics about the South having more than its share of overweight people, you'll have a better understanding of why this is. This region has some of the best food on the planet—hands down!

High Class Shepherd's Pie

Shepherd's Pie has gotten a bad rap! Well you know what? Done right, it can definitely be a thing of beauty. Stay with me here… A well-seasoned layer of thick saucy meat, beautiful al dente carrots and baby peas (not mushy veggies!), and a layer of fluffy brown butter mashed potatoes with a sprinkling of white cheddar and some fresh thyme. Oh yeah! And not to mention a great representation from all the food groups and a great way to stretch a budget!

Shepherd's Pie is a traditional dish with a meat base and a mashed potato topping. The Irish made it with ground lamb, hence the name. Where I live, ground beef is much easier to come by; however, if you prefer lamb, go for it! Another great thing about this is that you can assemble it on the weekend and pop in the oven on a busy weeknight. My husband, who had definite opinions on how it did and did not need to be made, reported that it was the best he had ever had. *Hmmm…* So keep an open mind and keep reading!

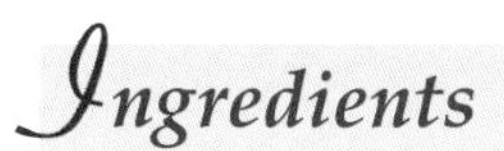

Ingredients

For the Meat Layer

- 3–4 large carrots, finely diced
- 1 cup diced onion
- 2 cloves garlic, minced
- 1½ lbs russet potatoes (for the potato layer)
- 1 tsp kosher salt
- 1½ lbs lean ground beef
- 1 tsp black pepper
- 1 cup dry red wine
- 2 Tbsp Worcestershire sauce
- 2 Tbsp tomato paste
- 3–4 sprigs fresh thyme, finely chopped
- 1 cup beef stock
- 2 Tbsp all purpose flour
- 1 cup frozen peas

For the Potato Layer

- 1½ lbs potatoes (See meat layer list)
- 2 Tbsp unsalted butter
- ½–1 cup half-and-half
- 1 tsp kosher salt, to taste
- ½–1 tsp ground black pepper, to taste
- ½–1 tsp garlic powder
- Fresh thyme leaves
- About 1 cup Vermont white cheddar

How to...

Start by prepping all the veggies. Chop your carrots, onions, and garlic. And while you are at it, peel and cut the potatoes and get them on to boil in some salted water.

Brown the ground beef in a skillet, breaking it up into small pieces. When it's about halfway cooked through, add the chopped onions. Cook them down for several minutes until they are soft and translucent. Now add the garlic. Once the meat is cooked through, add your seasonings. Start with the kosher salt, black pepper, then add in the chopped carrots. The reason I add them after the meat is already basically cooked is that I don't want them cooked down to mush. I want them to retain their shape and some texture.

Now let's work on making a beautiful red wine gravy for this. Add in the red wine, Worcestershire sauce, tomato paste, fresh thyme leaves, beef broth, and flour. Bring the sauce up to a boil (so the flour will do its job as a thickener), then bring it down to a simmer for a few minutes. We want it to be wonderfully saucy—but NOT runny! When it reaches that "saucy" point, turn off the heat.

If you didn't already do this, get those potatoes going! Start off with cold water to cover. Don't forget to add the salt. You need each step of the process to be seasoned. Once they are boiling and fork-tender (about 10–12 minutes depending on how small you cut them)—NOT mushy—drain them. Just throw the strained potatoes back into the hot pot.

Notes:

In a small saucepan, melt your butter. We want it to get slightly brown. Browned butter tastes really nutty and wonderful and completely different from plain butter, so please don't skip this step. To the slightly browned butter, add the half-and-half. Bring this mixture up to a simmer. *You basically just want to get it nice and warm before you add it to the potatoes.* Then, add the hot cream mixture to the potatoes.

> **Note:** *My husband thinks that fresh chives or green onions would be great in the potatoes. I promised that I would pass that along.*

Give them a nice stir by hand and season them up using kosher salt, black pepper, and garlic powder. Add them to a ricer if you have one. Passing them through the ricer makes them really light and fluffy!

At the last minute, add the frozen baby sweet peas to the meat mixture. Stir gently. I do NOT want to cook them ahead of time as I don't want them to be all starchy and mushy. The heat from the meat and cooking them in the oven will be PLENTY enough heat, believe me.

We are now ready to turn this into a masterpiece! Go ahead and preheat the oven to 400°F. Start by adding the meat mixture into the bottom of your cooking dish, casserole, baker, or whatever you are using.

Now put those great fluffy potatoes into a dessert decorator and pipe them out to make a super-pretty top layer. I like all those little ridges so they get sort of brown and crusty. If you don't have one, you can drop the potatoes by the spoonful and perhaps use a fork to make ridges. Add a little fresh thyme (or chives) to the top of the potatoes. Now this beauty is all ready for the oven!

Bake the casserole for about 30 minutes or until the top is golden brown. In the last 15 minutes, you can add some freshly shredded Vermont white cheddar cheese. You could certainly use yellow cheddar if you want to, or even some Parmigiano Reggiano. The cheese gives it a beautiful sheen on top, yet I can still see the fresh herbs and all those great little ridges.

Now we have taken something really mundane and ordinary and made it extraordinary! I think it would be absolutely adorable baked and served in individual ramekins. And just another note... it makes great leftovers for your office lunch the next day after all those flavors sit in there together. ***Score!***

> **Food Nerd Notes:** *Cottage Pie, or Shepherd's Pie, came into use in the late 1700's when the potato was being introduced as an edible crop affordable for the poor. The dish was a means of using leftover roasted meat of any kind, and was both lined and topped with mashed potatoes. The term "Shepherd's Pie" did not appear until 1877, and since then it has been used synonymously with "Cottage Pie," regardless of whether the principal ingredient was beef or lamb. The home cook should feel free to use the protein of his or her choice.*

Sesame Shrimp and Asparagus Stir-Fry

I've been looking for some lighter dishes to make with everyone struggling to get into their clothes after the holidays. I adapted this recipe from one I found one day in a *Good Housekeeping* recipe. It's very simple, adds a big serving of veggies, and is much lower in fat and calories than take-out! Additionally, you could make this faster than driving to your favorite Asian take-out restaurant.

Ingredients

- 1 lb asparagus, trimmed and cut into 2-inch pieces
- 1 Tbsp peeled and grated ginger
- 1 pint cherry tomatoes, halved
- 2 Tbsp soy sauce
- 1 Tbsp rice vinegar
- 1 Tbsp sesame seeds
- 2 Tbsp canola or vegetable oil
- 1 tsp sesame oil
- 1 lb large shrimp, cleaned
- 1 cup long-grain white rice, cooked

Notes:

How to...

For Prep: Trim the asparagus, grate the ginger, cut the tomatoes, make the sauce, and toast the sesame seeds. For prep ahead of time, you could actually even cook the shrimp and store them in the fridge. When you add the shrimp later, just cook them for 1 minute to heat them through.

For Sauce: Combine soy sauce, rice vinegar, and grated ginger in a small bowl. Set aside.

In a 12-inch skillet, toast the sesame seeds over a medium-high heat for about 4 minutes. Transfer them to a small dish. In that same skillet, heat the vegetable oil over medium-high until hot, and then add the asparagus. Cook the asparagus until they are tender-crisp, about 4–5 minutes. Add the tomatoes and cook 1 minute. Stir in the soy sauce mixture and shrimp into the asparagus and cook about 2–3 minutes. It will NOT take the shrimp long to cook. Once they turn pink and opaque, they are done.

Remove the skillet from the heat and stir in the sesame oil. To serve, spoon the shrimp mixture over rice and sprinkle with the toasted sesame seeds.

PLEASE don't forget the sesame seeds like I did! (I was not very happy with myself.)

Spinach Artichoke Dip Stuffed Chicken Breasts

I just LOVE spinach artichoke dip, and that got me thinking about trying to use it as a filling. When it is really good, it has many of the elements we prize in a dish: color, texture, flavor, creaminess, and complexity. So why not use that to dress up our poor little "blank slate" chicken breasts? Sounds like it might be worth a shot, huh?

I suppose this could get a little complicated, but we are going to take some shortcuts here to making this delicious spinach artichoke chicken quickly—as in "you just got off of work and need to make dinner, shuttle kids to games, and help with homework" quick. Rather than make my spinach artichoke dip from scratch, I am just going to pick up a prepared container of it at the market. I know, I know. Please don't shake your head in disappointment. This is an after-work recipe! ***Stay with me!***

Ingredients

Skinless, boneless chicken breasts, trimmed of fat
Prepared spinach artichoke dip
Salt, pepper, dried basil, garlic powder, all to taste
1 can of medium artichoke hearts (packed in water), drained
1 pint of cherry tomatoes, halved
3 Tbsp olive oil
2 Tbsp all-purpose flour
2–3 large cloves of garlic, minced fine
Handful of freshly grated Parmesan cheese
2 cups grated mozzarella cheese
Handful of fresh basil, cut into ribbons

Notes:

How to...

Preheat oven to 400°F. Use a sharp knife to create a pocket into each chicken breast, being careful to not slice all the way through it. Stuff each pocket with a large spoon of spinach artichoke dip. I didn't measure it. *It will depend on the size of each of your chicken breasts.*

Use two toothpicks to close up each breast and to contain the dip. Season each breast liberally with kosher salt, black pepper, dried basil, and a little garlic powder. Arrange them in an oven-safe casserole dish that you have sprayed with a little cooking spray. In a medium-sized bowl, combine the drained artichoke hearts with the halved tomatoes, olive oil, flour, minced garlic, dried basil, salt, and pepper. Top the chicken breasts with the artichoke tomato mixture.

Bake the chicken uncovered until an internal thermometer in the thickest part of the chicken reads about 155°F. The time will depend on how large or thick your chicken breasts are! *They are NOT cooked yet!* Remove the chicken from the oven, top the whole dish with the grated Parmesan and mozzarella cheeses, and then return it to the oven uncovered until the internal chicken temperature reaches 160–165°F. Top the chicken with fresh basil ribbons.

Alternate Method

I used the oven to cook the chicken and vegetables because it may be a better "busy mom/dad" option for those of you who may be helping with homework or school projects. But if you have two hands available to you, another idea would be to cook the stuffed, seasoned chicken breasts in a searing-hot black iron skillet in a little olive oil and butter first. Then, I would deglaze with a little white wine or chicken broth to make a lovely sauce. Then reduce the heat and add the tomatoes and artichoke hearts to the sauce! This is what makes cooking fun: being able to do things however you want to! Don't care for artichokes? Try fresh asparagus spears or zucchini.

Pasta alla Tuscana

This pasta dish comes together in about 15 minutes start to finish, and it just makes me happy each time I have it. Tender angel hair pasta is blanketed in the sweet tomatoes bursting with their juices, flavored simply with the garlic and olive oil and finished off with ribbons of sweet-spicy basil and nuggets of melting fresh mozzarella.

Optional changes: This particular dish is vegetarian. However, in the past I have added a handful of crumbled bacon (or pancetta) to the dish. You could certainly add in some grilled chicken strips if your family balks at the idea of a meatless dish… or add in some fresh shrimp in the last couple of minutes! I have also had this in the past with fresh baby spinach. I just add the spinach in the beginning while everything is sautéing, and they wilt right down, adding lots of nutrition and great color. And lastly, it is fairly common for Tuscan pastas to be served *all'arrabbiata*, which means spicy! So you could add in some red pepper flakes or a minced jalapeño if you want to go that route.

Italian cooks rely chiefly on the quality of the ingredients rather than on elaborate preparation. Ingredients and dishes vary by region; however, many dishes that were once regional have proliferated with variations throughout the country. Simplicity is central to the Tuscan cuisine, with many dishes having peasant origins. Having visited the area a couple times myself, something that becomes immediately clear is the theme of Tuscan chefs using simple, seasonal, top-quality ingredients.

Ingredients

- 1 pint mixed yellow and red grape heirloom tomatoes, cut in half
- 2–3 large cloves of garlic, finely minced
- 2 Tbsp extra virgin olive oil
- Kosher salt and cracked black pepper, to taste
- 1 tsp dried basil
- ½ box angel hair pasta
- Fresh mozzarella, cut into small cubes (quantity up to you!)
- A handful of fresh basil, cut into thin ribbons

How to...

Get a pot of water started for the pasta because this comes together VERY quickly!

Sauté tomatoes and garlic in hot olive oil for a couple of minutes. Season them simply with kosher salt, black pepper, and dried basil. Now add the angel hair pasta to the boiling water—these will only cook for about 4 minutes. At this point, turn the tomatoes down all the way to the lowest setting, as they are done. Add the ribbons of basil to the tomatoes. You don't want to add fresh herbs in during the cooking process because they will lose flavor. We are adding them just at the end, where they will perfume the dish and get warmed by the sauce. The juice from the tomatoes and the olive oil create the "sauce" for the dish. *If it seems to need a little more, add a little extra olive oil and cook on low a couple of minutes for the flavors to marry. But this is very light and simply dressed pasta. It shouldn't be dripping in sauce.*

Drain the pasta and serve the tomato sauce over the fresh, hot pasta. Add some chunks of fresh mozzarella to the sauce and let them start melting. Garnish with a little extra basil ribbons and some fresh cracked pepper.

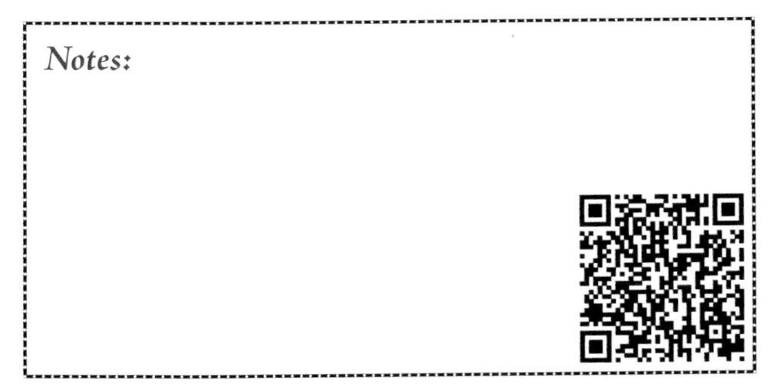

Super Easy Stuffed Shells

This one is definitely kid friendly, fast, and super easy! My little ones love to help out in the kitchen, no matter where we go. The first time we made this was on a week-end trip to my mother's house, where every herb imaginable grows in abundance and little hands are always welcome in the meal prep. No doubt, that is where my culinary point of view comes from!

This recipe is mostly staple items that you likely have in your pantry already. We cook with lots of fresh herbs here in this part of the country (They have a bright, vibrant taste, are huge money savers, and teach the kids more principles than I can list here), but you could certainly use dried herbs from the spice rack if you have them on hand.

Ingredients

1 box large dried pasta shells
1–1¼ lbs ground beef

Seasonings of Your Choice

Salt, pepper, garlic powder, dried basil, dried oregano, Italian seasoning, all to taste

Cheese Filling

1 cup ricotta cheese
1 cup shredded mozzarella cheese
1 tsp dried basil
1 egg

Spaghetti sauce of your choice

Toppings

1 cup shredded mozzarella
¼ cup Parmigiano Reggiano
Italian seasoning, to taste

Tip: *To make this super quick and easy, you could have your meat browned ahead of time. Also, for those of you who get home late from work and still need to make dinner for the family, the whole thing could be made ahead of time and kept in the fridge. In that case, you could walk in from work, take it out of the fridge, pop it in the oven, and let it heat up along with the oven.*

Notes:

How to...

Boil large dried pasta shells according to directions in a large pot of salted water. Drain, rinse in cool water, and let cool.

Brown the ground beef. Season it to your liking—salt, pepper, garlic powder, basil, oregano, and Italian seasoning.

Make an easy filling of ricotta, shredded mozzarella, salt, pepper, dried basil, and an egg. Distribute the filling into the shells.

Spoon some of the meat mixture into each shell. Then arrange the stuffed shells in the casserole dish on top of a bit of the sauce. The sauce in the bottom will keep them from sticking or getting all dried out. You don't really want them to form a "crust" on the bottom. We want tender pasta. I personally like them really "saucy," but make them according to your family's taste.

Add the rest of the sauce over the top of the stuffed shells. Sprinkle shredded mozzarella over the sauce and then a little freshly grated Parmigiano Reggiano. Sprinkle with additional fresh or dried herbs if you would like. *Cover and put in the fridge now if you are making this ahead of time for tomorrow's after work meal.*

Bake for 10–15 minutes or so. Everything is already cooked; now you are just getting everything hot and melty and gooey! *If you are taking it out of the fridge to bake, you will obviously need to bake it longer. In that case, leave it covered until hot, maybe 25–30 minutes, and then uncover for about 5 minutes, or so to let the cheese brown just a bit.*

Creamy Chicken Piccata

Piccata is actually a method of preparing food in which the meat is sliced, lightly coated in flour, sautéed, and served with a sauce made of the pan drippings along with the addition of butter, lemon juice, capers, and stock or wine. The dish originated in Italy using veal, but here in the United States, chicken is a popular variation of this.

Follow me in a step-by-step prep of this classic Italian recipe. I promise I will take all the perceived difficulty out of cooking this chicken dish, and you will end up with a creamy, tangy sauce that is simple but heavenly... and certainly worthy of "date night" or having company over.

In Italy, veal piccata is a *secondo*, which would be served after the pasta (or starch) course. Here in the United States, it is usually served *with* a starch, such as pasta. I like to take my piccata a couple of steps further with the addition of chopped sun-dried tomatoes and heavy cream. The cream tones down the acidity and makes the sauce oh-so-silky on your tongue (while maintaining the tartness of the lemon), and the sun-dried tomatoes are chewy and tangy, balancing the creaminess very well. They add texture, color, flavor, and an extra nutritional punch.

I have to admit—I'm not a huge fan of piccata in a restaurant because all I taste is the acidity of the lemons. With my recipe, I feel that this flavor is more balanced with the cream in the sauce.

Ingredients

- 1¼ lbs chicken breast tenders, *or 2 boneless, skinless chicken breasts, butterflied and sliced in half*
- Kosher salt and fresh cracked black pepper, to taste
- Flour
- 2 Tbsp extra virgin olive oil
- 4 Tbsp butter, divided
- Linguine pasta
- ⅓ cup white wine, chilled, *a medium to dry wine–not sweet*
- 1 cup low-sodium chicken broth
- ⅓ cup lemon juice, freshly squeezed
- 2 Tbsp capers, drained
- 2 Tbsp sundried tomatoes, chopped
- ½–1 cup heavy cream
- 1 Tbsp Italian parsley, chopped for garnish
- 1 fresh lemon for garnish

How to...

To speed up your prep, consider using pre-cut chicken tenders. If using whole breasts, slice chicken breasts diagonally into medallions (approximately 3–4 each).

Pound chicken pieces between plastic wrap until very thin and even thickness. Season the chicken with salt and pepper. Dredge the chicken pieces lightly in flour and shake off the excess. Add the 2 Tbsp EVOO and 2 Tbsp butter to a pan. When they start sizzling, add in a few of your prepared chicken pieces. Sauté the chicken on medium-high heat for about 3 minutes on each side until they are light brown. Since they are so thin, they will cook pretty fast. Remove and keep warm. You don't want to crowd the pan, so it takes a few pans full to get it all done. I can usually get about 3 pieces of chicken per pan in each batch, depending on the size of the pan.

At this point, you can start heating your water for the linguine. When the water comes to a boil, add pasta and cook according to package directions, about 10–11 minutes.

On medium-high heat, add ⅓ cup of white wine to deglaze the pan that the chicken was cooked in and reduce. *Feel free to just deglaze with additional chicken stock if you prefer not to use wine.* Scrape up all the fond (browned bits stuck to the bottom) to incorporate all the flavors into the sauce. Add in the chicken broth, lemon juice, capers, and sun-dried tomatoes. Bring to a boil, and then reduce the sauce by half.

Notes:

Next add in the remaining 2 Tbsp cold butter and ½–1 cup heavy cream. Adjust seasonings as needed.

Your sauce will start off fairly watery and very fluid. Bring to a boil, and then reduce the heat to about medium. Give the flour, butter, and cream a chance to thicken the sauce. This time could vary according to the amount of heat, the type of pan, etc. I'd say anywhere from about 5–10 minutes. I usually let it go until my linguine is about ready to drain.

Tip » *What we are looking for: reduction in volume, a slight color change, and bubbles that actually change in character. When the sauce is still really liquid, the bubbles are small and burst easily. When it starts to really become the reduced sauce we are looking for, the bubbles are larger and more "elastic" looking, and they linger longer before popping.*

When your sauce has become reduced and silky, you have two options. If there are no kiddos around, add the chicken back to the sauce. Place the chicken and sauce over your drained linguine, adding parsley, and thinly cut lemon slices for garnish. The second option is easier with little ones underfoot. Add the drained linguine directly to the sauce and stir to incorporate. Then add the chicken and remaining ingredients. Garnish before serving.

Tip » *Please do yourself a favor and use fresh lemons—the ones that came from a tree—NOT the stuff that comes from a squeeze bottle! Roll the lemons a few times on the table under firm pressure to get more juice out of them. You can also pop them in the microwave about 15 seconds before you juice the lemons.*

Let's review—Fast (30 minutes), easy (step-by-step—you can do this!), kid friendly, but still impressive enough for guests!

Entrees

Mmm...

Menu Musings

crafty cuisine

The Main Event

Side Dishes

SIDETRACK YOUR FAMILY INTO EATING THEIR VEGGIES!

Black Bean and Corn Salsa

Roasted Green Beans

Southern

Style Cornbread Dressing

Stuffed Baby Artichokes with Lemon Vinaigrette

I made these for my parents when I visited the fishing camp way down in Southern Louisiana, near the Gulf of Mexico. It is one of my favorite places in the world. It's a place where you leave the real world behind as you sit out on the deck and watch the shrimp boats heading down the canal into the Gulf to troll for their catch all night. And my parents are just the best—it doesn't matter what I dream up to cook, they always seem to be up for it! Before our fishing weekends, we stop and load up on groceries along the way. I found these adorable baby artichokes! And my, oh my... were these delicious!

These are not immature versions of the larger ones but actually fully grown in their own right. Ask your grocer, as they are not the normal globe artichokes. They are mostly edible except for the outer leaves and barely have a choke (the fuzzy stuff you scrape out) at all. And they are so cute and delicious!

Notes:

Ingredients

A few lemons for acidulated water
1 pack baby artichokes
½ cup freshly grated Parmigiano Reggiano
1 cup bread crumbs, store-bought or homemade
Salt and pepper, to taste
1 large clove garlic
A few sprigs of fresh thyme
2 Tbsp extra virgin olive oil plus extra for drizzling
3–4 Tbsp milk or cream
A bit of water for the bottom of the pan

Lemon Vinaigrette

Lemon zest of a large lemon
4 Tbsp fresh-squeezed lemon juice
2 Tbsp extra virgin olive oil (EVOO)
Salt and pepper, to taste
Fresh parsley, chopped

Tip: Heat the lemon about 20 seconds in the microwave before cutting it. This will give you a lot more juice.

How to...

Go ahead and preheat the oven to 350°F. Make sure you have some acidulated water (water with lemons) ready. As soon as you cut the artichokes, you will want to put them in the bath so they don't oxidize and turn brown. These will brown faster than an apple or banana, so let them bathe!

Trim off about an inch of the stem and the outer third or so of the leaves, the prickly parts. Cut off the tops of the artichokes—about an inch and a half. Let them swim around in the lemon water while you prepare your filling.

When you are ready to stuff them, cut the little guys in half and immediately rub the cut edges with a lemon to prevent browning. Scoop out the choke (any fuzzies in there) and make more room for the topping! A small (⅛-tsp) measuring spoon is about exactly the right size to scoop out a nice round spot. A small melon baller would also work.

Combine all ingredients for the topping: freshly grated Parmigiano Reggiano, fresh bread crumbs (We just threw some French bread into the blender. They were perfect), salt, pepper, a clove of finely chopped garlic, and a few sprigs of thyme, stripped from the stems. Moisten the mixture with a couple of tablespoons of extra virgin olive oil and a few tablespoons of milk or cream. You just want it to stick together and be kind of crumbly.

Stuff the topping between the leaves and into that cavity that you created. Then add more on top. Arrange the stuffed artichokes in black iron skillet or casserole dish. Drizzle a little more extra virgin olive oil on top. Add a little water to the bottom of the pan to help steam them, and throw them into the oven. Bake the artichokes uncovered for 15 minutes at 350°F. While they are in the oven, prepare the lemon vinaigrette (Mix all the ingredients together). After they come out of the oven, drizzle the lemon vinaigrette over the artichokes, if desired. If you are dining with someone who doesn't appreciate the lemon as much, you can just serve it on the side.

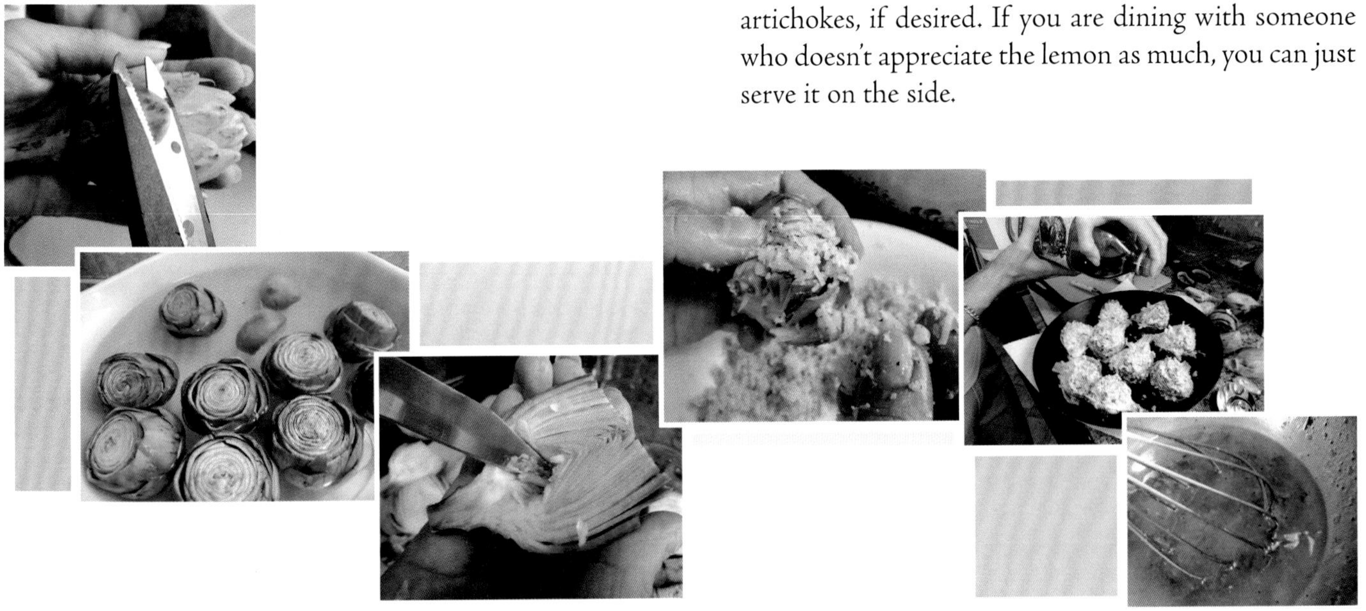

Lily's Maple Bacon Green Beans with Slivered Almonds

I'm almost embarrassed to put a green bean recipe in here, but since I received so many inquiries over the ones I make for Lily, I acquiesced. Coming from a country family in Southern Louisiana, this is food I grew up with, and it is absolutely my daughter's favorite! I have a list of about a half dozen folks who have told me that they never would eat green beans until they tried them this way. Wow! I am super excited about that. These are really fresh and delicious... and I hope you'll try them, too!

I should preface this by saying that I cannot stand to eat green beans out of a can. They just have that weird canned flavor. We ALWAYS use fresh green beans. Secondly, when Lily was younger, and had limited kitchen skills, this gave her about 20 minutes of "snapping" time, where I could focus on some other aspect of the meal. Also, if you have a recipe where your kids will eat practically a half pot of veggies, you embrace it!

Ingredients

Several (maybe 4–5) pieces of maple flavored bacon
A handful of diced onion
A big bag of green beans, picked fresh
Flaked sea salt, large restaurant pepper, garlic powder, all to taste
A handful of sliced almonds

Note: *Lardon is a small strip or cube of pork fat used in a wide variety of cuisines to flavor savory foods and salads. In French cuisine, lardons are also used for larding by threading them with a needle into meats that are to be braised or roasted. Lardons are not normally smoked, and they are made from pork that has been cured with salt.*

Notes:

How to...

Cut the bacon into "lardons" (about ½-inch pieces). Cut the onions into a small dice. Trim the stem-end of the beans off, and find a kid to snap your beans—the size doesn't really matter—or just leave them long and elegant.

Start a pot of water to boil for the beans. Once boiling, add the beans until they are about 90% done. Drain the beans when they reach this point.

While you are blanching the beans, sauté the bacon over medium-high heat until about done. It's important that you do NOT put the onions in with the bacon at the beginning. If you do, the water in the onions will prevent the bacon from browning and crisping properly. Once the bacon is almost crisp, add the onions. Sauté the onions with the bacon until they are soft and translucent.

Add the blanched green beans to the crisped bacon and onions. You can use a kitchen spider or a slotted spoon or drain in a colander. Stir the beans into the bacon mixture to ensure that a little of the maple bacon grease has coated all of the beans. Adjust the seasonings by adding salt, pepper, garlic powder, and slivered almonds.

Cook for maybe a couple of minutes more for the flavors to incorporate and then remove from heat. The beans should still be firm (not mushy), salty, mapley, peppery, crunchy from the bacon and almonds, and sweet from the tender onions.

Mmmm! Enjoy!

Black Bean and Corn Salsa

If you are looking for something a bit healthier to snack on while you watch those big bowl games, this is one of my family's favorites. It's very healthy, low in fat, and high in fiber and vitamins. We love it as a dip with tortilla chip scoops while some members of the family enjoy it as a side dish. It's easy, colorful, and well balanced—the sweet corn of summer, the tang from the balsamic vinegar and lime juice, and the fiesta bite of fresh cilantro… *Mmm! Try it with the Creamy "Work Week" Chicken Enchiladas!*

Ingredients

- 1 can black beans, drained and rinsed well
- 1 can sweet corn niblets, *You can sometimes find these mixed white and yellow, extra sweet.*
- 2 Roma tomatoes, diced
- ⅔ green bell pepper, diced, *or a mix of green, red, and yellow bell peppers*
- ⅓ red onion, diced
- 1 small cucumber, seeded and diced small
- 2 small jalapeños, diced and seeded for mild, with seeds for spicy
- 1 handful fresh cilantro, cut into small pieces
- 2 large juiced limes
- Aged balsamic vinegar, to taste
- Extra virgin olive oil, to taste
- Kosher salt, to taste
- Fresh cracked pepper, to taste

How to…

Cut up and mix everything. Allow everything to marinate together for a while. That's all there is to it! BIG bag of tortilla chips!

If you have extra time, this is amazing with grilled corn!

Notes:

Creamed Spinach

I *love, love, love* fresh baby spinach, but for those cold winter evenings, I like something a little more comforting than a cold spinach salad. For these kinds of nights, creamed spinach is a lovely addition to any meal. For this recipe, the addition of the highly flavored, fresh Parmigiano Reggiano to the spinach really brings this cream sauce to life! Be sure to make more than you think you'll need. For one thing, the spinach cooks down so much that you have to start with a gargantuan pile to end up with enough. The second thing is that it is so delicious that you hope to have enough to go back for a second helping!

This recipe is so simple and easy that it's almost embarrassing.

Ingredients

- 2 Tbsp butter
- 1 Tbsp extra virgin olive oil
- 1 sweet yellow onion, minced
- 2 cloves garlic, minced
- 1 whole bag fresh baby spinach, stemmed and rough-chopped
- Salt and freshly ground black pepper, to taste
- ¼ tsp freshly ground nutmeg
- ¼ cup heavy cream, *Feel free to substitute half and half for the cream.*
- A few tablespoons of freshly grated Parmigiano Reggiano cheese

Notes:

How to...

In a medium sauté pan over medium-high heat, melt the butter and then add the olive oil. Mix in the onions and garlic; cook for 2 minutes until soft. Add the chopped spinach and warm through. It will wilt down quickly! Add the salt, nutmeg, and the heavy cream. Mix well. Cook until liquid reduces by half, roughly 3 to 4 minutes. Grate Parmesan into the spinach at the last minute. Stir and serve.

YUM! Sautéed garlic and onions, a creamy sauce, the tang of the Parmesan, the creamy spinach... ***you'll be back!***

Parmesan Zucchini Gratin

In the springtime, I sort of go into a "zucchini obsession," and that's just the way it goes. I had a dish similar to this one weekend in New York, and I just couldn't rest until I came home and made it! Yum—golden brown topping, soft and delicate vegetables, and a little sweetness from the tomatoes. ***It's a good bite!***

Ingredients

- 2 medium, slender zucchini, *Or switch it up by using 1 summer squash and 1 zucchini!*
- 3 Tbsp extra virgin olive oil
- ½ tsp salt
- ½ tsp pepper
- 3 cloves of garlic, minced fine
- ½ tsp fresh thyme leaves, chopped
- A handful of sweet grape tomatoes, *I used both red and orange.*
- ⅓ cup freshly grated Parmigiano Reggiano
- ¼ cup Italian breadcrumbs

Notes:

How to...

Wash and thinly slice the squash. Arrange the zucchini as you desire in a baking dish.

Combine the oil, salt, pepper, garlic, and thyme in a small bowl. Pour this dressing over the zucchini and work it down a little in between the slices. Chop the tomatoes and distribute evenly over the zucchini.

In another bowl, mix the cheese and breadcrumbs for the topping. Spread the topping over the vegetables.

Bake uncovered at 450°F for around 30–35 minutes until the topping is golden brown.

If you can, let it sit for about 10 minutes before serving. I couldn't quite wait that long before digging in!

Food Nerd Notes: *Gratin is a widespread culinary technique in food preparation in which an ingredient is topped with a browned crust, often using breadcrumbs, grated cheese, egg, and/or butter. Gratin originated in French cuisine and is usually prepared in a shallow dish of some kind. A gratin is baked or cooked under a broiler to form a golden crust on top and is traditionally served in its baking dish.*

A gratin dish refers to the shallow oven-proof container traditionally used to prepare gratins and similar dishes. The etymology of gratin is from the French language, specifically the words "grater," meaning "to scrape" (as in the "scrapings" of bread or cheese), and "gratiné," from the transitive verb form of the word for crust or skin. The technique predates the current name, which did not appear in English until 1846.

Roasted Green Beans

I don't know why I never thought to roast fresh green beans before! I love most veggies done this way, as roasting brings out the sweetness in a big way. These green beans are quickly dressed and roasted and end up tender-crisp with a slight caramelized edge on them. If for no other reason, it's a new way to try a great healthy vegetable!

Ingredients

Fresh green beans, trimmed on the stalk side,
You can leave the curly end.
Extra virgin olive oil
Kosher salt, to taste
Cracked black pepper, to taste
Garlic powder, to taste
Freshly grated Parmigiano Reggiano cheese

How to...

Preheat oven to 425°F while you trim the green beans. Dress them simply with olive oil. Sprinkle to taste with salt, pepper, and garlic powder.

Roast for 15 minutes. Gently shake them around to turn them over after the first 10 minutes. Grate Parmesan cheese over them right after removing them from the oven. Serve immediately. ***Yum!***

How easy was that? Almost embarrassingly so… so act like you worked hard on them.

Notes:

Food Nerd Notes: *Tender, flexible green beans are a delight of vegetarian lovers for their wholesome nutritional qualities. They are unripe or immature pods obtained from the bean plant belonging to common fabaceae family and known scientifically as* Phaseolus vulgaris.

Fresh green beans are very low in calories (31 kcal per 100 g of raw beans) and contain no saturated fat, but are very good source of vitamins, minerals, and plant derived micronutrients.

They are a very rich source of dietary fiber (9% per100g RDA), which acts helps to protect the mucous membrane of the colon by decreasing its exposure time to toxic substances as well as by binding to cancer-causing chemicals in the colon. Dietary fiber has also been shown to reduce blood cholesterol levels by decreasing re-absorption of cholesterol-binding bile acids in the colon.

Green beans contain excellent levels of vitamin A and many health-promoting flavonoid polyphenolic antioxidants, such as lutein, zeaxanthin. and ß-carotene, in good amounts. These compounds help act as protective scavengers against oxygen-derived free radicals and reactive oxygen species that play a role in aging and various disease processes.

Zeaxanthin, an important dietary carotenoid in the beans, selectively absorbed into the retinal macula lutea in the eyes where it is thought to provide antioxidant and protective UV light-filtering functions. It is conceivable, therefore, green beans offer some protection in preventing age-related macular disease in the elderly.

Fresh snap beans are a good source of folates, with 100g of beans providing 37 µg or 9% of folates. Folate along with vitamin B-12 is one of the essential components of DNA synthesis and cell division. A good folate diet during preconception periods and during pregnancy helps prevent neural-tube defects in the offspring.

They also contain good amounts of vitamin B6 (pyridoxine), thiamin (vitamin B1), and vitamin C. Consumption of foods rich in vitamin C helps the body develop resistance against infectious agents and scavenge harmful oxygen free radicals.

In addition, beans contain healthy amounts of minerals like iron, calcium, magnesium, manganese, and potassium, which are essential for body metabolism. Manganese is a co-factor for the antioxidant enzyme superoxide dismutase, which is a very powerful free radical scavenger. Potassium is an important component of cell and body fluids that helps control heart rate and blood pressure.

Eggplant and Herbed Goat's Cheese Stacks

Eggplant, known also as aubergine, is found in many vegetarian cookbooks as a meat substitute and has also been called the "poor man's cutlet" because it can be quite meaty in texture. I adapted this recipe from one found in the *Everyday Vegetarian Cookbook*. I love the tangy flavor of goat cheese, but you can feel free to substitute slices of soft mozzarella for the goat cheese if you prefer.

Ingredients

serves 4

Sun-Dried Tomato Relish

¼ cup sun-dried tomatoes
1 large clove garlic, minced
1 Tbsp white wine vinegar
2 Tbsp extra virgin olive oil
Handful of freshly grated Parmigiano Reggiano cheese (about 2 Tbsp)
1 Tbsp (rounded) basil leaves
Salt and pepper, to taste

½ cup extra virgin olive oil
2 large cloves garlic, crushed
2 small eggplants (aubergines)
2 ripe tomatoes
4 oz goat cheese with herbs
Salt and pepper, to taste
8 basil leaves

The sun-dried tomato relish is really a great recipe all on its own, even if you don't make the eggplant; it would be a great meatless topping for pasta or on a crusty piece of bread as a quick bruschetta. But as a topping for the eggplant and goat cheese, the bright tangy flavors in the relish cut through the richness of the dish.

How to...

Make the relish first. Throw all the ingredients in a small food processor and whirl away until you have a lovely paste. ***That's it!***

Now for the Eggplant

Mix the oil and garlic together. Either crush the garlic first or crush it INTO the oil.

I used a molcajete (mohl-kah-HEH-tay) (see Food Nerd Notes at right) that I picked up in Mexico on a recent trip, where I watched this little man known as "The Scorpion" make them on a foot-turned potter's wheel and then fire them in a homemade kiln in his backyard. He made an adorable little piggy dish as well.

Cut each eggplant into six ½-inch slices and then cut each tomato into four ½-inch slices. Cut the goat cheese into eight ½-inch slices. Brush the eggplant with half of the oil mixture. Heat a sauté pan and cook the eggplant in batches for 3–4 minutes each side, or until golden. Season with salt and pepper. Remove and keep warm. Brush the tomato with the remaining oil mixture. Cook for 1 minute each side, or until sealed and warmed through. Season with salt and pepper.

To assemble, place an eggplant slice on each plate. Top with a slice of tomato and then a basil leaf and a slice of cheese. Repeat with the remaining ingredients to give two layers. Then finish with a third piece of eggplant. Add a dollop of the sun-dried tomato relish and a basil leaf. Serve immediately.

Food Nerd Notes: *A molcajete is a stone tool, the traditional Mexican version of the mortar and pestle, used for grinding various food products. The molcajete was used by pre-Hispanic Mesoamerican cultures, including the Aztec and Maya, stretching back several thousand years. The matching hand-held grinding tool is known as a tejolote. Molcajetes are used to crush and grind spices and prepare salsas and guacomole. The rough surface of the basalt stone creates a superb grinding surface that maintains itself over time as tiny bubbles in the basalt are ground down, replenishing the textured surface. As the porous basalt is impossible to fully clean and sanitize, molcajetes are known to "season" (much like cast iron skillets), carrying over flavors from one preparation to another. Salsas and guacamole prepared in molcajetes are known to have a distinctive texture, and some also carry a subtle difference in flavor from those prepared in blenders. Molcajetes can also be used as a cooking tool, where it is heated to a high temperature using an open fire or hot coals and then used to heat its food contents. Molcajetes are also used as serving dishes in restaurants and homes. While recipes are usually not stewed or otherwise cooked in them, the molcajete stays hot for a very long time, and it is not unusual for a dish to still be bubbling a half hour after serving.*

Balsalmic Roasted Brussels Sprouts with Pine Nuts and Parmesan

Fresh Brussels sprouts have really been gaining a lot of popularity lately as a healthy and delicious side dish. Roasting them really changes the flavor profile, and of course, adding a wonderful supporting cast of other yummy flavors (toasted pine nuts, Parmigiano Reggiano, and aged balsamic vinegar) certainly adds a little pizzazz to them for your pickier eaters.

Here are some things to remember. First, you need to start with really nice, fresh, young vegetables. Second, remember that the better the quality of the ingredients, the better your dish will be. That means using the real deal Parmigiano Reggiano, using a good aged balsamic vinegar, etc. Using junky ingredients will give you a junky dinner!

Ingredients

- 1 lb fresh Brussels sprouts, trimmed and cut into quarters
- 2 Tbsp olive oil
- 1 Tbsp balsamic vinegar
- Kosher salt and black pepper, to taste
- 1 Tbsp pine nuts, toasted
- 1½ Tbsp Parmigiano Reggiano, freshly grated

Notes:

How to...

For the Brussels sprouts, I used the smaller ones, as I think they are less bitter and more tender. Obviously, the first order of business is to remove them from the big stalk first.

Cut them into halves or quarters, and then toss them into the extra virgin olive oil and some aged balsamic vinegar. Sprinkle them with salt and pepper. Arrange the coated vegetables on a baking sheet. Roast them in a 450°F oven, uncovered, for about 20 minutes. They will start getting brown, and the edges will get crispy when they are roasted.

As soon as they come out of the oven, toss them with the toasted pine nuts and sprinkle the cheese over the top. Serve them hot.

Food Nerd Notes: *The Brussels sprout is a cultivar of wild cabbage grown for its edible buds. The leafy green vegetables are typically around 1–1½ inches in diameter and look like miniature cabbages.*

Forerunners to modern Brussels sprouts were likely cultivated in ancient Rome. Brussels sprouts as we now know them were grown possibly as early as the 13th century in what is now Belgium. The first written reference dates to 1587. During the 16th century, they enjoyed popularity in the southern Netherlands that eventually spread throughout the cooler parts of Northern Europe. Production of Brussels sprouts in the United States began in the 18th century when French settlers brought them to Louisiana. Thomas Jefferson grew them at Monticello. The first plantings in California's Central Coast began in the 1920s with significant production beginning in the 1940s. Currently there are several thousand acres planted in coastal areas of California, which offer an ideal combination of coastal fog and cool temperatures year-round. The harvest season lasts from June through January. They are also grown in Baja California, Mexico, where the harvest season is from December through June.

Brussels sprouts, as with broccoli and other brassicas, contain sulforaphane, a chemical believed to have potent anticancer properties. Brussels sprouts and other brassicas are also a source of indole-3-carbinol, a chemical that boosts DNA repair in cells and appears to block the growth of cancer cells. Although boiling reduces the level of the anticancer compounds, steaming, microwaving, and stir-frying does not result in significant loss.

To ensure even cooking throughout, buds of a similar size are usually chosen. Whatever cooking method is employed, it is important not to overcook them, which will render them gray and soft. Overcooking releases the glucosinolate sinigrin, which has a sulphurous odor. However, they taste best when sautéed or roasted.

Spicy Fried Cauliflower Bites

These spicy little bites will make you forget you are eating veggies! I had two kids walk in shortly after these were done, pop them in their mouths, and heard a satisfying, "Mm... these are good!" That, my friends, is the sound of success! I protested (with a secret smile, of course), "That's not kid food!"

So if you are looking for a way to wake up your cauliflower and try something different, this might just do the trick!

Ingredients

- 1 5.3-oz container plain Greek yogurt
- 4 green onion tops
- Juice of half of a large lemon
- 1 tsp sugar
- 2 tsp Sriracha, or hot sauce of your choice
- 1 tsp rice wine vinegar
- ¼ tsp celery salt
- A head of cauliflower
- Eggs and water
- Bread crumbs, *I used Panko Bread Crumbs.*
- Salt and pepper, to taste
- Garlic powder, to taste
- Cornstarch
- Canola oil

How to...

Sauce. Combine yogurt, 3 slivered green onion tops, lemon juice, sugar, Sriracha chili sauce, rice wine vinegar, and celery salt. Set aside.

Cut cauliflower into small florets. Whisk eggs with a little water. In a zip top-bag or produce bag, mix Panko bread crumbs with salt, pepper, and garlic powder to taste. Then add corn starch. Heat oil with thermometer to 350°F in a heavy pot or fryer. Add some florets to the egg wash and then into the spicy sauce and then into to the bread crumb mixture. Add some air to the bag and shake until florets are coated with the bread crumbs.

Add the coated florets to the hot oil. Fry at 350°F for 3–4 minutes or until golden brown. Remove with a spider or slotted spoon to a paper towel lined plate to drain. Season with additional salt (depending on how much salt you added to bread crumbs). Top with a little extra sauce and the other green onion and serve hot and crispy!

Notes:

Note: I had a hard time deciding on a "seasoning theme" for these. They lend themselves to so many different things, like a blank palette. I chose the spicy chili sauce of Sriracha with the rice wine vinegar and lemon, but feel free to choose your own flavor profile.

- *Mexican—Add cumin to the bread crumbs and sauce… Perhaps dip in spicy ranch with lime?*
- *Italian—Add Italian seasoning, basil and oregano to the bread crumbs and dip in spicy marinara?*
- *Indian—Add curry to the dip?*
- *… and then add your favorite cold beverage!*

Carrot Soufflé– just like at Picadilly!

Picadilly is a restaurant that we Southerners are well familiar with, and they happen to make a carrot soufflé that is just to die for! I don't know where this recipe came from, but I'm glad it fell into my hands! This soufflé is so sweet, light, and airy that there is a really good possibility that you will be able to sneak it onto your kids' plates without a fight. Admittedly, this isn't the healthiest version of a carrot, but it is darned good and very easy to make! You probably have all this stuff in your kitchen right now as a matter of fact.

Ingredients

- 2 cups baby carrots
- ¼ cup water
- 1–1½ cups sugar
- 1½ tsp baking powder
- 1½ tsp vanilla
- ⅓ cup bread flour
- 4 eggs
- ½ cup melted butter
- A sprinkle of confectioners' sugar

Notes:

How to...

Cook the baby carrots with the water in the microwave for 10 minutes, covered. Remove them from the water with a slotted spoon (to drain them) and transfer them into a food processor along with the next six ingredients. Blend until smooth. Pour carrot puree into a greased casserole dish and bake at 350°F for 1–1½ hour (depending on the size of the dish and depth of the batter). For individual dishes, reduce cooking time. Sprinkle with confectioners' sugar to serve. ***That's it!***

Keep in mind that this is the quick and dirty version of a soufflé. For the real deal, you would use beaten egg yolks and fold in the egg whites, which have been beaten to a soft peak meringue. This would be really light and airy. So that basically makes this recipe a mock soufflé, but that's okay.

Wouldn't this be darling baked and served in little pumpkins at Halloween?

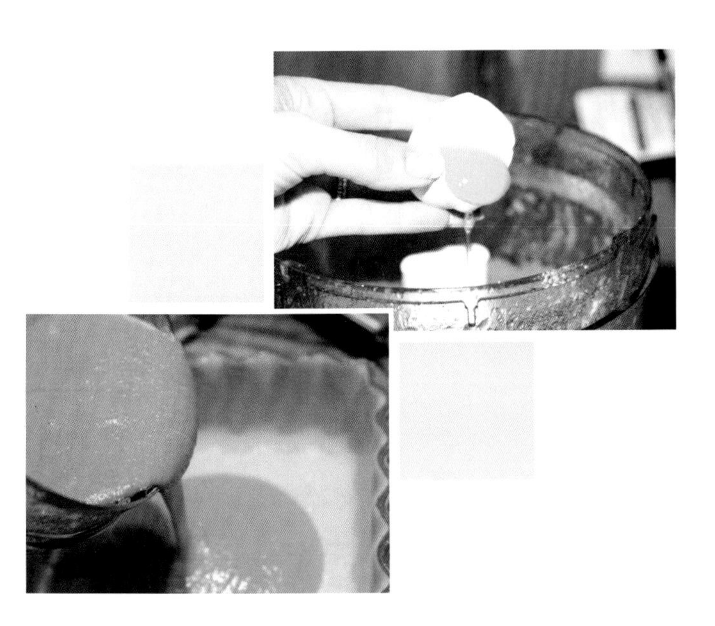

Food Nerd Notes:

- *A soufflé is a lightly baked cake made with egg yolks and beaten egg whites combined with various other ingredients and served as a savory main dish or sweetened as a dessert. The word soufflé comes from the French verb "souffler," which means "to blow up" or more loosely "puff up"—which is a description of what happens to this combination of ingredients.*
- *When it comes out of the oven, a soufflé should be puffed up and fluffy, and it will generally fall after 5 or 10 minutes (as risen dough does). Soufflés can be made in containers of all shapes and sizes, but it is traditional to make soufflé in individual ramekins.*

Secret Ingredient Mac and Cheese

Well, let's see. Recently, I had a call from someone asking me to come up with a mac and cheese recipe that was more "substantial" and wouldn't just "run all over the plate" when you ate it. I was looking through the fridge and pantry to see what was what, and I also saw that there were some carrots that needed to be used. It got me thinking. "Hmmm... I wonder if I could add these carrots to the mac and cheese where no one would know they were in there. It certainly would increase the nutritional level of the dish. And they're even the same color!" And that is how an idea is born. Of course, one idea led to the next, and by the time I finished my morning run, I decided that cauliflower would work great too, as both of these are super mild. Between the time the idea was hatched and the time I got back from the grocery, I had somewhat of a plan. I would roast both of the vegetables (and you don't lose nutrients to boiling) and then puree them and add them to the cheese sauce. I convinced myself that my kids would never know it. That idea became the challenge.

The only problem was Lily, who I had just picked up from preschool on the way back from the grocery. Once she smelled the vegetables that had just finished roasting, she, of course, wanted a piece of the action. Suffice it to say that I didn't exactly finish with the same amount of vegetables that I started with. She demanded a bowl of them, which she polished off while watching a movie. Yes—not chocolate, not chips, not cookies for this little girl. Roasted veggies! So I guess I can't complain about that, right? Besides that, the movie time gave me the chance to puree the rest and add them to the sauce without her seeing me.

The verdict—no one knew. It was delicious! So smooth and creamy, and yes, substantial! I seasoned it up with some more secret savory ingredients to offset the sweetness and give it more depth of flavor and topped it with some delicious toppings. Yes, it's true. I like garnishes on my foods. They make the dish very pretty and give it more interesting textures and flavor combinations. You think I may have food ADD at all? I love comfort food, but I still don't want it to be boring.

Notes:

Ingredients

- 2 cups chopped carrots
- 1 head chopped cauliflower
- Olive oil plus kosher salt
- ½ cup water
- ¾ cup chopped onions
- ½ cup butter
- 2 large cloves garlic, finely minced
- 1 1-lb box of rotini pasta
- 3 Tbsp all-purpose flour
- 3 cups milk
- 1 Tbsp Worcestershire sauce
- 1 tsp ground mustard powder
- 1 tsp kosher salt
- ½ tsp black pepper
- ½ lb low-fat (2% milk) cheese, cut into chunks (I used Velveeta.)

Garnishes: *1 cup sharp grated cheddar cheese, French fried onions, chopped cooked smoky bacon, and crispy fried sage leaves*

How to...

Chop and season the vegetables with a little olive oil drizzled over the top, plus kosher salt. Roast the vegetables at 400°F for around 30 min. Stir around after about 20 minutes. Purée the roasted vegetables in a food processor (or a blender), and add ½ cup water to thin them out.

In a medium saucepan, sauté the ¾ cup chopped onions in the ½ cup butter. Let them cook several minutes, and then add the 2 cloves of finely minced garlic. While your onions are cooking down, you will probably want to start your water boiling. When it does, salt the water and add a whole box of twisty pasta. *That's what Lily calls them.* Cook 9 minutes. Drain. They should still be a little *al dente* because you will finish them in oven. When onions and garlic are soft, add 3 Tbsp all-purpose flour. Cook for an additional 3 minutes or so, and then start whisking in the milk.

Tip» *If your milk is room temperature rather than cold, it will have less of a tendency to clump up.*

I also tried baking the mac and cheese in individual ramekins. In case you are wondering, this works just as well! They make an awfully cute presentation for dinner guests, and in the case of someone like me who LOVES mac and cheese—it's also portion control!

For the critics who will inevitably write and say that this is not mac and cheese if you use rotini rather than macaroni, I invite you to just breathe deeply, live a little, and lighten up. You can smile knowing that you added all those extra nutrients and a ton of fiber to one of your family's favorite dishes!

Add in the milk, Worcestershire sauce, ground mustard, kosher salt, and black pepper. It should get thick pretty quickly. Next, add in the Velveeta, which you cut into chunks, and the pureed vegetables. Adjust your seasonings, and then pour your sauce over the cooked, drained noodles.

Spray a casserole dish with cooking spray and add the mac and cheese. Top the casserole with fried onion strings, cooked and chopped bacon. I fried the sage leaves in a little butter for a minute or so and then drained them on a paper towel and set aside. The fried, crispy leaves are awesome. They just crumble in your mouth and are much less pungent than the fresh leaves. Bake your casserole at 350°F for about 20 minutes or so. Keep an eye on it so it won't over-brown. Once the casserole is out of the oven, top it with the sage leaves.

Keep in mind that if you made this in advance and had it refrigerated, it will obviously take longer than this to heat through. In that case, you may want to tent it with aluminum foil until heated through, and then remove the cover to brown slightly at the very end. Don't let the foil touch the top, because it will stick to your cheese. Heaven forbid we should lose any of the cheese!

Tomato, Zucchini and Ricotta Tarts

Oh, how beautiful the veggies are in the summer! This tart is super simple to prepare and is the perfect light and crisp side dish for your summer grilling menu. We served the tomato zucchini tarts with Jamaican jerk grilled shrimp kabobs over a bed of saffron rice. How's THAT for "Summer Lovin'?"

Ingredients

4 tarts

Thinly cut slices of zucchini and tomato
Kosher salt and black pepper, to taste
1 Pillsbury premade, rollout pie crust cut into quarters

Filling

3 Tbsp ricotta
3 Tbsp fresh mozzarella cut into small pieces
Kosher salt, black pepper, dried basil, all to taste

1 clove finely minced garlic
1 Tbsp extra virgin olive oil

Notes:

How to...

Prep the veggies first by slicing them and sprinkling them with salt. Blot them dry after 30 min, or put something heavy on top with paper towels to remove excess liquid before adding to tart pans.

Cut the pastry dough into quarters. Press the dough into tart pans. With a paring knife, cut the dough off level with the top of the pan. Fill the pastry first with the cheese filling. Next, add the prepped vegetables, alternating thinly cut slices of zucchini and tomato. Combine the finely minced garlic with the olive oil and sprinkle it over the vegetables. Season with salt and pepper.

Bake uncovered at 425°F about 35–40 min. Veggies will start browning and cheese will get bubbly. Serve with a garnish of freshly cut basil.

Butter-Pecan Sweet Potatoes

I adapted these somewhat from something I found on the Martha Stewart website. Let's face it. What CAN'T you find there?! This just may be my favorite sweet potato recipe EVER! First of all, they are gorgeous and festive. BEST of all, however, they are unbelievably good! The inside is all soft and buttery; the outside is just crispy enough from the roasting and the caramelization of the sugar with the nuttiness and crunch of the pecans and just a hint of a bite of heat from the cayenne pepper! ***Oh My!*** We kind of felt like neglecting everything else on the plate.

I included approximate measurements on the spices, but actually, I just went by feel on the amounts. I added lots of brown sugar, etc. because I wanted a really nice candied exterior on my potatoes. My personal recommendation is to use the ingredients, but as far as measuring, just do what feels right!

Ingredients

serves 4

2 large sweet potatoes (or one medium per person)
Extra virgin olive oil (maybe ⅓ cup)
Coarse salt
3 Tbsp cold butter, cut into small pieces
A whole handful of light brown sugar (maybe ⅔ cup)
Handful of pecan pieces (maybe ½ cup)
¼ tsp cayenne pepper (approximate)

See Food Nerd Notes *below.*

Notes:

How to...

Preheat oven to 400°F. Peel potatoes and halve lengthwise; slice crosswise ½-inch thick. On a baking sheet, toss potatoes with olive oil (just use your hands, people!) and then season with salt.

If doing a lot of potatoes, it may be necessary to transfer half the potatoes to a second baking sheet; cook both baking sheets until potatoes are tender, tossing occasionally, 25–30 minutes. You want to have some space between each of the potatoes or else you will have steaming rather than roasting.

Sprinkle the partially cooked potatoes with butter, brown sugar, pecan pieces, and cayenne pepper, dividing evenly. Bake until sugar is caramelized and hard, about 15 minutes. Toss gently; serve immediately.

For a dinner party, etc., you could roast them ahead of time, cool and refrigerate, and then do the final step about 20 minutes before serving time.

So here's sort of a pop quiz. You DO remember that I told you that sweet potatoes ranked #1 among all vegetables in total nutrition, right?! (My students know that I continually haunt them with information that I've taught them in the past.) Well I'm about to throw another one at you…

Food Nerd Notes: Cayenne Pepper—*maybe the King of medicinal herbs! Cayenne pepper* (Capsicum annuum) *is also known as the Guinea spice, cow-horn pepper, aleva, and bird pepper. The Capsicum genus is in the nightshade family* (Solanceae) *and has many acclaimed health benefits. Many cultures around the world recount amazing results from using cayenne pepper for both simple healing as well for battling challenging health problems.*

Cayenne pepper powder comes from red hot chili peppers. These are not only good to eat but also incredibly healthy. The peppers are especially potent when taken in powdered form. To make the powder, the fruit or body of the peppers are dried, then ground down, pulped, and baked into cakes and then sifted to make the spice known as cayenne pepper.

In addition to being a popular spice in food (primarily ethnic cuisine), cayenne pepper has been used for centuries as a medicinal herb. Cayenne is said to have originated within the city of Cayenne in French Guiana. However, it's now produced in many parts of the world. It was used quite extensively by the Aztecs and Mayans, with historians asserting that it was a staple of the Aztec diet. Cayenne is also revered in the alternative health community, and by medicinal herbalists, for its remarkable array of health benefits.

So what are these health benefits? According to various sources, cayenne pepper, through the instrumentality of its secondary metabolite capsaicin (pronounced cap-say-sin), may have the power to kill prostate cancer cells, among other fantastic health benefits. Other naturopathic practitioners have used it for years to prevent heart attacks, remove arterial plaque, rebuild flesh destroyed or harmed by frostbite, heal hemorrhoids, rebuild stomach tissue, heal stomach ulcers (that's counter-intuitive, huh?), and fortify overall health. Other health benefits include improving circulation, rebuilding blood cells, lowering cholesterol, emulsifying triglycerides, and removing toxins from the bloodstream… and it's even a great insect repellent. It immediately equalizes blood pressure in your system and heals the gall bladder too. It can be used as a diuretic as well, helping in eliminating both urine and built-up fecal matter in the intestines. It even has proven anti-fungal properties.

As far as heat, cayenne pepper is generally rated at 30,000 to 50,000 Scoville units. As an herbal supplement, it was mentioned as far back as the 17th-century book Complete Herbal *by Nicholas Culpeper. Cayenne pepper is high in vitamin A and also contains vitamin B6, vitamin E, vitamin C, riboflavin, potassium, and manganese. Cayenne pepper has been hailed as an aphrodisiac because the capsaicin increases blood flow to all parts of the body. It is known in many cultures to be a potent libido-enhancing aid that increases euphoric endorphins in the blood stream.*

So there!

Southern Style Cornbread Dressing

While folks in other parts of the world are having savory bread dressings and rice dressings and various bread stuffings for Thanksgiving, the people in the South are VERY adamant about having cornbread dressing as a necessary side dish to the holiday turkey! In fact, this may be THE quintessential Southern side dish of the holiday season!

This is not exactly a make-at-the-last-minute dish, but it *is* one that you can certainly make a day ahead of time and refrigerate or freeze until you are ready to pop it into the oven for the big meal. And that turns out to be a big plus when you have so many other things going on with family, food to make, and other activities that need your attention.

Ingredients

- 1 pan cornbread
- Chicken broth
- Chicken meat
- Salt, pepper, garlic powder, poultry seasoning, all to taste
- 2–3 ribs celery, chopped (about 1 cup)
- 1 large onion, chopped (about 1½ cups)
- 1 Tbsp butter
- 2–3 cloves of garlic
- Green onions, chopped (about ¼–⅓ cup)
- Fresh sage, chopped (about 2 tsp)
- 2 raw eggs

How to...

Prepare a pan of your favorite cornbread. Prepare your chicken broth. If using a whole chicken, once the meat is cooked, remove it to another bowl so it won't be overcooked and dry. Crumble the cornbread. Strain the broth to separate it from the bones, skin, etc. Add the cooked, chopped chicken back into the broth to get all juicy again.

Sauté the celery and onions in butter. I start with the celery first for a few minutes since it will take longer to soften than the onions. After another few minutes, add in the garlic. Add the vegetables to the crumbled cornbread. Add the chicken from the broth. Add as much or little as you like. I used about 2 cups of meat. Add the broth to the mix. I had 2 cups of the final broth that I added here.

Mix. It will be VERY soupy, but this is good. The cornbread will soak up a LOT, and you don't want the final baked dressing to be dry. Stir in some chopped green onions. Add in some chopped sage. Careful! It's pretty strong and floral. Taste and season at this point. Add the salt, pepper, poultry seasoning, etc. Add in the two beaten eggs. This will help the dressing stay light and fluffy.

Bake the dressing at 350°F for about 30–45 minutes. Yes, that is a BIG range, but it depends on the quantity that you are baking. Most likely closer to 45 minutes for a large casserole dish, but significantly less for an individual casserole dish or smaller ramekins. You want the top to be golden brown and nice and crusty and the inside cooked through and set—not jiggly.

Now then. Doesn't that make everything better? Sure is good to live in the South!

Braised Baby Carrots with Rosemary Infused Maple Pecan Glaze

Occasionally, I get treated to a fantastic meal by the man of my dreams. Eat your heart out, ladies! This particular time, all I was in charge of was making a couple of side dishes. My husband was making the most scrumptious peppercorn-encrusted grilled steak topped with a honey and blue cheese topping. So I made some garlic and Parmesan mashed potatoes and these absolutely delightful braised baby carrots. They were a great juxtaposition of sweet and savory all at the same time!

You'll notice that the measurements aren't all that specific. You're right. This is sort of one of those touchy-feely recipes, but also super simple to make to your liking.

Ingredients

1 lb baby carrots
2–3 Tbsp butter
Sprinkle of cinnamon
2–3 Tbsp maple syrup
Handful of chopped pecans
3-in sprig of rosemary
Freshly cracked black pepper, to taste

Option: *For another variation, rather than the pecans, add a chiffonade (long, thin strips) of a few fresh sage leaves at the very end of cooking.*

Notes:

How to...

Add the baby carrots to a pot of simmering-boiling water and cook until about done. Gently drain the carrots, being careful not to break them.

In a small seasoned black iron skillet, add a couple of pats of butter. Cook on medium-high until butter is very hot and bubbly. Add the carrots. Cook in the butter until the butter gets a little brown color. Now lower heat to medium.

Add a sprinkle of cinnamon over the carrots. Add 2–3 Tbsp maple syrup and a handful of chopped pecans over the carrot. Add part of a sprig of rosemary (or sage) of about 3 inches worth that has been stripped and chopped.

Allow the liquid to reduce down to a glaze. Turn off the heat and allow them to sit and thicken a bit.

CAREFULLY remove them to a plate. They will be very tender now and will break easily. Spoon the glaze and pecans over individual portions. Add a final sprinkling of cracked black pepper to finish these off. Something about that bite of the pepper really brings out the flavors in this dish.

Food Notes: *Braising is a (usually slow) cooking method that is begun on the stovetop and then followed by simmering in liquid. Braising is a popular way to cook less tender cuts of meat. When cooking vegetables, the method is an effective way to infuse them with the flavor of the braising liquid.*

Roasted Carrots and Parsnips

Yay! My favorite time of year is when the parsnips are starting to show up again in the grocery store. It means fall is here, and roasted vegetables will be turning up on everyone's menu soon. Since they are delicious, healthy, and easy, isn't it time for you to give these guys a try?

Parsnips may be a little foreign to some of you. They are related to the carrot and actually look like white carrots, but are a little spicier and when cooked, a little sweeter than carrots. They are often picked after the first frost, so this is why we are just beginning to see them again. These roasted vegetables are both rustic and elegant at the same time, and make a lovely side for a roasted chicken or Cornish hens. The carrots, parsnips, and even the onions, will turn deliciously sweet as the starches convert to sugar during the roasting process.

Ingredients

- ½ bag carrots
- ½ bag parsnips
- ½–1 sweet onion
- Drizzle of extra virgin olive oil
- Salt, to taste
- Freshly cracked pepper, to taste
- A sprig of fresh thyme, *optional*

How to...

Peel and cut the carrots and parsnips into thick French fry shapes or however you want to cut them as long as they are all the same size and shape for even cooking. Peel and cut the onion into medium-to-thick rings (from the root or stem side). Arrange all veggies in a single layer on cookie sheet. You don't want them overly crowded or piled up because this will cause them to steam rather than roast. You can line with foil for easier cleanup if you'd like. Drizzle with extra virgin olive oil and season with salt and pepper. Add stripped thyme leaves if desired.

Roast in oven about 400°F for about 45–50 minutes (depending on your oven) or until insides are fork tender and outsides are crispy, turning every 20 minutes or so. If the carrots still taste carroty, then they are NOT ready yet. They will get really sweet when ready. Give them time!

Notes:

Food Nerd Notes: *While parsnips can be eaten raw, they are more commonly served cooked. Parsnips can be boiled, roasted, or used in stews, soups, and casseroles. In some cases, the parsnip is boiled, and the solid portions are removed from the soup or stew, leaving behind a more subtle flavor than the whole root has and contributing starch to thicken the dish.*

The parsnip originated in the Mediterranean region and originally was the size of a baby carrot when fully grown. When the Roman Empire expanded north through Europe, the Romans brought the parsnip with them. They found that the parsnip grew bigger the farther north they went.

Parsnips are not grown in warm climates since frost is necessary to develop their flavor. The parsnip is a favorite with gardeners in areas with short growing seasons. Seeds can be planted in early spring, as soon as the ground can be worked. Harvesting can begin in late fall after the first frost and continue through winter until the ground freezes over. More than almost any other vegetable seed, the parsnip seed significantly deteriorates in viability if stored for long, so it is advisable to use fresh seed each year.

In Roman times, parsnips were believed to be an aphrodisiac. In the United States, this plant was introduced by British colonists as a root vegetable. In the mid-19th century it was replaced by the potato and consequently escaped from cultivation.

The parsnip is richer in vitamins and minerals than its close relative, the carrot. It is particularly rich in potassium with 600mg per 100g (that means it can help you manage that blood pressure). The parsnip is also a good source of dietary fiber. And 100g of parsnip contains 75 calories (230 kJ) of energy.

Desserts

STRESSED
SPELLED
BACKWARDS

Double Chocolate

Praline Bundt Cake

Bananas Foster Cake

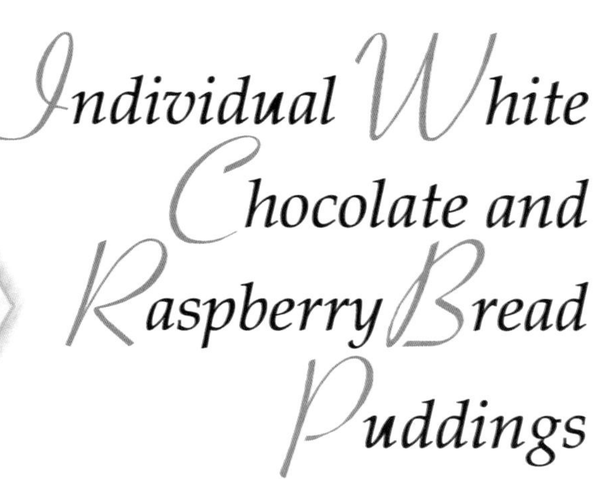

Individual White Chocolate and Raspberry Bread Puddings

Somehow there seems to be a mystique about making bread pudding. In reality, however, it's basically the same batter that you make for French toast. Nothing to it! This recipe takes that basic bread pudding concept and kicks it up just a couple of notches with the addition of creamy white chocolate and fresh, juicy raspberries… an amazing combination, according to my husband.

I made these individually. Why? Well this works for a variety of reasons. Let's think of a few: The individual servings will cook faster, they are super cute to serve, they provide built-in portion control, and they are very easy to transport. This also means the extras are easy to send to work with my husband or share with my coworkers.

Ingredients

- 5 cups bread, cut into 1-in cubes
- 4 Tbsp butter, melted
- 8 oz white chocolate (divided)
- 2 cups milk
- ⅔ cup sugar
- 1 vanilla bean, *optional*
- ½ tsp clear vanilla
- 4 eggs
- ½ pint fresh raspberries

Raspberry Sauce

- ½ pint fresh raspberries
- ½ cup sugar
- Juice from one lemon

Notes:

How to…

Prep: Preheat oven to 350°F. Cut the French bread into 1-inch cubes. Let them sit out for a while. The dried-out bread will soak up the liquid better than really moist bread. Choose a muffin tin that has 6 of the "jumbo-sized" wells, rather than the standard size (The ones I used accommodate about ¾ cup each). To each muffin well, add some of the melted butter, divided equally. Chop half of the white chocolate into little pieces, and add it to the bread cubes. Just mix it loosely to combine. Add the bread cubes and chocolate pieces to the wells, and then set aside.

Make the Batter: To a heavy saucepan, add the milk and sugar. Heat until the sugar is melted, but don't boil the milk. If you are using a vanilla bean, add the seeds now. To do this, split the bean lengthwise and scrape out the "caviar" with the edge of a knife. Add to the warm milk. If you want, just split and throw the whole thing in there. You can strain it out later. All those fragrant little vanilla bean specks are lovely in the batter! Also, add the clear vanilla now. Once the sugar is melted and the vanilla beans are dispersed, you can turn off the heat. Stir in the remaining half of the white chocolate until melted. Hold aside one or two squares of white chocolate for the garnish. Strain the hot milk mixture through a fine sieve if you threw the vanilla bean pieces in there.

In a medium bowl, beat the eggs. To the eggs, begin to add the warm milk mixture, *slowly*, while whisking them furiously as you add the milk. In other words, you need to temper the eggs, or else you will end up with scrambled eggs! NOT good! Pour the egg and milk mixture over the bread cubes. You may need to push the bread cubes down into the mixture just to get them all immersed in the liquid. Allow them to sit for 10–15 minutes just so the bread can soak up all the batter. The warm batter will begin to melt all those chocolate pieces. Yum! Add a handful of raspberries to the top of each of the wells containing the bread pieces. Push them down into it if you want, or just let them rest on top. It's your choice.

Bake: Set the muffin tin into a larger pan, and add water halfway up the wells. We are creating a water bath. Bake the bread pudding, uncovered, about 40–45 minutes at 350°F. It should have stopped being "jiggly" by now, and the top should be a nice golden brown. Don't overcook it, as you don't want it to be dried out.

Make the Sauce: While the bread pudding is baking, make the raspberry sauce. I use the rest of the pint of raspberries. Add the raspberries, sugar, and lemon juice to a small saucepan. Heat until the berries have broken down and the sugar is melted. Mash the raspberries. I use a potato masher. I wanted my sauce to be slightly chunky, but make it to your preference.

Serve: Serve the bread pudding, still warm, with some of that warm raspberry sauce and fresh mint leaves. I shave some white chocolate into curls on the top. To make the curls, just run a vegetable peeler along the edge of the chocolate squares. ***Easy-peasy!***

Apple Praline Bundt Cake

I adapted this recipe from my husband's great-grandmother's recipe. He said he grew up with his mother making it, but wasn't exactly sure where it came from. I had to trace it back just a bit, but it was worth it! I hope that she would have been proud. I am certainly humbled to have been entrusted with this treasured family recipe. The things that I changed were to cut some of the fat and calories from the original recipe and add some touches just to make it my own, but I tried to keep to the authentic spirit of the dish. These are things that I encourage all of my readers to do, as the process of making something your own is one of the true beauties of cooking in your own kitchen.

There may seem like a lot of steps, but this made-from-scratch dump cake is very easy. Just follow along with me step-by-step, and YOUR house can smell like apples and warm spices soon!

Ingredients

Cake

- 1 cup granulated sugar
- 1 cup chopped pecans, toasted
- 1 cup light brown sugar, packed
- ¾ cup canola oil
- ¾ cup cinnamon applesauce
- 3 large eggs
- 3 cups cake flour, *You could use sifted all-purpose flour.*
- 1 tsp baking soda
- 1 tsp baking powder
- 1 tsp salt
- 1 tsp cinnamon
- 1 tsp ground nutmeg
- 2 tsp vanilla
- 3 cups chopped Granny Smith apples
- 2 Tbsp praline syrup, *optional*

Praline Glaze

- ½ cup brown sugar, packed
- ¼ cup butter
- ¼ cup milk
- 1 tsp vanilla
- 1 cup confectioners' sugar

Garnish

Glazed pecans, *I purchased them in a bag.*
Mint leaves

How to...

First, decide on the type of apples you will use. Some apples are best for eating in hand while others hold up better to the heat of cooking. It may depend on what area you live in and the time of year, so ask your grocer to recommend some best for cooking. I had two kinds that I was considering: Honeycrisp, which is one of our favorites, and Granny Smith. I ultimately decided on the Granny Smith apples for this. They are really crisp, produce a nice amount of juice, and do not turn to mush when you cook them.

Prepare the Bundt pan with cooking spray and then granulated sugar (or flour). Start toasting the pecans. I put them in the oven for about 8 minutes on 375°F. You need to shake them around every couple of minutes. Mix together the sugars, oil, and applesauce.

TIP » *If you have no applesauce, you can use a full 1½ cups canola oil. But using the applesauce cuts fat and calories while still giving a tender, moist cake.*

Add eggs and beat well. Mix the dry ingredients together, and then add them to the wet egg mixture. Fold in vanilla, apples, and toasted pecans. Batter will be fairly stiff. The juice from the apples will thin it out as it bakes. Bake at 350°F for 75 minutes or until a long wooden pick comes out clean from the middle. Allow to cool at least 15 minutes in the pan. Then turn it out onto a cooking rack. If desired, brush a praline-flavored syrup (or a simple syrup) over the warm cake so it will soak in and keep everything nice and moist.

Notes:

TIP » *Praline syrup can be found in any gourmet coffee shop or the area of your supermarket that has flavored syrups. You can also just make a simple syrup by dissolving equal parts sugar and water and boiling it for a few minutes. I like the praline syrup because it tastes like sweet Southern pecans and goes well with the flavor profile of this cake.*

While the cake is cooling, make the praline glaze. Stir together brown sugar, butter, and milk into a heavy saucepan. Bring to a full boil and cook about 2 minutes, stirring continually. Remove from heat. Stir in vanilla and confectioners' sugar. Pour over cake immediately before it sets up. Garnish the praline glaze while it is still wet with glazed pecans so they will stick.

Oreo Heath Bar Cake

This beauty is a chocolate fudge cake with Oreos baked into batter and Heath bar pieces mixed into the filling and decorating the top. It's very decadent, but super simple to make. I made this cake for the first time when my (now) husband moved to my city. I had a meal prepared for the whole family and everyone who came to help him move. There was not one speck of it left by the end of the night! Give it a shot! You're sure to love it!

Ingredients

- 1 box chocolate fudge cake mix (I used Duncan Hines.)
- 3 large eggs, room temperature
- 1 cup water
- ⅓ cup vegetable or canola oil
- 1 tsp vanilla
- 30 Oreos

Vanilla Buttercream frosting

- 6 cups confectioners' sugar
- 2 sticks softened butter (16 Tbsp)
- 2 tsp vanilla
- 5 Tbsp half and half

Decoration

- 1 bag Heath bar pieces
- 4 full-sized Heath bars

Melted chocolate for added garnish

Notes:

How to...

Prep: Take out your eggs so they can come to room temperature. Sometimes I cheat and heat up a cup of water in the microwave and let them sit in the warm water while I get everything else out. Room temperature eggs will give you a fluffier cake than cold eggs. Prepare your pans with cooking spray sprinkled with granulated sugar. Add a circle of parchment paper to the bottom of each to ensure that your cakes won't stick. Preheat the oven to 325°F.

Mix: For the cake, I used Duncan Hines (my all-time favorite brand) chocolate fudge cake mix. After pouring the prepared batter into the pans, I gently mixed in two rows of Oreos (about 30 Oreos in total) that I roughly chopped into quarters.

Bake: Bake at 325°F for 24 minutes. You do not want to overbake the cake or else it won't be moist. Allow the cakes to cool in the pans about 5 minutes before turning them out onto cooling racks. Remove the parchment paper!

Frosting: Combine frosting ingredients in a stand mixer and whip until fluffy. Try to keep the kids out! My goodness, it's delicious!

Decorate: In between the cooled cake layers, I added about half of the bag of Heath bar pieces (the tiny ones that come pre-chopped in a bag in the baking aisle) on top of the frosting and then topped with the second layer.

For the topping, I bought a bag of (full-sized) Heath bars and Lily rough-chopped four of them into pieces that were approximately the size of a quarter and piled them on top. Around the edges, I spooned more of the small pieces from the bag.

On top of the vanilla icing and the larger candy pieces, I drizzled melted chocolate. I actually used melted chocolate-flavored Almond Bark since it is so easy to work with.

Cream Cheese Stuffed Pear Dumplings with Praline Sauce

One day, we had such a lovely time planting our spring garden out in the gorgeous weather. Of course, I had help! Afterwards, we scrubbed the dirt from our hands and sat out on the front porch swing and enjoyed these amazing stuffed pear dumplings. These may look fancy, but they are super simple to make. Just peel, core, stuff, wrap, and bake the pears. I'm sure apples would work just as well, if that is your preference.

You could also top them as you choose—it's YOUR dish! My first topping is a praline sauce. By all means, if you have any leftover, save it for topping your ice cream. DELISH! The second topping, because I have a little girl who adores berries, is a mixed berry sauce (This one would be fabulous over pancakes as well). And who knew that they would work so well together! One is silky, creamy, and sweet, and the other has a slight tartness to brighten up the bite.

As always, I'll take you through each step of what I did. By the way, the sauces could easily be made ahead of time and stored in the refrigerator until you need them. Just heat them up before serving. These would be SO ELEGANT for a dinner party!

How to...

Mix your filling before preparing the pears so they won't sit and oxidize (brown). Mix the softened cream cheese and the confectioners' sugar together. That's all there is to it!

Peel the pears. Do NOT remove the stem! Remove a small slice from the bottom of the pears so they will sit flat. Core the pears from the bottom to remove as much of the core and seeds as you can without disturbing the stem. I found that a melon baller worked great for this job.

Unroll the pie crust on a lightly floured surface. You'll want to roll it out a bit larger than it already is, but don't get it too thin. Cut out a circle in the dough using a paring knife. I used a bowl because I doubt I could cut a perfect circle by eye! Do whatever works for you.

Fill the pears with the cream cheese mixture using a narrow spoon. I think I may have used a child-sized spoon. A pastry bag may work well for the job, too.

Wrap the pear in the pastry crust circle one side at a time, brushing lightly with the egg wash so it will stick together. For the egg wash, just mix together an egg white and water. Continue in one direction around the pear until it's all wrapped up. Sprinkle with large decorating sugar. The crystals just make it so pretty! I knew that I'd better do it over a bowl or else it would be everywhere!

Now out of any leftover pastry crust, cut out some "leaves" with a paring knife. Apply them using the egg wash to glue them to the crust. Sugar them as well so they won't feel left out. Set the pears in a baking dish that you have lined with parchment paper. You do not want them to stick, and this will make your cleanup a snap!

Cover the stems with little bits of aluminum foil. You don't want them to burn. Bake at 400°F for about 40 minutes.

For the last 10 minutes, I covered the tops loosely with aluminum foil so the bottom parts would brown a little more.

Ingredients — for 4 pears

Pears

- 8 oz reduced-fat cream cheese, softened
- 4 Tbsp confectioners' sugar
- 4 red d'Anjou pears
- 1 box Pillsbury roll-out pie crust
- 1 egg white and 1 Tbsp water for an egg wash
- Decorating sugar

Praline Sauce

- 4 Tbsp butter
- ¾ cup brown sugar
- ½ cup canned evaporated milk, *Or you can use heavy cream.*
- ½ tsp vanilla (I always use clear Mexican vanilla.)

Berry Sauce

- 1 cup frozen mixed berries
- 2 Tbsp raspberry preserves
- ½ cup granulated sugar

Notes:

For the Praline Sauce

Melt butter into a saucepan. Add brown sugar and let it all come to a nice bubbling mess! Add in the evaporated milk or cream. Add in the vanilla. Bring to a nice boil, and the thickeners will start to do their work. Then you can bring the heat back down to maybe medium, letting it bubble gently until it has reduced and thickened to a nice syrup. This will probably take about 10 minutes. You don't want to overcook it, or you will actually make praline candy. Set it aside and let it cool a bit or you will blister someone's mouth! You want to serve warm, not hot.

Now for the Berry Sauce

Grab a bag of frozen mixed berries from the freezer and dump some into a saucepan. Yes, you can certainly use fresh if you have them on hand. Add in the preserves. They will act as a thickening agent because of the pectin in them. Add in some sugar if you want the berries to be a bit less tart. Allow them to come to a boil and cook down for a while. I used a potato masher to break up the larger berries. It's still a little bit chunky, but the strawberries were huge. The consistency of the final sauce is totally up to you. Allow them to cook down and reduce until syrupy. Then set aside to cool.

Serve

Top the baked pears with a bit of each sauce. You can make a bed of the berry sauce, and then drizzle the praline sauce over the top, if you wish. Or serve either one alone... or serve them totally naked! The point is to have fun with it and please the palates of whomever you are serving. Garnish with extra fresh berries and sprigs of mint.

Enjoy them with someone you love.

Apple and Cherry Danish Tarts

These gorgeous beauties will help you pretend to be a baker, even if you aren't! You don't have to spend all your time perfectly arranging the fruit as you would in a tarte Tatin or making the perfect crust or braiding the pastry or any of those other somewhat laborious techniques of other tarts and Danishes. You essentially just cut the puff pastry, pile on the toppings, and bake. So… is it a Danish, or is it a tart? I don't know. Somewhat of a hybrid, I suppose. At the bottom of the recipe, we'll have a look at the semantics.

Ingredients

½ box (1 sheet) of frozen puff pastry
1–2 large, firm, crisp apples, *I used the Honeycrisp variety.*
2 Tbsp butter
2–3 Tbsp brown sugar
Apple pie spice
Cinnamon
1 Tbsp corn starch
1 can cherry pie filling
¼ cup softened cream cheese
2–3 Tbsp confectioners' sugar
½–1 tsp vanilla
1 egg white
About ½ cup large sparkling (coarse) sugar
About ¼ cup all-purpose flour to roll out pastry
2 Tbsp apple jelly

How to…

Remove the pastry from the freezer and allow to thaw until the creases are pliable. Preheat oven to 375°F. Prepare your baking sheet with parchment paper or a Silpat (nonstick baking sheet).

Peel and dice the apples and cook down for several minutes in a small saucepan with the butter, brown sugar, apple pie spice, and cinnamon. I only wanted to soften them, not cook them totally down to a mush. Once the juices are coming out of the apples, add a

Notes:

little corn starch to tighten up the sauce. Alright, I cheated on the cherry filling—this came straight out of the can, as my daughter is a big fan. I told you that you are just *pretending* to be a baker for this recipe, right?

Prepare the cream cheese filling: Combine softened cream cheese, confectioners' sugar, and vanilla in a small bowl. You only want it slightly sweetened, as the rest of the filling will be pretty sweet.

On a well-floured board, roll out the pastry into a rectangle a bit larger than it already is after you unfold it. Using a pizza cutter or a knife, divide the dough into 9 squares (or whichever shape you desire). One at a time, brush one side of each pastry with the egg white (all the way out to the edges) and then dip in a plate of the large sugar, pressing gently. This large sugar can be found in the cake decorating section of your favorite store. Allow any excess sugar to fall back into the plate. Place the pastry, sugar side up, in the prepared pan. Repeat with the other pieces.

Add a dollop of sweetened cream cheese filling to the center of each pastry. Then mound up about ½ cup of fruit topping onto each. Leave about ½ inch of exposed pastry around the sides. *For the cherry topping, be careful to not get TOO much of the gooey filling. Too much of that will run all over the pastry and be somewhat of a mess.* Of course, you are probably thinking to yourself, "Hey, why don't I just use apple pie filling too?" You are certainly welcome to do that. My only

criticism of the pie filling is that there is too much of the gel stuff and it is a little bit TOO wet for the dough to rise and puff as much as I'd like it to. So if you do that, use mostly fruit and only a bit of the gel.

Bake for 15 minutes at 375°F. Then reduce heat to 350°F and continue to bake for another 15–20 minutes longer or until the edges are golden. Remove the baking sheet and cool for just a few minutes, and then transfer the tarts to a cooling rack. If you leave them in the pan too long, they will start to stick. Once cool, transfer them to a tray. Warm the apple jelly a bit in the microwave or small saucepan until liquid enough to use as a glaze. Brush the liquefied apple jelly over the apple topping. It gives them a pretty sheen. This is not necessary for the cherry topping.

All you need to accompany these is a nice hot cup of tea or coffee to ease the stresses of the afternoon. I assure you, the edges of the pastry crust on these little guys will not go uneaten. Crispy, crunchy, flaky layers that practically melt in your mouth, the little crackle of the sugared edges, the tartness of the fruit, the sweet creaminess of the cream cheese filling... ***Mmmm.*** But perhaps wipe a little flour over your brow and act like you've really done something hard in case anyone should question you!

Food Nerd Notes:

- *A tart is a baked dish consisting of a filling over a shortcrust pastry base with an open top not covered with pastry. The filling may be sweet or savory, though modern tarts are usually fruit-based, sometimes with custard.*
- *A Danish pastry is a sweet pastry that has become a specialty of Denmark and the neighboring Scandinavian countries. The Danish pastry is made of a yeast dough that has been rolled out thinly, coated with butter, and then folded into numerous layers. This is repeated several times to create a dough that is fluffy, buttery, and flaky—essentially a laminated dough with many flaky layers. The Danish can be topped with chocolate, sugar, or icing and may be stuffed with fruit fillings, nuts, or custards. In the US, Danish pastries are typically given a fruit or sweet bakers' cheese filling prior to baking.*

Raspberry Swirl Cheesecake Minis

These adorable, portion-perfect Raspberry Swirl Cheesecake Minis will be just the ticket to end your meal on a sweet note without blowing your entire diet! Fresh raspberry sauce is marbled through the decadent and creamy cheesecake, which tops off a crunchy, chocolate cookie crust. ***How sweet it is!***

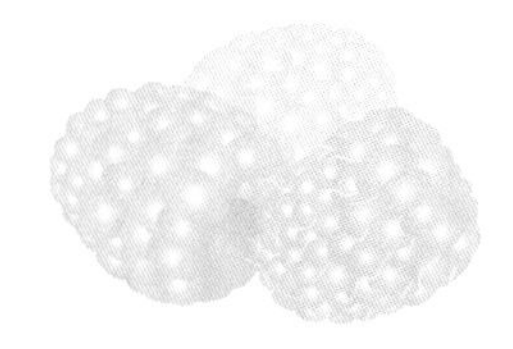

Ingredients

1 dozen

Crust

1 cup chocolate cookie crumbs
About 13 chocolate sandwich cookies
1 Tbsp granulated sugar
5 Tbsp melted butter

Raspberry Sauce

6 oz (a slightly rounded cup) fresh raspberries
3 Tbsp granulated sugar
1 tsp corn starch

Filling

2 8-oz blocks of full-fat cream cheese, room temperature
⅔ cup granulated sugar
⅛ tsp table salt
1 tsp vanilla, *I like the clear, Mexican vanilla the best.*
½ tsp lemon zest (about 1 lemon)
2 large eggs, room temperature
½ cup full-fat sour cream, room temperature

Notes:

How to...

Begin by taking out all of your cold filling ingredients so they can come to room temperature. Preheat oven to 300°F.

Crust: In a food processor, mix all ingredients until they resemble wet sand... umm... dirt. Press 1 Tbsp of the cookie crust into each cupcake liner that you have set into standard muffin pan. Press the crust down with your fingers. Cover the entire pan and place in the refrigerator to harden.

Raspberry Sauce: Mix all ingredients in a cold saucepan, and heat until bubbling. Break down the raspberries by mashing them. I used my potato masher for this. Remove from heat when thicken. Transfer to a glass container and cool in the refrigerator until needed.

Filling: Mix all room temperature ingredients in a stand mixer on low. You don't want to mix on high because it will put too much air into the batter. Using an ice cream scoop, fill the cupcake papers. I found the ice cream scoop to be the perfect amount of batter.

Next, add three drops of the cooled raspberry sauce on top of the filled cheesecake batter. I used a baby spoon for this. Use a chopstick or knife to swirl the raspberry sauce into the cheesecake batter.

Cook's Note: *This recipe makes more filling than you will need for a dozen cheesecakes. So either you can save the filling for another time in the refrigerator or make more crust and raspberry sauce! I think it's really nice to have filling left over for another time. The concept of this recipe is to have a nice, sweet ending to your meal but in a portion-controlled manner.*

Bake: Bake at 300°F for 18–22 minutes. The center should still be a little bit jiggly and still slightly moist looking. Remove and allow them to cool. Cover and refrigerate overnight or for several hours.

Tip » *When releasing the papers from the pan after chilling overnight, you may find that they stick down. The paper liners allow the melted butter to bleed a little, and with chilling, the butter can tend to stick to the pan. If this happens, set the whole pan in a larger pan (or sink) of warm water for a few minutes to warm that butter up again. To circumvent this issue, you can use an outer foil liner. I didn't want to bake the cheesecake in foil liners, as I have heard they impart a metallic taste (yuck). But if you use an inner paper liner and an outer foil liner, this may do just the trick!*

Chocolate Covered Cherries Cake

While on vacation in Mazatlan, Mexico, one year, the resort made this amazing chocolate cake that we all loved. At first it appeared to be a standard chocolate cake with buttercream filling. But then there was that certain something in the background. It was the taste of cherries with the chocolate. Chocolate covered cherries! So of course this cake would NOT leave my mind until I came home and attempted to create my own version. Some people come home with sand dollars and t-shirts. I come home with recipes that haunt me!

Several years later, this is still my son's favorite birthday cake. And we still talk about our wonderful vacation together. Food does that. It brings back memories.

Ingredients

The Cherry Simple Syrup

1 cup Kirsch, *See* Food Nerd Notes *at bottom*
½ cup sugar

Chocolate Cherry Cake

1 box dark chocolate fudge cake (I used Duncan Hines.)

Ingredients as called for on box for the cake, also adding

- 1 tsp vanilla
- 1 Tbsp Kirsch
- 1 can of cherry pie filling

Chocolate sticks (I used 4 jumbo packs of Kit-Kat chocolate bars.)
Mint leaves for garnish

The Chocolate Cherry Buttercream Filling

½ cup butter
Pinch of salt
1 tsp meringue powder
3½ cups confectioners' sugar
½ cup heavy whipping cream
1 tsp vanilla
2 Tbsp strong coffee
1 Tbsp unsweetened cocoa powder
2 tsp Kirsch

The Ganache

1 cup heavy whipping cream
12 oz semisweet chocolate chips

How to...

First, start with the Kirsch syrup.

Personally, 90 proof is just WAY too much alcohol for me, as I only wanted the flavor, not to have my toddlers walking around tipsy! So I made a simple syrup of the Kirsch and sugar and boiled it for 5 minutes to boil a majority of the alcohol off. Stir until sugar completely dissolves. Allow it to cool completely.

Make cake mix as directed on package, adding additional vanilla and Kirsch. The vanilla should be the best you can find. I use Mexican vanilla, as it has a great flavor! One tip I have for the cake is to bring your eggs to room temperature before mixing them into the cake mix. This gives you a fluffier cake. Somehow, I can never remember this ahead of time though, so I usually just cheat by putting them in warm water for several minutes. Bake as directed (325°F for 33 minutes in my case, for two 8-inch pans). Please do not overbake your cakes!

Notes:

Let's move on to the buttercream. Your butter should be softened, but not melted. Beat the butter until it is light and fluffy. Add in a pinch of salt and the teaspoon of meringue powder. I did not measure the salt. I literally pinched it. Add the confectioners' sugar in small bits at a time on LOW speed (or else it will be all over your kitchen). After adding half of the sugar, I added the cold, heavy whipping cream. Then add the remainder of the sugar. To avoid having a flat taste, I added an additional teaspoon of Mexican vanilla to the buttercream as well. We're trying to mirror the major flavors of each component. Add 2 Tbsp of strong, cold brewed coffee. It will not taste like coffee, but the coffee does bring out the chocolate flavor better. Next, add in 1 Tbsp of unsweetened cocoa powder. Believe me, the cake will be PLENTY sweet! After it's all nice and fluffy, pop it into the fridge. You want the butter to stay cold.

Now back to the cake, which we have allowed to cool on wire cooling racks. Paint some of the Kirsch simple syrup onto the cake tops. Just use a clean paintbrush. I keep one just for pastries. I painted it on pretty thick. This will soak into the cake and keep it really moist, as well as add the cherry flavoring to the cake. Then put the cakes into the freezer to firm up for a while. When the cakes are nice and firm, cut them in half. Take about half of the can of cherries, and split

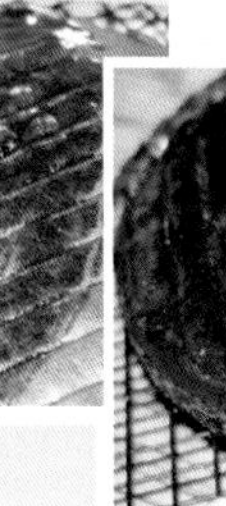

them in half. We will use the gel stuff as well at this point. To the bottom half of the bottom layer, add a crumb coat of the buttercream filling. Add the other half of the bottom layer, and to this, add the split cherries and cherry sauce. This goopy stuff will soak into the cake, too… so moist! Repeat with the top 2 layers. Finally, add the remainder of the buttercream to the top. Now go and put the whole thing back into the freezer.

Now let's make the ganache. Add the heavy whipping cream to a saucepan. Bring it just up to a boil, not even, just to the point where it's considering a boil. Then reduce to low. To the scalded cream, add in the semisweet chocolate chips. Stir or whisk over low heat until the chocolate is smooth and dissolved. It will get smooth and glossy. Then remove from the heat.

Go get the cake out of the freezer. Set the cooling rack over a sheet pan. You will need something to catch the drips! Starting in the middle of the cake, pour the warm ganache in a smooth stream, allowing it to flow over the edges of the cake. It really looks like a mess, doesn't it? That's okay. Now go and put it all back in the freezer again. If you are wondering about all the freezer time, it's because I was so paranoid that the ganache would melt the buttercream and the whole cake would start sliding off. I would rather cool in between each step than to have that happen and have wasted an afternoon of dirty dishes and quiet nap time!

So, after the ganache is set but still sticky, I took it out and began arranging the Kit-Kats (in pairs) around the cake. These are much less expensive (and more fun) than those fancy (and high-priced) chocolate sticks that some websites sell. And you may as well have some fun with this!

Tie a pretty red ribbon around the Kit Kats.

Drain the remaining half of the can of cherries and rinse them in cold water. Arrange them around the perimeter of the cake with a few in the center.

Shave part of a block of white chocolate over the center. This is so simple. Just use a standard vegetable peeler.

And voila! It suddenly becomes a piece of art! Oh, and don't forget the mint leaves!

Food Nerd Notes:

- Kirsch (Kirschwasser) (*keersh-vahs-ər*), *German for "cherry water," is a clear, colorless cherry-flavored fruit brandy traditionally made from double distillation of morello cherries, a dark-colored cultivar of the sour cherry. It is now also made from other kinds of cherries. The cherries are fermented complete, including their stones. Unlike cherry liqueurs and so-called "cherry brandies," Kirschwasser is not sweet. The best Kirschwassers have a refined taste with subtle flavors of cherry and a slight bitter-almond taste that derives from the stones. It is not to be confused with crème de kirsch, a sweet cherry liqueur.*
- *Because morellos were originally grown in the Black Forest region of southern Germany, Kirschwasser is believed to have originated there. Kirschwasser is colorless because it is either not aged in wood or is aged in barrels made of ash. It may have been aged in paraffin-lined wood barrels or in earthenware vessels.*
- *Clear fruit brandies made from distilled, fermented fruit are very popular in southern Germany, Austria, Switzerland, and France. In France and in English-speaking countries, these beverages are known as eaux de vie. The European Union sets a minimum of 37.5% ABV (75 proof) for products of this kind; Kirschwasser typically has an alcohol content of 40%–50% ABV (80–100 proof). About 22 pounds of cherries go into the making of one 750 ml bottle of Kirschwasser! No wonder it's pricey!*

Hello Dolly Bars (aka Magic Cookie Bars)

You may have heard these called Hello Dolly Bars, or Magic Cookie Bars, but either way, this recipe goes WAY back to the 1960's (See *Food Nerd Notes*). Something that enduring must have something going for it, right? Well truthfully, if you have a sweet tooth, what's not to love? Coconut (God's gift straight to me), chocolate chips, and sweet Southern pecans, all made into a moist, chewy cookie bar? Gracious goodness. You'll be sorry if you don't make these this instant!

There are a couple of really cool things about these bars: (1) You mostly likely have all the ingredients on hand right now. (2) They take all of 10 minutes or less to throw together. (3) They are AMAZING, just the perfect thing to hit the spot on a nice Sunday afternoon!

Ingredients

- 1½ cups graham cracker crumbs
- ½ cup butter, melted
- 3 Tbsp sugar
- 1 10-oz bag pecans, chopped
- 1 cup shredded coconut
- 1 12-oz bag semisweet chocolate chips
- 2 cans sweetened condensed milk

Notes:

How to...

Preheat oven to 350°F.

In a small bowl, combine the graham cracker crumbs, butter, and sugar. Press firmly into the bottom of a 9 × 13-inch baking pan. Spread the chopped pecans over the crumbs, followed by the shredded coconut and chocolate chips. Pour the condensed milk evenly over the top.

Bake 35–40 minutes or until the edges are golden brown. I put aluminum foil around just the edges for the last 5–10 minutes so I could get equal browning on the middle section without over-browning the edges. Cool before slicing. Makes about 18 servings (but they are so rich that I actually cut them into 36 squares).

Food Nerd Notes: *To the best of my knowledge, Eagle Brand condensed milk was the first place this recipe could be found. Over 150 years ago (1856), the sweetened condensed milk was invented by Gail Borden. His creation had little to do with baking, but rather his goal was to invent a stable milk product to address the lack of refrigeration. He later began selling the product from the back of a pushcart in New York City for 25¢ a quart, and people were mainly using it in coffee, tea, and cocoa. Throughout the Civil War and both World Wars, Eagle Brand became a precious source of milk and sugar, which were both in short supply.*

Post-WWI prosperity brought refrigeration to most kitchens and desserts to many family tables. Eagle Brand was then reinvented as "the dessert-maker," with many sweet applications. In 1931, the Borden kitchens began offering homemakers $25 for their original recipes and received over 80,000! The "Magic Cookie Bar" or "Hello Dolly Bar" was one of these recipes that debuted in the 1960s.

Pumpkin Upside Down Cake

Oh my gosh… for the life of me, I can't figure out why I waited until the holidays were here to make this amazing cake. This is one of my favorite cakes, and with the availability of canned pumpkin all year long, you could make this any time you choose. We've made this cake for years now starting in October, and it gets rave reviews from folks in each age group!

The method of making it may seem a little strange to you, but it's pretty hard to mess up. So if you are looking for something festive to bring to your holiday party (anywhere from Halloween through the Christmas season)—this is for you!

This recipe came from *The Secret Ingredients Recipe Book.*

Ingredients

24 servings

Cake

- 1 16-oz can pumpkin, *not pumpkin pie filling*
- 1 12-oz can evaporated milk
- 1 cup granulated sugar
- 3 eggs, room temperature if possible
- 2 tsp cinnamon
- 1 2-layer box of yellow cake mix (I used Duncan Hines.)
- 1½ cups chopped pecans, *or more if you prefer!*
- 1 cup butter, melted

Topping

- 8 oz cream cheese, softened
- 1 cup granulated sugar
- 12 oz nondairy whipped topping
- ⅓ cup toasted chopped pecans

Notes:

How to...

Preheat oven to 350°F. Line a 9 × 13-inch baking pan with waxed paper. I like to spray both sides of the waxed paper with nonstick cooking spray.

Combine the pumpkin, evaporated milk, sugar, eggs, and cinnamon in a bowl and mix well. Pour into the prepared pan. Sprinkle the cake mix over the pumpkin mixture. Sprinkle the pecans over the cake mixture. Drizzle the butter over the layers. Bake at 350°F for 60–65 minutes. It will still be a little bit jiggly, but it will firm up when it cools.

Cool in the pan about 30 minutes before turning it out onto a flat platter. Loosen the sides of the cake from the pan by passing a knife between them. *Do not try this while the cake is still hot.*

For the topping, combine the cream cheese, sugar, and whipped topping in a bowl and mix well. Spread over the top of the cooled cake. Top with toasted chopped pecans. To serve, cut into 2-inch squares (it's pretty rich). For serving to a crowd, it works well to put the squares into cupcake liner papers. For Halloween parties, top each square with a plastic spider ring. ***These are a huge hit!***

Bananas Foster Cake

I adapted this from one of the *Southern Living* Christmas cookbooks, which was given to me by one of my sweet students. It has all the luscious flavors of the traditional Bananas Foster dessert thanks to a brown sugar rum glaze on each layer, but this one won't melt right before your eyes. As a matter of fact, this one is best savored slowly, maybe with a nice cup of coffee.

In addition to the moist cake and brown sugar rum glaze, there are layers of bananas between the layers and a silky cream cheese frosting on top. And if THAT isn't enticing enough, it's topped off with pieces of sweet, nutty Southern pecan pralines! Can this go wrong?

Now I need to be perfectly honest and tell you that this is a special occasion cake. It does require quite a few steps, although each of them is simple to perform. Just give yourself ample time. I got busy with other duties of the holidays and ended up making the cake on Christmas Eve and the pralines on Christmas Day due to a time crunch. That was another story entirely, as the recipe calls for store-bought pralines. HA! This was not going to happen on Christmas Eve or Christmas Day. There were none to be found when I needed them, so I ended up having to make my own. You could shave quite a few of these steps off of the recipe using store-bought pralines... although the extra pralines that I made were very much welcomed by my guests!

Notes:

Ingredients

Cake

3 cups all-purpose flour
¼ tsp salt
1 tsp baking soda
1 cup butter
1 cup granulated sugar
1 cup firmly packed light brown sugar
5 large eggs
1 cup milk
3 ripe bananas, mashed
1 tsp vanilla extract
Cooking spray for baking, *with added flour*
2 firm, ripe bananas, sliced

Brown Sugar Rum Glaze

6 Tbsp light brown sugar
1 Tbsp light corn syrup
3 Tbsp water

1 Tbsp butter
2 Tbsp dark rum
¼ tsp ground cinnamon

Cream Cheese Frosting

2 8-oz packages softened cream cheese
1 cup butter, softened
2 16-oz packages powdered sugar, sifted
2 Tbsp milk
4 tsp vanilla
2 firm, ripe bananas, sliced
Garnishes: cinnamon sticks, praline pieces

Classic Southern Pralines:

2 cups packed brown sugar
1 cup heavy cream
1 tsp vanilla
2½ cups lightly toasted pecan halves

How to...

Method for Cake

Preheat oven to 350°F. Combine sifted flour, salt, and baking soda. Beat butter and sugars at medium speed with an electric mixer until fluffy. Add eggs, 1 at a time, beating until blended after each addition. Add flour mixture to butter mixture, alternating with milk, beginning and ending with flour mixture. Beat at low speed until blended after each addition, stopping to scrape bowl as needed. Stir in mashed bananas and vanilla.

Pour batter into 3 (8-inch) round cake pans coated with cooking spray for baking. These will generally say "with added flour." I also like to cut rounds of parchment paper and place these in the bottom of the pans for extra insurance. Bake at 350°F for 25 minutes or until a wooden pick inserted in center comes out clean. Run a sharp knife around the edges of pan. Cool cake layers in pans on wire racks for 5 minutes; remove from pans to wire racks, and cool completely (about 1 hour).

Meanwhile, Prepare Glaze

Bring brown sugar, corn syrup, and 3-Tbsp water to a boil in a small saucepan, stirring constantly. Cook, stirring 1 minute or until sugar dissolves. Stir in butter, rum, and cinnamon.

Prepare Cream Cheese Frosting

Beat cream cheese and butter at medium speed with an electric mixer until smooth. Gradually add powdered sugar, beating until smooth; stir in milk and vanilla.

Note: *My ingredient list represents a double portion of the frosting suggested by the recipe. I can never seem to make a "single" portion ice a cake the way I believe it should be. So I doubled it.*

Pierce cake layers with a wooden pick (I used a wooden skewer); drizzle with brown sugar rum glaze. Let stand for at least 10 minutes.

Spread a little cream cheese frosting on one cake layer; arrange half of banana slices over frosting. Repeat procedure with a second cake layer with frosting and remaining half of banana slices. Top with the third cake layer. Frost top and sides of cake with remaining frosting. Garnish with praline pieces and cinnamon sticks.

Method for Pralines

Prepare a sheet tray by covering it with waxed paper. Combine brown sugar and cream in medium heavy-bottomed saucepan over medium-high heat. Stir with a wooden spoon until sugar is dissolved. Then do not stir any more. Insert candy thermometer and boil until the sugar reaches 240°F (soft-ball stage). Remove from heat and stir in vanilla. Continue to stir until mixture thickens and becomes opaque. Stir in all pecans and drop by teaspoonful on prepared sheet tray. Allow to cool completely at room temperature before removing from waxed paper. Now that we have the pralines, break them into large chunks and use them as garnish.

Food Nerd Notes: *The term* praline *refers to a confection made from nuts and sugar syrup whether in whole pieces or a ground powder. Pralines differ around the world in texture as well as ingredients. Originally a French recipe, they were made using almonds. Pecans were native to the New World and thus were originally not ingredients in European pralines. The European chefs typically used almonds, as they were available locally and were relatively cheap.*

French settlers brought this recipe to Louisiana, where both sugar cane and pecan trees were plentiful. During the 19th century, New Orleans chefs substituted pecans for the original almonds, added cream to thicken the confection, and thus created what became known throughout the American South as the praline. They are usually made by combining brown sugar, butter, and cream in a pot on medium-high heat and stirring constantly until most of the water has evaporated and it has reached a thick texture with a brown color. Then it is usually dropped by spoonful onto wax paper and left to cool. Pralines have a creamy consistency similar to fudge.

Homemade Snickers Bars

Just WOW! After making these, I promptly brought them to work to pawn them off on my co-workers and students… because this kind of thing is WAY too dangerous to have around the house! My perception *could* be off, but even some of my students said these are better than the real thing! While they do take a bit of time to make (allowing each layer to cool in between), each step is really easy; and the result is pretty spectacular! I'd be willing to bet that most of the ingredients are in your pantry already.

Ingredients

makes one 9 × 13 pan

- 2½ cups milk chocolate chips
- ¾ cup honey-roasted, creamy peanut butter (I used Peter Pan brand.)
- ¼ cup unsalted butter
- 1 cup granulated sugar
- ¼ cup evaporated milk
- 1 jar (about 1½ cups) of marshmallow fluff
- 1 tsp high-quality vanilla
- 1 cup honey roasted peanuts, rough chopped
- 1 bag (about 11–14 oz) of caramel bits
- ¼ cup heavy whipping cream
- ⅛–¼ tsp cayenne pepper, *optional*

How to…

Layer 1–*peanut butter, chocolate ganache*

I used a Take-Along disposable pan from Rubbermaid because they are flexible enough to turn over and pop all the candy out at the end; and you can turn them over right onto the lid. Thoroughly grease your baking pan before you begin. I used nonstick spray.

Notes:

Bottom chocolate layer

- » *1¼ cups milk chocolate chips*
- » *¼ cup honey-roasted creamy peanut butter*

Melt the ingredients together in a saucepan or the microwave (which is what I did). Then pour into the baking dish and spread until even. Let this cool and harden completely in the fridge.

Tip » *If you are using the microwave, heat them in about 30-second intervals and stir well in between. If melting them on the stovetop, be sure your utensils and pot are clean and dry. You can't let even one drop of water get in this mixture.*

Layer 2– *the nougat layer*

- » *¼ cup unsalted butter*
- » *1 cup granulated sugar*
- » *¼ cup evaporated milk*
- » *1¼ cups marshmallow fluff*
- » *¼ cup creamy, honey-roasted peanut butter*
- » *1 tsp high-quality vanilla*
- » *1 cup honey-roasted peanuts, rough chopped*

Melt the butter in a saucepan over medium heat. Add in the sugar and milk, stirring until dissolved, and bring to a boil. Let cook for 5 minutes, stirring occasionally. Add in the marshmallow fluff, peanut butter, and vanilla, stirring until smooth. Turn off the heat and fold in the peanuts. Then pour over the bottom chocolate layer. Let the nougat cool completely in the fridge.

Layer 3– *the caramel cream layer*

- *1 bag caramel bits*
- *¼ cup whipping cream*

Combine the ingredients in a saucepan over low heat. Let melt, stirring occasionally until smooth. This will take a while (maybe around 10 minutes). Pour the caramel cream sauce over the nougat layer and let it cool completely in the fridge.

Layer 4– *spicy peanut butter chocolate ganache*

- *1¼ cups milk chocolate chips*
- *¼ cup creamy, honey-roasted peanut butter*
- *⅛–¼ tsp cayenne pepper,* optional

Melt the ingredients in a saucepan or microwave. Then pour over caramel and spread until even. Let this layer cool and harden completely in the fridge. With the lid ON, turn them over and gently press the bottom of the pan. You will see them slowly releasing. ***Ta da!*** You can let your breath out now. Cut them into bars or squares.

Note: *You'll want to keep them in the fridge, as they get soft fairly quickly.*

Mississippi Mud Puddles

We had a family reunion at my mother's house one particular Fourth of July. My kids suggested we make a Mississippi Mud Pie. Well, you *KNOW* we can't just make something *ordinary*, so we opted for individual servings, thinking that might be easier for folks to just pick up and eat rather than wrangling a piece from a larger casserole dish, as it's usually done. My oldest child (who rarely cooks with us but almost always offers… ahem… constructive criticism and serves as our tasting critic) argued that this wouldn't really be a Mississippi Mud Pie if we offered it in individual servings. He said, "Those would be more like Mississippi Mud *PUDDLES* in that case, Mom." So here they are!

Ingredients

The Crust

1 cup flour
1 stick melted butter
1 cup chopped pecans

Bourbon Ganache Layer

1 package semisweet chocolate chips
1 pint heavy cream
1 Tbsp bourbon

The Cream Cheese Fluff Layer

1 8-oz package cream cheese, softened
1 cup powdered sugar
1 cup cool whip

The Pudding Layers

1 large box instant chocolate pudding plus 2½ cups whole milk
1 large box instant French vanilla pudding plus 2½ cups whole milk
Extra Cool Whip! Because it needs its own layer!

Garnishes

White and milk chocolate curls
Toasted pecans
Swedish fish, *optional*

Notes:

How to...

Prepare all the components, and then begin assembly.

The Crust: Combine ingredients. Press in a 9" × 13" pan. Bake for 15 min at 375°F. Then let it cool.

Bourbon Ganache Layer: This bourbon ganache layer goes on top of the pudding layers. Melt chocolate and cream together over double boiler, stirring until silky. Add bourbon and cook another minute or two. Cool before adding to layers. You can put the pot over an ice bath to cool faster. The alcohol will cook out, but you can certainly leave it out if you don't want the bourbon in there.

The Second Layer: Combine ingredients in a stand mixer (or hand mixer) and whip until smooth and creamy.

The Pudding Layers: This is a little less milk than the packages call for, but results in a little bit stiffer product, which works well here. Some recipes call for mixing both puddings together, but I separated the layers because I thought it would look prettier. Mix with a stand or hand mixer until smooth. *If you use the "cook and serve" type instead of the instant, MAKE SURE they are cooked before layering!*

Create an assembly line:

1–Crust
2–White cream cheese fluff
3–Chocolate pudding
4–French vanilla pudding
5–Ganache
6–Cool whip
7–Optional garnishes.

Begin assembly when all components are accounted for. To begin, you will spoon some of the crust into the little dessert cups. Just crumble it up. It makes a pretty, crunchy layer. We used clear plastic dessert cups, as they were appropriate for people walking around with them inside/outside at the family reunion. *I used 9 oz cups, which were pretty, but for a dessert this rich, you could probably do a smaller-sized cup. We found that 9 oz of this is a LOT!*

Layer as indicated. Garnish as desired. I added white and milk chocolate curls and toasted pecans to the top. To make the chocolate curls, just pull a vegetable peeler along the side of a block of chocolate, and it will curl up. Ta da! It's that easy!

After assembly, the mud puddles need to be refrigerated until you are ready to serve

Note: *The chocolate curls are quite breakable, so if you need specific placement, use a toothpick to lift them into position. We just gathered them up and tossed them on. You can also "curl" the chocolate right over the dessert and just let them fall.*

Strawberry Cream Cheese Cobbler

Cobbler has got to be one of the easiest "throw together" desserts there is. One night, the little ones and I were home alone for the evening and we had—yes, I admit it—frozen pizza! I know, kind of hard to believe, isn't it? I tried to resign myself to the idea, but I just couldn't let the night go by with frozen pizza being the sum total of my children's culinary experience. That brings me back to cobbler—a dessert made up of stuff you most likely have on hand this very second! This at least made me feel a little less guilty about the frozen pizza.

So without further delay, let's see how to make it. Then you'll have a culinary curve ball in your back pocket for some day when you just want to throw something together.

Ingredients

- 1½ cup granulated sugar
- 1½ cup self-rising flour
- 1½ cup milk, *regular or 2%*
- 1 tsp vanilla
- 1½–2 cups fresh strawberries, stems removed, washed, and cut into quarters
- ½ stick (4 Tbsp) butter, melted
- 4 oz cream cheese (regular or reduced-fat)

Notes:

How to...

The basic batter for a cobbler is just a 1:1:1 ratio of sugar, self-rising flour, and milk. Then you get to throw whatever additional flavorings and berries you'd like. The Mexican vanilla gives everything an amazing flavor (just throw that imitation stuff down the sink!), and the fresh sweet berries speak for themselves. My favorite part, however, is the crust. The butter bakes up around it, making it so buttery and crunchy. ***Yum!***

Note: *By using a self-rising flour, we eliminate the need of adding leavening ingredients, making this super fast and easy to put together.*

Mix together the sugar, self-rising flour, and milk. Add in the vanilla, then whisk together. Prepare the strawberries by rinsing them, removing the stems, and cutting them into quarters. Prepare the pan by melting 4-Tbsp butter and pouring it into the bottom of a 9 × 13 × 2 casserole dish. Pour the batter right over the butter. Add the fresh berries right on top of the batter. Now get your cream cheese ready. All I do is cut it into little cubes. Add the cream cheese cubes onto the top of the cobbler and push them down a bit with your finger. Bake the cobbler, uncovered, for 1 hour at 350°F.

Tip » *You can vary the texture and depth of the crust by changing the size of the casserole dish. Try a smaller, square, or round dish for a deeper, doughy drust.*

Food Note: *For those of you not familiar with this Southern favorite, cobbler refers to a variety of dishes consisting of a fruit or savory filling poured into a large baking dish and covered with a batter, biscuit, or pie crust before being baked. Cobblers originated in the early British American colonies. Apparently, the English settlers were unable to make their traditional puddings due to lack of suitable ingredients and cooking equipment, and this is what they came up with.*

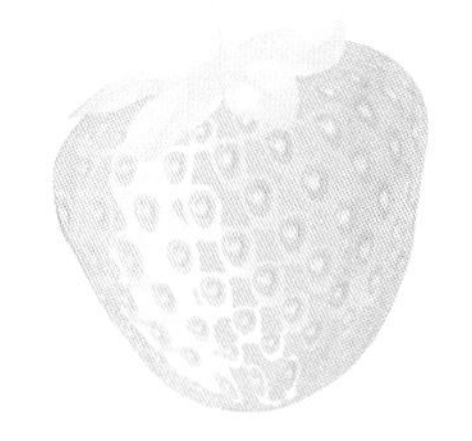

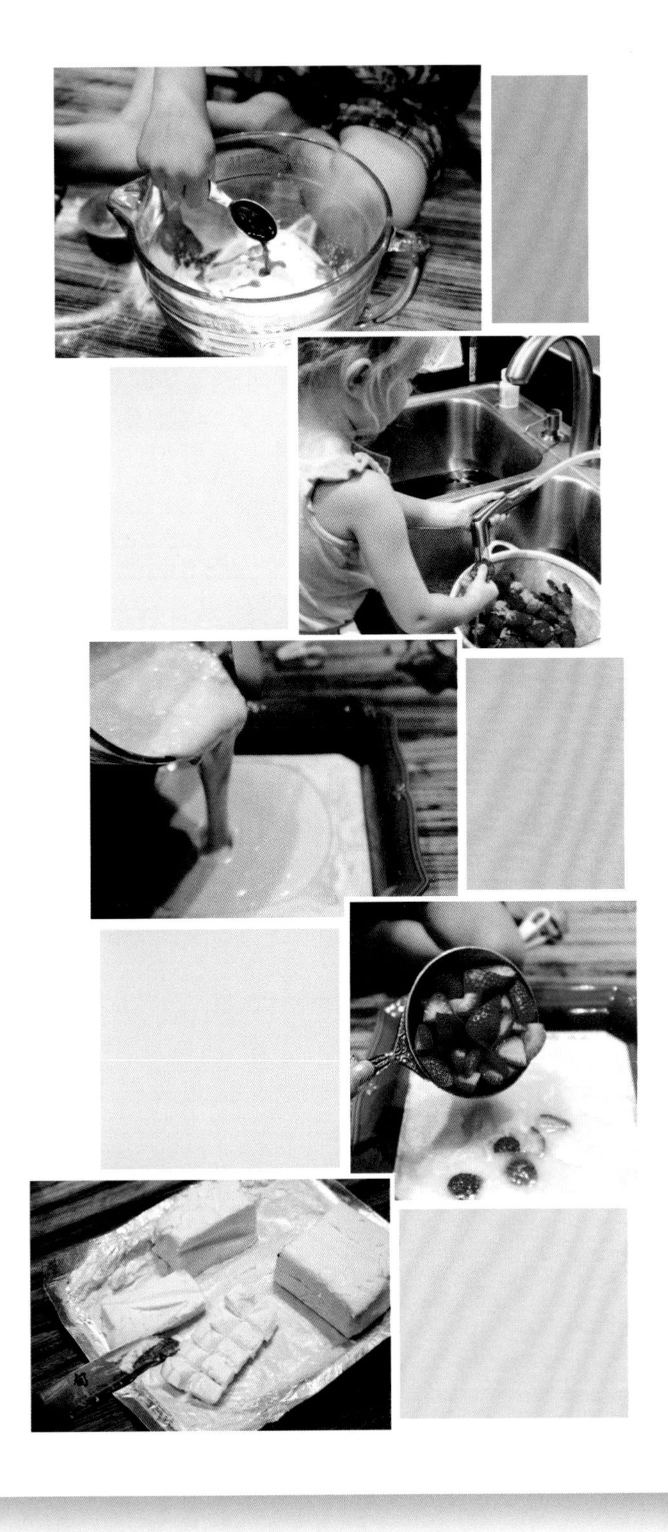

Blueberry Lemon Bars

These dainty Meyer lemon bars are made extra special with the addition of fresh blueberries and a toasted coconut shortbread cookie crust!

There are so many recipes around for lemon bars that it's really hard to know where to start! This one is a hybrid of a couple of different recipes, with toasted coconut in the crust and a big handful of fresh juicy blueberries. They add a wonderful color and texture balance and just a hint of tartness to balance out the sweet lemony filling. Keep in mind that Meyer lemons are not quite as tart as regular lemons and are a little sweeter. They are a like a cross between a lemon and a mandarin orange.

Ingredients

Crust

- 1 cup shredded coconut, toasted and cooled
- 2 cups all-purpose flour
- ½ cup granulated sugar
- ½ tsp salt
- 12 Tbsp (1½ sticks) chilled butter, cut into ½-inch cubes

Filling

- 1½ cups granulated sugar
- 4 eggs
- 3 Tbsp lemon zest, *I used 4 Meyer lemons.*
- ½ cup lemon juice, *I used Meyer lemons.*
- 2 tsp all-purpose flour
- 1 tsp baking powder
- ⅛ tsp salt
- ¼ cup fresh blueberries plus 1 tsp flour to dust, *or cornstarch*

Note: *Meyer lemons are not as sour and tart as regular lemons. If you are using regular lemons, you may want to either cut back on the amount of lemon juice or add more sugar.*

Notes:

How to...

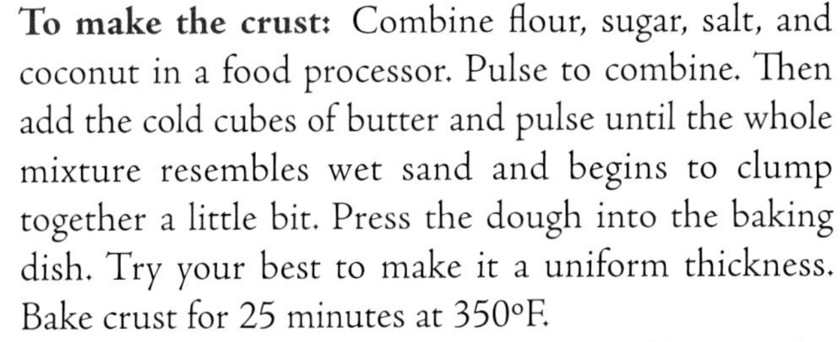

Preheat the oven to 350°F. Line the bottom of a 9" × 13" baking dish with parchment paper, allowing it to come up the sides. *Later, we will use that to pull the whole dessert out of the dish.* Add the coconut into a rimmed pan and broil to toast (around 6 minutes total), shaking the coconut around every couple of minutes. Watch it carefully!

To make the crust: Combine flour, sugar, salt, and coconut in a food processor. Pulse to combine. Then add the cold cubes of butter and pulse until the whole mixture resembles wet sand and begins to clump together a little bit. Press the dough into the baking dish. Try your best to make it a uniform thickness. Bake crust for 25 minutes at 350°F.

While the crust is baking, make the filling. In the food processor (clean first, please), combine sugar, eggs, lemon zest and juice, flour, baking powder, and salt. Process this mixture on low until well mixed and smooth. In a small bowl, dust the blueberries in a little flour and shake the excess off. The flour will help to keep the blueberries from bleeding.

Pour the filling over the warm crust, add the floured blueberries, and return the dish to the oven. Bake for another 25 minutes uncovered. Cool completely and garnish with powdered sugar. *I actually let mine cool overnight in the fridge.* Use a sharp knife to go around the short ends of the dish where the filling is in contact with the dish, and then use the parchment to lift the whole thing out. Cut into squares or bars.

German Chocolate Brownies

Alright, so after making these, I promptly brought them to the office. WAY too dangerous to keep around the house. I like the topping on a German chocolate cake, but not usually the cake itself. That type of chocolate just seems too light for my tastes. So for these, I purposely sought out the darkest, fudgiest brownie mix I could find. So if you are into dark, rich chocolate brownies and coconut, these may be just the thing for you, too!

We're going to file this under the semi-homemade category. I made them after work, so I shaved some time and effort off of them by using a brownie mix. I made them my own, however, with this to-die-for, creamy coconut-pecan topping. If you have a favorite made-from-scratch brownie recipe you want to use, knock yourself out. But for an easy, but decadent, dessert that people will rave over without a lot of stress, follow my step-by-step photos.

Ingredients

Brownies

- 1 pkg dark chocolate brownie mix
- ¼ cup water
- ½ cup canola oil
- 2 large eggs, *Bring to room temperature.*
- ½ tsp pure vanilla extract

Notes:

Coconut Pecan Frosting

- ½ cup chopped pecans, toasted and cooled
- ½ cup flaked, sweetened coconut, toasted
- ½ cup half and half, *or evaporated milk*
- ½ cup granulated sugar
- 1 egg yolk, beaten
- 4 Tbsp butter
- ½ tsp pure vanilla extract

Note: *My daughter is just starting to learn to read, so she "read" the instructions off of the box before we began. It was priceless and included that I should "put the mixed-up ingredients" into a "short bowl" to bake them in. Well, our short bowl is a casserole dish. Yes. I really do let them take all that time to try and read the directions and stuff.* This IS our quality time together.

How to...

Preheat oven to 350°F. Rather than spray my stone baker, I lined it with parchment paper so that I could just lift the brownies out of the dish. Mix brownie batter according to package directions. Pour batter into a prepared casserole dish. Bake according to directions. I used a 9" × 9" stone baker and cooked for 34 minutes. A toothpick inserted into the batter should come out clean, but don't over bake or they will dry out.

To prepare for the frosting, toast the pecans and the coconut. I dry toasted the nuts about 7 minutes in the 350°F oven, shaking them around a couple of times. I just used a lower rack while the brownies were cooking. Same thing for the coconut—dry toast them in a pan in the oven, mixing them around every couple of minutes or so until pretty and brown. Watch the coconut carefully so that it doesn't burn.

While brownies are baking, let's prepare the coconut pecan frosting. Combine the remaining ingredients. Carefully bring to a boil, then reduce heat to medium low, and cook for about 5–7 minutes so that it will thicken. Remove from heat, and then stir in the toasted pecans and coconut.

Spread the frosting over the warm brownies. Let the brownies and frosting cool a while before lifting out. Then cut the brownies. To do so, just carefully lift out the parchment paper from the dish. ***Ta Da!*** No more digging out the brownies!

There IS no other word to describe these than decadent! The darkest, fudgiest brownies I could find and a coconut pecan praline-esque topping over that?!! ***YES!***

Chewy Oatmeal Sandwich Cookies with Candied Ginger Crème Filling

These beautiful chewy oatmeal sandwich cookies have a little something up their sleeve! The sweet crème filling is dotted with spicy-sweet bits of candied ginger. I really enjoy having something traditional that has a bit of a new twist to it!

These may look like something you would have to special order, but they are crazy easy to make. Just follow along with me, and we'll make them together, step-by-step! And you probably have most of these ingredients on hand already.

Ingredients

for 6–7 large sandwich cookies

Cookies

- 1¼ cups old fashioned rolled oats
- ¾ cup all-purpose flour
- 1 tsp ground cinnamon
- ½ tsp baking powder
- ½ tsp table salt
- ½ cup (1 stick) butter, softened
- ¾ cup granulated sugar
- 2 Tbsp molasses
- 1 large egg
- 1 tsp vanilla
- 1 cup pecans, finely chopped

Notes:

Filling

- 1¼ cups confectioners' sugar
- ¼ cup vegetable shortening (I used Crisco)
- Pinch of salt
- ½ tsp vanilla
- 1 tsp cold water
- 1½ Tbsp chopped candied, *crystallized*, ginger

Note: *Let me first note that you can make both the cookie dough and the filling ahead of time. Just pop it all in the refrigerator and take some out to make as many cookies as you wish.*

Note: *If you go to my blog, Menu Musings, you will see probably more steps than necessary, but I wanted to illustrate the point that kids are quite adept in the kitchen. My daughter is 4, but in one of the photos, you will see her carefully leveling off her dry ingredients for a correct measurement.*

Let's Work on the Cookie Dough First.

First, combine the oats, flour, cinnamon, baking powder, and salt in a large bowl.

In a separate bowl, add the butter, sugar, and molasses. Beat these together on medium-high until fluffy. This may take several minutes. Now mix in the egg and vanilla until smooth. Reduce the mixer speed to LOW and add the flour/oats mixture. Beat until combined. Stir in the pecans by hand. Cover the cookie dough and refrigerate until chilled. Overnight is fine.

Filling

Beat together the confectioners' sugar, vegetable shortening, salt, and vanilla. The mixture will seem dry and crumbly, but should come together in the end. If not, add a bit more water to it. Mix to combine. It will look like coarse sand. Chop the candied ginger into small bits and add to the crème filling. Stir to incorporate. If you aren't using the filling now, you can cover and refrigerate. If you're making the cookies now, there's no need. *If you are sensitive to the candied ginger, I'm sure these would be amazing with candied cherries or some other fruit!*

Okay, Back to the Cookies.

Line two baking sheets with parchment paper for easy release. Form the dough into 12 balls of about 2 Tbsp each. It is pretty important that your portions are equivalent because we need the cookies to be the same size to make sandwiches out of them. Arrange them with plenty of room between them to accommodate spreading. Flatten them a bit with the backside of a fork. *You have to watch this dough carefully. It tends to disappear when you turn your back!*

Bake for 15 minutes. Halfway through, I switched the position of the baking pans, since I'm always worried that the top pan and bottom pan may cook differently. Allow them to cool for a while on the baking pan just to firm up, and then you can transfer them to cooling racks to cool completely.

Assembly

When the cookies are cool, we are ready to put these together. Transfer the ginger crème filling to a sheet of plastic wrap and form it into a log. Slice the crème filling into 6 equivalent portions.

Roll each piece of filling with a rolling pin until approximately the same size as the cookies. It will be quite stiff, and it is not really spreadable, so rolling works great here. Now it's just a matter of topping each of the cookie bottoms with some ginger crème. Then top with the second cookie. Gently press them together.

Double Chocolate Pecan Pie

Since pecan pie was my grandfather's (Papa's) favorite and he worked away from home, I'm told my mother made him one weekly for when he returned. Someone close to me was away working for a week, this was a welcome home dessert. In addition to the nostalgia of this dessert, this particular pie has a little something extra with the addition of chocolate—glorious chocolate!

Ingredients

- 1 unbaked 9-inch pie crust (contains 2 crusts), *Or you can make your own.*
- ½ cup butter, melted
- 1 cup sugar
- 1 cup light corn syrup
- 4 eggs, beaten
- 1 tsp vanilla
- ¼ tsp salt
- ¾ cup semisweet chocolate chips
- 2½ cups chopped pecans

Garnishes: *heavy cream and chocolate*

Notes:

How to...

The Crust

Okay, so it's no secret that I am intimidated by making pastries. I'm not the biggest fan of preformed pie shells, either. Use one crust for the pie plate and the second for the braid. To assuage my guilt over not making the crust from scratch, I try to do a little something extra to it to pretend that I actually did something. This little braided edge is one way to make it my own.

Roll out the crust on a lightly floured surface. Cut the pastry into strips of ⅛"–¼" wide. Braid them together, gently. Wet the edges of the braids together to bond them to each other. It took me about 3½ braids worth to go around the 9-inch pie plate. Then, just simply glue the braid to the pastry in the pie plate by brushing it with a little water and applying a little gentle pressure.

The Filling

Combine butter, sugar, and corn syrup in a saucepan.

> **Tip »** *If you spray the measuring cup with nonstick spray first, the syrup will just slide right out.*

Cook over low heat, stirring constantly until all the sugar dissolves. Remove from heat and allow it to cool slightly.

Whisk together the eggs, vanilla, and salt. SLOWLY temper the eggs by adding *small amounts* of warm syrup to them, whisking like crazy as you do. This will bring the egg temperature up slowly enough that you won't end up with scrambled eggs. I think a ladle is very handy to do this. Mix well!

Fill and Bake.

Pour the filling into the unbaked pie shell. Add ¼ cup chocolate chips, half of the pecans, another ¼ cup chocolate chips, the rest of the pecans, and then the last ¼ cup of chocolate chips.

Bake at 325°F for 50–55 minutes (covering the edges with foil after the first 30 minutes). *For making this foil shield, trace a circle on the foil around the bottom of the pie plate with a pen. Fold foil into quarters and cut an arc into it a about an inch smaller than the circle. You will have a circle when you open it.*

Allow the pie to cool to at least room temperature or colder before serving. Garnish with a dollop of sweetened, whipped heavy cream, and some chocolate shavings.

Peanut Butter Cups—just like Reese's!

On the 7th anniversary of Hurricane Katrina, we were all home, off from school and work because of Hurricane Isaac. This seems to be the magical time of the year for these terrible storms. I am indeed my mother's daughter, however, and find it impossible to just sit still and do nothing. We had spent the last two days playing card games, Scrabble, Monopoly, building Legos, making projects, watching movies, and just manning the fort.

That's what brought me to make this recipe—because keeping little ones entertained is a fairly ambitious job sometimes. I was looking for something to make with my daughter while the boys all played "boy stuff," and it needed to be something that was no bake and simple in the event that our electricity went out. I have a gas stove, so that's not a problem. The wind was very gusty outside and we were having significant rain, so our cooking project needed to come from pantry staples that did not require a trip to the grocery store. We decided to make peanut butter cups. These are so simple that you'll wonder why you've just been buying them forever!

The lowdown: Extreme simplicity and awesome taste. Kid/teen comments: "These DO taste JUST like Reese's!" That's good enough of a testimony for me! It appears as though Lily and I had another successful day.

Ingredients

Filling

- 3/4 cup creamy peanut butter (I used Peter Pan Honey Roast Creamy peanut butter.)
- 1/3 cup confectioners' sugar
- 1/4 cup butter, melted
- 2 Tbsp graham cracker crumbs

Chocolate Shell

- 1½ cup semisweet chocolate chips
- 2 tsp shortening
- 1 Tbsp peanut butter

Now admit it. You have all that stuff already, right?

Notes:

How to...

Line 12 regular-sized muffin tins with cupcake papers. Set aside.

Mix all the filling ingredients together. Set aside.

Melt the chocolate shell ingredients together, stirring frequently over a double boiler (or a pan set over a simmering pan of water). Spoon some chocolate in each of the paper shells. Use the back of a spoon to gently slope the chocolate about ⅓–½ way up the sides of the shells. Place in the freezer 6–7 minutes to set. Spoon some of the filling into each chocolate shell. I dipped my finger into a little vegetable oil to pat and smooth down the peanut butter (so it wouldn't stick to my finger). Spoon more of the chocolate (Reheat if necessary) on top of the peanut butter and spread around so that you can no longer see any of the peanut butter. Put them back into the freezer to set. ***That's it!***

These are best chilled right out of the freezer. They do tend to get a little melty, so it's best to leave them in the freezer or fridge until ready to serve. If you need them to be room temperature, you could add a little paraffin to the chocolate as it melts.

But seriously, these were super simple and delicious! It made our rainy hurricane day a little brighter, that's for sure.

Macaroon Kiss Cookies

So one day, I was browsing the Internet, and I came across some macaroons with a chocolate candy kiss on them. I knew right away that I just had to make some! I changed up the recipe a bit to suit my own tastes, and let's just say they didn't last very long when I took them to work! These are not the typical egg white-meringue type of confection. They are a soft and chewy, cream cheese-based cookie heavily laden with coconut inside and out—definitely not overly sweet. Oh! It's Heaven if you enjoy coconut. They are very simple to make, and the dough can be refrigerated and baked as needed (which could be a problem!). The Hershey's Kiss in the middle takes them over the top, and the whole thing is just waiting to be enjoyed with a nice cup of hot tea or coffee.

Ingredients — makes 4 dozen cookies

- 2½ cups all-purpose flour
- 1 Tbsp, plus 1 tsp baking powder
- ½ tsp table salt
- ⅔ cup butter, softened
- 6 oz cream cheese, softened
- 1½ cups granulated sugar
- 2 egg yolks
- 1 Tbsp good quality vanilla
- ¾ tsp almond extract
- 1 Tbsp, plus 1 tsp fresh orange juice
- 10 cups sweetened flaked coconut, divided into one 6-cup and one 4-cup portion
- 48 chocolate kisses (I used Hershey's Kisses.)

How to...

In a medium-sized mixing bowl, sift together your flour, baking powder, and salt. Set these aside for later. Sifting makes the flour oh-so-fluffy and avoids it being "packy," as over time it can become compacted.

In your stand mixer, beat together the butter, cream cheese, and sugar until light and fluffy. Now add the egg yolks, vanilla, almond extract, and freshly squeezed orange juice. Beat until smooth.

Notes:

In 1-cup increments, mix the flour mixture into the butter mixture. Once the flour is incorporated, add in the 6 cups of coconut. Mix well to combine. Cover and refrigerate your dough for about an hour.

While you are waiting, go ahead and unwrap your Hershey's Kisses. I would recommend buying more than needed. Invariably, someone is going to pass through the kitchen and grab a few from your stash!

Now that our dough is chilled, let's get down to business. Get your oven preheated to 350°F. Prepare your pans with parchment paper for easy release. Scoop the dough out using a 1-Tbsp measuring spoon. This will give you balls of about 1½ inches. Roll them in your hand into a smooth ball and roll in the remaining 4 cups of coconut.

Arrange them on the parchment paper leaving ample room between them. They will spread a bit. I was able to put 1 dozen cookies on each pan at a time. Bake at 350°F for 12–13 minutes. The cookies will be puffy and lightly browned.

After the baking time, remove the cookies and immediately press a Hershey's Kiss into the center of each cookie. Then place them BACK into the oven for another minute. Then remove them and set them out on a cooling rack for about 10 minutes or so. They will firm up a bit.

The chocolate will stay soft for quite a while; so let them cool completely before packaging them up. I put them in an airtight container to take to work. I can tell you they didn't last long at the office!

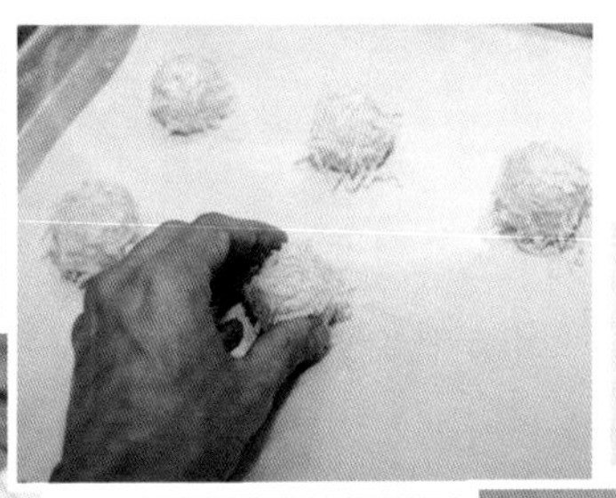

Lily's Blackberry Cobbler

We have been blessed with an abundant crop of blackberries around the wooded areas of our neighborhood. On an after-dinner walk with Canon and Lily, we picked a bounty of juicy plump blackberries just begging for something special. Last night, Lily helped to transform these blackberries into a fabulous cobbler, telling you how simple this recipe is.

This recipe can be used with any type of berries, even a bag of frozen mixed berries. If you use the frozen type, be aware that you may need to cook them just a bit longer. So basically, this is a throw-together dessert made up of pantry and freezer staples that you probably have on hand this very second! This makes it perfect for unexpected guests. You just mix it together and throw it in the oven, and after you've had time to clear the dinner plates, dessert is ready for a big scoop of ice cream and a house full of little purple mouths!

Ingredients

Just remember the 1:1:1 ratio, and you can change the quantities as you need to.

1½ cup sugar
1½ cup self-rising flour
1½ cup milk
1 tsp vanilla
4 Tbsp butter, melted
A bunch of juicy berries!

Notes:

How to...

Preheat oven to 350°F. For this super-easy dessert, you start by just mixing together sugar, self-rising flour, milk, and vanilla for the batter. (Give it a taste. ***It's yummy!***) Melt butter in the bottom of a baking dish. Pour the batter over the butter. The butter will come up around the sides of the batter and make it crispy, crunchy, and golden! Add the fresh or frozen berries right over the batter as little or as liberally as you like. There is no need to even mix them into the batter. The batter will cook up around the berries as it rises. This is SUPER simple! Bake for about an hour, and serve with a big scoop of ice cream!

Honey Vanilla Bean Lemondrop M

Toasted

Salted Caramel Appletinis

Blueberr ade

Drinks and Libations

HELP FOR THE PARCHED!

Pumpkin Pie Spiced Marti

Blueberry Lemonade

I had this for the first time at the wedding of one of my former students, who is now making us all proud as a successful medical student. It was served with and without rum, and OH MY, was it ever delicious! Shortly after that, my mother and my daughter and I were having lunch at a cool, artsy little cafe, and there it was AGAIN! My daughter absolutely fell in love with it, and I considered it all a sign that I needed to come home and make some. Blueberries are one of the big superfoods out there, as they have one of the highest amounts of antioxidants of any berry. It's so much fun to make something that your kids love when it's also a way to get extra nutrition in them! We'll leave the spiking to the grownups. ***Please enjoy responsibly.*** There is nothing hard about it, and the payoff has been pretty sweet!

Ingredients

Simple Syrup, makes one cup

- ½ cup sugar
- 1 cup water
- 1 vanilla bean, seeded (keep the pod)

- 1 12-oz bag unsweetened, frozen blueberries, thawed
- 1 12-oz can frozen lemonade concentrate, thawed
- 3–4 cups water/ice

Optional Garnishes

Lemon curls, mint leaves, and fresh blueberries

Notes:

How to...

Make the simple syrup first by combining sugar, water, and vanilla bean seeds and heating until the mixture comes to a boil and thickens slightly. Strain and set aside to cool.

Add the berries to a food processor and blend until all fairly smooth. Pass them through a fine mesh sieve to remove all the blueberry pulp and skins. Otherwise, your lemonade may be gritty. We really only want the juice from them.

Combine the lemonade concentrate, processed berry juice, simple syrup, and water (or ice). Stir to combine. Serve over ice with garnishes, if desired.

Salted Caramel Appletinis

One fall, I had an absolutely crazy week! There were final exams to be given and graded, students to be counseled and registered, final class rosters to be turned in, publishers to be met with, school fall festivals to be attended, and snack helper days and Halloween fun to be had! By the time evening came on Friday, I was looking forward to a fun cocktail to celebrate the successful completion of the week. This cocktail seemed just right as it embodied the flavors of fall... after all, who can turn down caramel apples?!

Ingredients — makes 2 martinis

A martini shaker of ice cubes
4 oz caramel vodka
4 oz green apple vodka
4 oz apple cider
1 oz praline or caramel syrup

Garnishes

Caramel apple dip
Kosher salt
Cinnamon apple chips

Tip: *The praline syrup can be purchased in the specialty coffee area of your grocery or at most coffee shops.*

How to...

Fill your martini shaker with ice cubes. Add the other four ingredients and shake vigorously for at least a minute so the liquid will get really, really cold. Strain out into a martini glass, which should be rimmed with caramel apple dip and a sprinkling of large kosher salt granules. Garnish as desired. ***Please enjoy responsibly.***

Notes:

Pumpkin Pie Spiced Martini

I am always so very thankful when the cooler weather finally reaches down to kiss the South and gives us a break from the heat and humidity. The crisp weather, the changing foliage, the emergence of pumpkins, the bales of straw, and the scarecrows on everyone's porches… I just LOVE it!

The autumn season is also when we start pulling out our favorite pumpkin recipes. Some of them are old and handed down, and some of them may be brand new to us. This Pumpkin Pie Spiced Martini may just be pumpkin perfection if you enjoy the spices of fall. It's creamy and decadent with the richness of the pumpkin and just a hint of the warm spices that we love this time of year. But why wait for Thanksgiving? It's pumpkin pie in a glass!

Ingredients

makes 2 martinis

A martini shaker of ice
- 2 oz vanilla vodka
- ½ oz coffee-flavored rum-based liqueur (I used Kahlua.)
- 1½ ounce pumpkin pie creme liqueur (I used Fulton's Harvest brand.)
- 1 ounce crème de cocoa
- 2 oz half and half
- 1 Tbsp canned pumpkin pie mix
- ⅛ tsp pumpkin pie spice

Optional Garnishes

Cane sugar for rimming the glass
Whipped cream
Crushed cinnamon graham crackers
Ground nutmeg or pumpkin pie spice
Cinnamon sticks

Notes:

How to...

Add all seven drink ingredients over ice in a martini shaker. Shake vigorously at least one minute until very cold. *Optional: rim the glass by dipping in crème de cocoa or Kahlua and then dip into raw cane sugar crystals.* Strain the drink out into prepared martini glasses and serve immediately. You may also garnish with whipped cream, crushed cinnamon graham crackers, a bit of ground nutmeg, and a cinnamon stick.

Please enjoy responsibly!

Honey Vanilla Bean Lemondrop Martini

Yes, of ***course*** you can just make this for the family without the alcohol! But even if you do, remember—everything is more fun when you serve it fancy with the lemon slice and the mint and the sugar rim. Even the fancy lemonade version will make the kids excited!

Ingredients — about ½ gallon

- 5 large lemons, *You need 1¼ cups freshly squeezed lemon juice.*
- 1 cup granulated sugar
- ¼ cup honey
- 1 cup water for the simple syrup
- ½ of a vanilla bean
- Cold water to make up the rest (up to ½ gallon)
- Garnish: *large sparkling sugar for the rim, additional lemon slices, mint leaves*

Extra Ingredients for the Martini Version

Vanilla vodka (I used Smirnoff.)

Notes:

How to...

First, squeeze the lemons! You'll need about 5 large lemons. Add the freshly squeezed lemon juice to a pitcher.

In a medium pot, combine sugar, honey, and water. Heat it until all the sugar has dissolved. Add the vanilla beans and seeds to the simple syrup you have just made.

Bring the syrup to a boil and let it boil for 4–5 minutes until it is slightly thickened and reduced. Remove from heat and let it cool. This also gives the vanilla beans time to perfume the syrup.

Remove the vanilla bean pods from the syrup. Add the syrup to the lemon juice. See the specks of vanilla bean in there?! Yum! Add cold water up to about half a gallon or the strength you would like it. Add some fresh lemon slices to the top. And there you have it!

Ahhh, summer in a glass!

And Now Just for the Grown Ups...

Add 2 parts vanilla vodka to a shaker filled with ice.

Add 4 parts of the awesome honey vanilla bean lemonade that you just made.

Shake, shake, shake! Strain out into a martini glass that you have rimmed with sparkling sugar crystals. I used honey around the rim to glue the sugar on.

Garnish with a fresh lemon slice and some fresh mint.

Please enjoy responsibly.

Toasted Coconut Martinis

On one gorgeous spring day, there was a plethora of activities to keep us all busy. My husband and our oldest three ran in a 5K race early in the morning, and then I took the youngest two on a 5K ride on the lovely Longleaf Trace close to our home. Then there were the requisite home chores and errands to be run, groceries to be bought, dinner to be planned, fishing to be had on the lake out back, and some friendly ping pong competitions. You know the Saturday drill. By late afternoon, we deserved a little happy hour!

These yummy and decadent Toasted Coconut Martinis fit the bill exactly! They take only a few minutes to mix up, and the payback is oh so good! Why should you wait until you go out to a fancy restaurant to have something like this? There is absolutely nothing wrong with sitting out on the back deck, or the porch swing for that matter, with your sweetheart or a few friends and enjoying something so sublime! ***Please enjoy responsibly.***

Notes:

Ingredients for 2 martinis

- 2 oz plain white rum (I used Bacardi "Rock Coconut" rum.)
- 4 oz coconut rum (I used Malibu.)
- 3 oz Whipped Cream vodka
- 2 oz coconut cream, canned
- 2 oz pineapple juice

A drizzle of white chocolate liqueur (I used Godiva.)
Toasted coconut, *Honey makes it stick to the rim.*

Note: *Please make this drink into whatever form you want. If you don't care for toasted coconut around the rim or in your martini, then skip that. I happen to like it. The beauty of making these at home is the freedom of individualizing them to your liking. The other great thing is that you won't need a designated driver.*

How to...

Into a martini shaker, mix together the alcohols, cream of coconut, and pineapple juice. Add ice and shake for a minute or so until cold. Strain the drink out into toasted coconut-rimmed martini glasses. Drizzle some of the Godiva white chocolate liqueur over the top and garnish with a bit more toasted coconut if you'd like.

To toast the coconut, I just put a big handful into a round cake pan and popped it into the oven under the broiler a few minutes. You do have to keep an eye on it and move it around every couple of minutes. Do NOT turn your back on it. It will burn in a heartbeat if you aren't paying it any attention! Then, to rim the glasses, I ran a bead of honey all around the rim and inverted the honey-rimmed glass down into toasted coconut firmly.

Index

A

B

C

D

E

Q

R

S

T

V

Y

Z